SKILFULLY DRILLED

A History of
the Australian
Instructional Corps
1921-1955

Roland Millbank

ECHO BOOKS

First published in 2015 by Barrallier Books Pty Ltd,
trading as Echo Books

Registered Office: 35-37 Gordon Avenue, West Geelong, Victoria 3220, Australia.

www.echobooks.com.au

National Library of Australia Cataloguing-in-Publication entry.

Author: Millbank Roland, author.

Title:Skilfully drilled : a history of the Australian Instructional Corps, 1921-1955 /
Roland Millbank.

ISBN: 9780646477909 (paperback)

Notes: Includes index.

Subjects: Australia. Australian Army. Australian Instructional Corps--History.
Military education--Australia--History.

Dewey Number: 355.50994

Book and cover design by Peter Gamble, Ink Pot Graphic Design, Canberra.
Set in Garamond Premier Pro Display, 12/17 and Minerva, Small Caps.

www.echobooks.com.au

Cover Photo: *Chief instructor weapons wing, Lieutenant S. P. Mowbray (standing), with Warrant Officer 1 Druitt and Warrant Officer 1 A. A. Whitton. They are preparing to fire the Projector Infantry Tank Attack Mk 1 during a test of the missile against Japanese pillboxes. Sogeri Valley, New Guinea. 1943.* (Australian War Memorial 057112)

Contents

TABLES AND IMAGES

ACKNOWLEDGEMENTS

In the fourteen years it has taken to write this history of the Australian Instructional Corps 1921-1955 I have received considerable assistance from a large number of people. A complete list of contributors and respondents is set out in Appendix 9, however a number of special people provided very important inputs and without them this work would never have been completed.

From the former members of the Corps I always received encouragement, assistance and great help, especially from Arthur Newton, Tom Dawson, Frank Guest, Colin Macpherson and Guy Fawcett. Sadly as the time has gone on they are no longer with us. At Central Army Records Office, Melbourne, the friendship and help of Jim Allen was greatly appreciated. On visits to Canberra Albert Palazzo at the Australian Defence Force Academy (ADFA) always gave unstinting help and encouragement. Jeffrey Grey of ADFA provided me with the basic tools to write my masters research thesis, which has morphed to become this book. In more recent times Ian Gordon has put my words and pictures into a format that I trust shows the debt the Army owes to these old soldiers of the Corps. Julie Reid has been with me on this long journey, much longer than either of us ever realised! Julie has provided lots of the necessary literary touches to make this history 'readable'. Finally I owe an enormous debt of gratitude to Cathy McCullough and Ian Gordon. As my editor, Cathy's unstinting help has added the 'colour' to my writing to make these exemplary soldiers come alive once more. Ian as publisher provided the soldierly leadership all field officers always desire.

I am a child of war (born 1938) and have experienced hardship caused by enemy action. My reading, and later understanding, of the difficulties facing Australian soldiers between the wars has given me immense admiration for the members of the AIC who 'soldiered on' despite lack of funds and obsolete equipment. I can only hope that my description does justice to the manner in which these consummate soldiers overcame problems.

Roland Millbank,
Newcastle-upon-Hunter, New South Wales, June 2014.

FOREWORD

Major General Gordon L. Maitland, AO, OBE, RFD, ED

Few of those who joined the Army during the Second World War would have had anything to do with the Staff Corps (the officers of the Permanent Force); however, in some way or another nearly every veteran heard of the Australian Instructional Corps—the AIC, comprising the senior non-commissioned and warrant officers of the Permanent Force.

As a platoon commander my first company commander was a member of the Darwin Mobile Force, and his successor didn't take long to tell me that he had received his weapons qualifications at the AIC's Randwick Small Arms School. It seemed as though everyone had been trained as an instructor by someone who had been trained by the AIC. The snowballing effect of the AIC's efforts was truly remarkable.

The training of the AIC engrained in its members a code of soldierly conduct that distinguished them. They were treated with callousness by the Army but they did not allow their treatment to diminish their performance. They were role models and in turn they made role models of those who sought to emulate them. There are sound grounds to claim that the AIC contributed significantly to the outstanding performance of the Australian Army in the Second World War.

The impact of the AIC was achieved not only through its individual members, but by what they preached—'Methods of Instruction'. Those methods were so simply, clearly and effectively constructed that everyone appreciated and accepted the methodology. The instructional techniques were so far ahead of practices outside the Army that many soldiers went on to develop training and consulting businesses based on their militarily acquired knowledge. Also many who served in the Citizen Military Forces received plaudits for the training they conducted of fellow staff in their civilian employments.

The AIC so distinguished itself that its story deserves to be told. Roland Millbank is to be commended for not only having both conceived the project and meticulously researched it, but for having the determination to press on to the very end by producing this work. It has been a labour of love for it will not be a bestseller. The Corps did not go to war as such and this account is one of dedicated service, not of colourful and exciting deeds. Furthermore the story is half a century old and the roll call of Second World War veterans is coming to an end.

On a more positive note, this work comprises an immense amount of material and so constitutes a valuable reference source. I myself have been grateful to use some of that material in writing an historical framework of the Army in Australia, and I sincerely thank Roland for it.

The Book's Title

Whilst the title of the book, as has been pointed out, only really highlights a very small aspect of the work of the warrant officers of the Australian Instructional Corps, it has been deliberately chosen.

Ian Kuring, the author of the magnificent tome on the Australian Infantry Corps, *Redcoats to Cams,* emphasized 'while drill was important, 'skilfully trained' was really far more descriptive, and would therefore be a much more accurate inscription, for use as the title of this book!'

Correct though this may be concerning the big picture, the title actually comes from a quotation used by Lieutenant Colonel Arthur Newton MBE writing in 1972 about his time in the corps. Colonel Newton used this title that is part of the catch cry of Army trainees captured by C.J. Dennis in his poem *The Push*:

> 'An' they've drilled us. Strike me lucky! But they've drilled us for a cert!

PREFACE

Thursday 14 April in the late autumn of 1921 was, for most people, a totally unremarkable day. But for Staff Sergeant Major Ernest William Latchford, it was a day that would totally change his career as a full-time soldier. Along with 599 of his colleagues who were professional soldiers, Ernest Latchford was transferred into the newly raised Australian Instructional Corps (AIC). These 600 selected staff sergeant majors were to become the quartermasters and instructors to the first divisional Army established in Australia following the Great War. The AIC was a brand new organisation, its members now distinguished from the earlier warrant and non-commissioned instructional staff of the Federation Army (1901– 1914) by virtue of its vastly different role. Previously, the assignment of instructional staff had limited their instructional duty to the five permanent Army Schools. In contrast, the task of the AIC was to provide all-corps instruction of the whole field Army. It was an enormously broadened role that would cover every aspect of practical training throughout the entire Army in all states and territories. In today's language the corps task would be described as 'training the trainers'.

Ernest Latchford was born on 24 January 1889 at Wahring, a small town on the Goulburn River weir near Murchison, Victoria, some 167 kilometres from Melbourne. He had been a 'printer's devil'[1] at Echuca, Victoria, when he joined the 12th Australian Infantry Regiment. This was to be a short engagement. Following six months' service he was discharged from the regiment, leaving the district to move to Melbourne where he worked as a bookseller at the famous Coles Book Arcade. Arriving at Auburn, Victoria, Ernest Latchford then enlisted once more, this time in the 1st/6th Australian Infantry Regiment where he served for three years and five months, reaching the rank of lance sergeant.

On 13 August 1910, at the age of 21 years 7 months, at a height of 5 feet 8 ½ inches and weighing 137 lbs, Lance Sergeant Latchford was enlisted in the Instructional Staff at Albury, New South Wales (NSW), for a period of five years and was given the regimental number 112. Eligibility for appointment to the Administrative and Instructional Staff came later through qualification at the No. 1 Special School held in Albury, New South Wales in 1911. For the next five years Ernest Latchford was the Area Staff Sergeant Major at Armadale and Moonee Ponds in Melbourne following the introduction of the Universal Military Training Scheme (UMT). He completed a series of regimental appointments until 1916 when he volunteered and was enlisted in the 1st Australian Imperial Force (1st AIF). As a staff sergeant major in the Permanent Military Forces (PMF), Ernest Latchford retained his substantive rank. In the 1st AIF he was commissioned as a lieutenant and platoon commander with the 38th Battalion, AIF.

Prior to seeing action in France, Lieutenant Latchford was posted to the British School of Artillery at Larkhill, England, where he trained the battalion gunners in the use of their new weapon, the Lewis machine-gun. As a captain at Messines he was awarded the Military Cross (MC) for 'conspicuous gallantry and devotion to duty'.

Following the Battle of Passchendaele in July 1917, Captain Latchford

---

1   A 'printer's devil' was a printer's apprentice who performed a number of tasks such as mixing ink and fetching the type for the printer.

was one of the 20 Australian officers selected to serve in Dunsterforce. This was a specialist force that operated in Persia, training irregular forces to block Turkish incursions into the country following the collapse of the Russian Army. With the disbandment of Dunsterforce in late 1918, Ernest Latchford volunteered to go to Russia with the British Military Mission in Siberia as a weapons instructor. Prior to returning to Australia, in England he was selected as a student to attend the British Army Small Arms School at Hythe (Kent) and the Machine Gun School Netheravon, (Wiltshire). This selection and the excellent grading he received were to later have a major impact on his career as an instructor. Returning to Australia in 1920, Captain Latchford, MC, reverted to his substantive PMF rank of staff sergeant major. Despite his 1st AIF commission, Ernest Latchford was not sufficiently senior (based on promotion) in the new AIC to be offered one of the 60 quartermaster (honorary) commissions available when the Corps was formed.

The story of the service of Staff Sergeant Major Latchford and that of his fellow professional soldiers, including the tasks and duties that they undertook, was to become a virtual history of the AIC over the next 34 years. When the AIC was formed, soldiers were appointed to the administrative position of staff sergeant major and then promoted to the rank of warrant officer.

In time the position of staff sergeant major would disappear and all members of the AIC would become warrant officers on promotion. Thus the AIC could be described as a corps of warrant officer quartermasters and instructors. These professional soldiers formed the backbone of the Australian citizen Army or Militia in the interwar years. The AIC's task was to train the instructors, who would then instruct the Militia officers and NCOs who would, in turn, would train their own units. Virtually unknown outside the Australian Military Forces (AMF) and largely unrecognised by a nation that was greatly in their debt in World War II, the staff sergeant majors/warrant officers of the AIC have disappeared almost without trace from the Army and into history.

When it was established in 1921, the AIC was a 'service corps' that provided training support to the combat arms of the Army (i.e. the infantry, cavalry, engineers and signals). Changes to the structure of the defence of Australia, including those that resulted from the Washington Naval Conference of 1922, the cancellation of compulsory military service obligations by the Scullin Government in 1931 and the raising of the Darwin Mobile Force (DMF) in 1938 were among the major changes that significantly affected the tasks and training of the Army and the AIC. These structure changes all form part of the narrative of this history. The life of the AIC ended when it was removed from the Australian Army's 'List of Corps Precedence' in 1955. Thus it is that the 34 years from 1921 to 1955 that constitute the life of the Corps, and thereby form the essence of this history.

The background to the story of the AIC is, in itself, fascinating and involves Federation Defence (1901–1914), the Great War (1914–1918) and the doctrine of Imperial Defence. Each of these developments influenced the progress of the AIC. The interwar years, characterised by economic deprivation and massive social change, deeply affected Australian society in general and the Army in particular. These conditions were to severely compromise the practical training role of the AIC. Yet, as the Second World War edged closer, members of the Corps staffed all the Army Schools without exception. Staffing also included and small specialised forces such as the DMF, whose members were trained by AIC warrant officers. It cannot be stressed too highly that AIC members played a huge important role in preparing the Australian Army for World War Two (WWII).

The AIC's most active years were those of the Second World War from 1939 to 1945 when its instructors provided a cadre of combat officers, quartermasters and instructors for both the PMF and the 2nd Australian Imperial Force (2nd AIF). As soldiers in the PMF the staff sergeant majors/ warrant officers remained members of the Corps and retained their seniority. However, by 1942 all AIC warrant officers were serving in units of either the 2nd AIF or the AMF. Wearing the uniform and badges of their AMF or 2nd AIF unit, AIC warrant officers became indistinguishable from their comrades at that time. This is the principal reason so many of their stories have remained unrecorded. The AIC did not go to war as a corps and because of this there is no war diary to record its members' exploits.

As the Australian Regular Army (ARA) emerged from the force known as the Interim Army in the decade 1945–1955, the AIC was to be transformed. Pre-war there had been five Army Schools; post-war there were 34 ARA schools. With the ARA concentrating on soldier training through its newly established post-war corps schools, the AIC lost its principal role. The introduction of examinations for quartermaster commissions compromised the AIC's secondary role. Loss of tasks would lead inexorably to the demise of the Corps in 1955.

Lieutenant Colonel Ernest William Latchford, MBE MC, who retired in 1949 holds a special place of honour in the Australian Army. Latchford Barracks at Bonegilla in Victoria, the final location of the Small Arms School from 1942–1945, has been named after him. Alone among his comrades-in-arms in the AIC, Ernest Latchford is singularly blessed. For the remainder of the over 2,000 permanent (regular) soldiers, who devoted their working lives to the service of the country, very little trace remains.

The transformation of the Regular Army saw the majority of warrant officers transferred from the AIC as the Corps Schools changed the style of instruction which for decades had transformed civilians into efficient fighting solders. The men who had left their mark on the world in two world wars had now become just another footnote in the relentless march of Australian military history. It was at this point that I became involved in the story.

'During the years after WWII, I have looked in vain for the publication of any history of my corps,' wrote an ex-member of the AIC to the editor of the NSW Returned and Services League Branch magazine *Reveille* in

November 2001.[2] The letter aroused my interest because I knew from my own service in the Army from 1973 to 1988 that the AIC no longer existed. My interest in the Corps had been awakened in 1995 with the discovery of a pair of AIC collar badges made into cufflinks in an antique shop in Ulverstone, Tasmania. Contact with the writer of the letter to *Reveille*, Mr. Tom Dawson of Kempsey, NSW, enquiries at the Australian War Memorial (AWM) and to the Army Historian, Mr. Roger Lee, confirmed that no history of the AIC existed. The lack of a documented history of the AIC presented a window of opportunity for me to research the Corps and ensure that its history be recorded.

Writing the history of the AIC involved solving a number of problems. I began with the reason behind the creation of the Corps—why did the Army require an Instructional Corps? I then progressed to researching the members of the Corps in a bid to ascertain precisely what manner of soldiers populated the AIC. In a natural extension of this question, I sought to discover what exactly AIC members did. I then examined the shape of the Corps and looked at its command and control structure. Having reasonably described the Corps, its role and members, I was left with the most poignant question of all: why was there no AIC when I joined the Army following the Vietnam War?

It took me some considerable time to answer all these questions and I quickly discovered that by far the most problematic issue concerned the membership of the Corps. Normally, the writing of a history of a military unit commences with the examination of the unit's Muster and Pay Roll and Nominal Roll. When I sought a Nominal Roll for the AIC from the Central Army Records Office (CARO) at Victoria Barracks in Melbourne I was told that none existed. CARO advised that, although for the past century the Australian Army has kept extensive records relating to the attendance and pay of soldiers in individual units, this form of roll-

---

2   Vol. 74, No. 6, November–December 2001.

keeping has never been the practice for such large diverse and scattered units as an Army corps.

The lack of an AIC Nominal Roll made writing a history incredibly difficult. A nominal roll will usually provide positive identification of individual AIC members at a particular point in their Army careers. An AIC Nominal Roll would have provided the structure to allow me to examine the work of Corps members in training the citizen Army from 1921 to 1939.

A nominal roll would also have provided the means to examine the careers of individual members and a mechanism to analyse how the AIC role of 'training the trainers' represented and reflected (initially) an imperial, rather than a national ambition. It would have provided a tangible illustration of the large increase in establishment numbers from the low of the interwar period to the peak of World War II, allowing some evaluation of the contribution of the Corps and its role in the defence of Australia.

In the absence of an official AIC Nominal Roll, I set about compiling my own from the various scattered and fragmented sources available. Over a period of 14 + years I have interrogated a large number of such sources, from the annually produced Army List of Officers (Staff and Graduation Lists) to the large numbers of Australian Army Orders (AAOs) housed at CARO and which, typically, could contain 300–500 separate orders for a single year. It was a considerable task, with full examination of the lists and orders taking me almost three years to complete.

I consulted a variety of other record sources including the National Archives of Australia (NAA) in Canberra (for records of the Military Board), Sydney (Villawood), Melbourne and Adelaide; the library of the Australian Defence Force Academy (ADFA), Canberra; the AWM and a large number of unit histories. The results of this research have produced a unique database currently containing over 1,800 names of AIC members identified through public records. Needless to say, the search continues.

While the AIC Nominal Roll is an important tool in compiling a history of the Corps, nothing was more important than speaking to ex-members of the AIC, their descendants and those who served with them. In writing this history, I interviewed over 100 former Militia and regular soldiers ranging from privates to major generals. Without exception, each commented on the exemplary manner, bearing and instructional technique of the AIC members. I hope this history can truly convey what consummate soldiers they were.

Roland Millbank
June 2014

CHAPTER ONE
THE CREATION OF A NEW CORPS

A Changed Australian Society

The Great War changed Australian society to such an extent that it was almost unrecognisable from even that of a decade earlier. Politically, Australia was in turmoil. Communism had arrived on the streets. North Quay in Brisbane on Sunday 23 and Monday 24 March 1919 saw a clash of the old and new cultures. Bolshevik supporters held a rally on Sunday, which was matched on Monday by a huge crowd of ex-soldiers rallying for 'King and Empire', and determined to boot the 'Commies' 'right out of Australia'.[1] However, the rise of Bolshevism in the streets was, in reality, an outward sign of internal struggles within the federal and state Labor Party where the rival branches of the Australian Communist Party had amalgamated and were attempting to change the course of socialism.[2] But Bolshevism/ Communism was only half the problem. The Australian economy was in crisis, faced with a huge post-war debt yet needing to spend heavily to create jobs and housing on a massive scale.[3] While the Great War was in progress, the economic doctrine of 'butter or guns' had been clearly resolved in favour of the guns. Now that the guns had fallen silent, the focus had turned solely to feeding the nation.

With the end of the 'war to end all wars', peacetime now stretched into the future and the situation concerning economic doctrine was reversed. This was the new environment in which the Australian Army, at that time known as the Australian Military Forces (AMF), had to operate. While the Australian Army was only one of many established organisations forced to change because of the demands of the nation's political leaders, it did face a number of unique problems.

The Federation Army and the Administrative and Instructional Staff

From its formation in 1901 until after World War II, the Australian Army consisted of a large, volunteer, non-permanent citizen Army that tended to fluctuate in numbers, from approx. 20,000 (1907) up to 50,000 each time war approached.[4] This citizen force, known initially as the Militia and later as the Citizen Military Force (CMF), was supported and administered by a small professional force of 1,600 known as the Permanent Military Force (PMF).[5]

The deliberate creation of a citizen Army based on part time service, rather than a full time regular or standing Army (read *Permanent Force)*, was created by the Australian political leaders to provide land defence of the continent at a moderate cost. The rejection of a large standing Army at this time had much to do with the unspoken fear of the largely British, Royalist supporting population. This was that a large standing Army could seize political power just as Oliver Cromwell had achieved in the 'Mother Country' several centuries earlier. The establishment of the Federation Army in 1901 brought into being a single organisation for national defence, where there had previously been six separate colonial armies. Being a part time citizen Army ensured only limited numbers of trained soldiers were available for 'imperial adventures' (as the Australian Labor Party and many Liberal politicians had viewed the South African war). While the upfront cost of a citizen Army was much less that that of a regular sized standing force, the real cost came in training. The vastness of the Australian continent demanded that the small permanent force had to be a training organisation employing very mobile, highly skilled instructors, capable of training the officers and NCOs of the citizen Army. In this scheme these citizen Army officers and NCOs would then, in turn, train their own citizen soldiers.

Within the PMF were the Administrative and Instructional Staff (A&I Staff). These were a cadre of permanent soldiers created at Federation to train and administer the Militia. Formed by Major General Edward Hutton under Section 32 (2) of the *Defence Act*. The A&I Staff consisted of permanent officers, warrant officers and non-commissioned officers (NCOs), but no rank and file. Its structure and roles were divided into two branches. The higher level administration and training conducted by officers at headquarters level, and the lower level (unit) instruction and administration delivered by warrant and non-commissioned officers. Following the Great War, the instructional staff of the Federation Army was to be the genesis from which the Australian Instructional Corps (AIC) would be raised.

Tasked with teaching drill, tactics, discipline and administration, officers of the instructional staff were attached to brigade headquarters. These officers reported to and were placed under command of the part-time brigade commanders.[6] Similarly, the tasks of instructional staff warrant and non-commissioned officers involved supervision and instruction of Militia and volunteer warrant and non-commissioned officers in their respective duties. In a similar manner to officers, the instructional members of the A&I Staff were placed under command of, and reported to, the commanding officer (CO) of the Militia unit to which they were attached.

The duties of all A&I Staff expanded in 1906 when the Commonwealth military forces took command of the six cadet forces previously under state organisation. Officers originating in these state organisations were taken into the broader system and became the A&I Staff (Officers) of the Commonwealth Cadet Corps.[7] This in turn led to the use of two distinct classifications of administration officers, with officers of cadets maintained on a separate list.

At the invitation of Prime Minister Alfred Deakin, Field Marshal Viscount Kitchener of Great Britain, then Commander-in-Chief of the British Army in India, visited Australia in 1909 to inspect Australia's state of military preparedness and provide advice on defensive measures for the young Commonwealth. Kitchener's report, submitted in February 1910, recommended the introduction of compulsory military training. Amendments to the *Defence Act 1903* legislated in 1911 saw the introduction of the Universal Military Training Scheme, known as the UTS. While the scheme bore Kitchener's imprimatur, it was designed and planned by a brilliant Army administrator, Colonel J.G. Legge.[8] The training program drafted by Legge received Royal Assent on 13 December 1909, the date from which Australian males aged from 12 to 26 were compelled to engage in military training.[9]

In 1910 the Army had three infantry brigades each of four infantry battalions (regiments became battalions in 1908) plus a garrison force of 18 battalions, a total force of 30 volunteer battalions.[10] In addition there were six Light Horse brigades (with three Light Horse Regiments) and a typical infantry brigade had a Light Horse Squadron.[11] The structure changed in 1911 when Australia was divided into six military districts (basically along state lines) comprising 219 training areas and the total force increased to 96 infantry battalions. Just over a quarter of the increased force was located in eastern Australia. The 1st Military District (Queensland and northern NSW) was allocated the first 12 infantry battalions. The 2nd Military District (most of NSW) raised the 4th to the 11th (inclusive) infantry battalions, a total of 28 infantry battalions.

The Military Districts were also allocated 'mixed brigades' which included both infantry and light horse regiments.

The introduction of the UTS in 1911 heralded a major expansion of the A&I Staff. To cope with the expected increase of approximately 92,000 Militia and cadet trainees, the Army proposed an A&I Staff establishment of 49 officers and 425 warrant and non-commissioned officers.[12] Accordingly, the officers of cadets were consolidated into the A&I Staff to give the staff a total of 99 officers.[13]

Prior to the introduction of UTS there was a marked deficiency of qualified warrant and non-commissioned officers. To rectify this shortage four additional Schools of Instruction were held, one annually from 1910 to 1913 inclusive.[14] A total of 318 soldiers qualified for promotion to staff sergeant major and were appointed to the instructional staff.

However useful UTS was for boosting the ranks of the A&I Staff, the training was, in fact, far from universal. According to historian John Barratt, 'Of about 155,000 boys who registered in 1911, only 59% (92,463) were finally liable for training.'[15] The UTS was generally accepted, but not totally popular. The scheme contained no provisions for conscientious objectors, as John and William Size of Oakbank in South Australia were to discover. In September 1913 the Size brothers spent 20 days at Fort Largs for refusing to drill.[16] Similarly, Tom Roberts from Brighton, Victoria, the son of Quaker parents, spent 21 days at Fort Queenscliff in June 1914. Roberts was described as 'totally uncooperative' and awarded seven days' solitary confinement by a military court.[17] The UTS was scaled back during World War I and lost its most junior trainees in 1922, but the bulk of the scheme lasted until 1929 when the Scullin Labor Government came to power. After the war the Government did not pursue UTS offenders with the same vigor as had occurred in the early years. One of the Scullin Labor government's first acts, was to suspend the UTS indefinitely, a move that was greeted with joy by many potential recruits. According to conscript Alexander Witt,

'When they chopped the compulsory out there was a lot of fella's who were damn glad to get out of it.'[18]

The last expansion of A&I Staff took place through individual appointments necessary to meet demand during the Great War when Australia fielded two armies. Fighting overseas was the volunteer expeditionary force known as the Australian Imperial Force (AIF), while at home the AMF/Militia citizen forces garrisoned Australia. As had been planned from the first days of Federation, the A&I Staff were used to bolster the ranks of the expeditionary force. Each of the units in the 1st Division, AIF, included a number of A&I Staff NCOs in key positions, many of the officers filling unit appointments such as adjutant, or assuming key roles on the staff of a brigade.

In addition, many A&I Staff were commissioned into the Militia forces at home in an effort to maintain the viability of the citizen force. But, by the end of 1915, Militia units and formations were feeling the deleterious effects of the loss of so many A&I Staff to the AIF. Among those who served overseas was Captain James Edward Newland, the only PMF warrant officer in two world wars to be awarded the Victoria Cross (VC).[19] More frustrating for permanent officers on active service, however, was a government decision to attempt to restrict them to the rank of major or below to avoid the creation of a top-heavy instructional cadre at the war's end. Although talented officers were thus effectively denied unit command, there were exceptions such as Lieutenant Colonel John McArthur, Distinguished Service Order (DSO) and Bar, who commanded both the 9th Battalion and later the 31st Battalion.[20] This government decision may well have contributed to the tensions that have existed between regular and Militia officers in the Australian Army since that time. Tensions that were most evident during World War II.

At the close of the Great War the strength of the Instructional Staff was 718.[21] The wartime experiences of the five AIF infantry divisions and two light horse (cavalry) convinced the government that a larger Army would be required after the war. A new divisionally based citizen Army was raised in 1921 based on the successful AIF model. The increased organisational demands of this much larger force required different administration and, as a consequence, the A&I Staff were disbanded. In its place two new corps were created. The A&I Staff officers became the Australian Staff Corps in 1920,[22] and the warrant officers and NCOs transferred to the AIC in 1921.[23]

By 1921 the pre-war Federation Army (1901–1914) that comprised formations of battalions and brigades had largely disappeared, absorbed into the expanded divisional Army. Soon after the outbreak of the Great War the Army's traditional structure of brigades was replaced by the much larger wartime divisional configuration containing up to 17,000 men. The Australian divisions became highly successful under several skilful leaders such as John Monash and Pompy Elliott. Although based on the European conflict model, the divisional configuration was adopted because it was seen by the country's leaders to be to Australia's advantage. With the earlier system, independent Australian brigades and units could be allocated to British divisions with the consequent loss of national identity. Thus the divisional structure offered Australia the benefit of a deployable organisation that (in theory) could operate as an independent structure complete with all arms and services.

Control and administration of the AMF/Militia and, in wartime, the AIF, was the responsibility of the Military Board that reported directly to the Minister for Defence. The Board consisted of four military members plus a civil member and a finance member. The first military member was the Chief of the General Staff (CGS), the Army's most senior officer. The second military member was the Adjutant General who was responsible for issues associated with personnel. The third military member was the Quartermaster General and the fourth the Chief of Ordnance.[24]

Throughout the Great War the Military Board had received unlimited support from Cabinet to pursue its aims. With the declaration of the Armistice in November 1918 and the advent of peace, however, this political *carte blanche* disappeared almost overnight.

Post-War Planning

Fresh from their triumphs in the Great War, the Australian generals planned a much bigger Army, ready to capitalise on the hard-learned lessons of that first, great conflict. The background planning for the much larger Army was derived from reports produced by two major committees in 1919 and 1920. The first committee, which sat in June 1919, comprised an expert panel assembled to advise the government on post-war defence expenditure. The committee consisted of Generals White, McCay and Legge and was chaired by the government's financial watchdog, the Hon. George Swinburne.[25] The committee produced a report that recommended the continuation of the UTS in a revamped form. The report envisaged that, by the mid-1920s, the citizen force created by the continuation of the UTS would comprise six infantry divisions and two mounted divisions and number some 180,000 men.

The Swinburne Report was supported by the Chauvel Report of February 1920. In January 1920, CGS Lieutenant General Sir Harry Chauvel chaired a Conference of Senior Officers to examine the future structure of the Army—its strength, organisation and equipment.[26] The committee's recommendations, published in February 1920 as the Report on the Military Defence of Australia—known as the Chauvel Report— identified Japan as Australia's 'only potential and probable enemy' and sought to provide a land force of 180,000 troops based on seven infantry and cavalry divisions to meet a possible Japanese invasion. While the World War I Armies (1st AIF and the AMF/Militia) had been depleted by combat and ravaged by the influenza epidemic of 1918–1919, the AMF/Militia continued to have its ranks bolstered by the influx of young men still bound by the UTS which had remained in force during the war years, albeit at a significantly reduced level. Compulsory military training was now regarded as the vehicle for taking the Commonwealth Military Forces (as the Army became known) into what General Chauvel described in a later report as the 'second phase' of the Army's development.[27] But there were few signs from the government that this force would become a reality. Defence Minister George Pearce, in his opening address, told the Senior Officers' Conference that 'finances were straitened'. It was a portentous statement.

The cost of the scheme proposed for Australia's defence was enormous. The Australian government was already saddled with a significant war debt. The defence budget, which now also included the enormous repatriation and pension costs and interest on war loans, amounted to some 20 times larger than the last pre-war defence budget at £77 million.[28]

Although the government was initially willing to approve the sizeable force recommended, it eventually opted for a token force of 38,000, reducing the UTS training requirement from fourteen days down to six days of camp training a year. Further economies followed. What the generals regarded as necessary, the Hughes Government merely considered desirable. Eventually the government settled for 'defence on the cheap'.

In 1921, as the Military Board completed its forward planning based on the Army's projections for 1922, it soon became apparent that continuing UTS recruitment would have significant consequences. The Board realised that the Army would face an enormous training liability in 1922 involving the induction of 72,000 Universal Trainees. This was a result of the suspension—rather than the cancellation—of the universal call-up for the years 1917–1918, 1918–1919, 1919–20. While these men had not commenced their military training during these years, their obligation remained. The Military Board also proposed that the quota for 1920–1921 be included with this mass of trainees, all of whom would complete 13 weeks' instruction.[29]

The vast size of this induction and the problems associated with training so many new recruits provided a strong case for the Military Board to create a new national training organisation.

The process to prepare the new divisional Army for the massive influx of conscripted recruits, who were to become Militia soldiers for the next four years, now began. The enormous UTS training liability would require a solid coterie of devoted trainers who would assure the delivery of quality instruction demanded by General Legge's original training program. Thus, in 1921, the Military Board set its mind to the task of securing the services of a corps of quality instructors who would fashion the conscripts into the modern Army envisaged by Kitchener.

A New Training Organisation Emerges

The push for change originated with the committee responsible for the Swinburne Report. They proposed substantial changes to the universal training scheme, their key recommendation that:

> Before the training of rank and file in accordance with the Committee's recommendations can begin, it will be necessary to organise a sufficient training staff of officers and non-commissioned officers, including the training as instructors of many of this staff, so as to ensure proper results when general training is resumed.
>
> It will take the greater part of the financial year 1919–1920 to carry out these preliminary arrangements that should be proceeded with vigorously, necessary provision being made in the estimates.[30]

In a much larger post-war Army, with more soldiers to be enlisted and trained, the need for a larger training organisation had quickly become apparent.

As has been outlined earlier, in 1921 the Army created a brand new corps with a modern training task that involved all-corps instruction of the field Army. The new corps had its origins in the previous military training system, the purview of the A&I Staff of the PMF created at Federation.[31] When the Commonwealth of Australia was established, the 'Federation

Army' had been led, administered and instructed by the A&I Staff. As previously stated the Administrative Staff were all commissioned officers, while the Instructional Staff were warrant officers. While numbers of both Administrative (99 officers) and Instructional Staff (425 soldiers) were low in actual terms, in relative terms they amounted to almost a third of the total force, given that the PMF numbered only 1,600. The Instructional Staff with, at its peak, an establishment of 425 warrant officers, worked entirely from the five Army Schools where they trained soldiers in battle and weapons skills. With the establishment of the AIC, a new era of soldier training was to commence. The task of the AIC instructors was to 'train the trainers' and this encompassed all soldiers from every corps in the Army.[32]

The carefully selected professional soldiers, colleagues of Staff Sergeant Major (Warrant Officer) Ernest Latchford, MC, were part of the AIC's total establishment of 600, consisting of 48 commissioned quartermasters and 552 staff sergeant major/warrant officers.[33] Ernest Latchford himself was to soldier on through World War II. As a Lieutenant Colonel he was to become the Chief Instructor at the Small Arms School (previously established as the School of Musketry), which was for many years the Army's premier establishment for training instructors in practical soldiering.[34]

The Instructional Staff professional soldier instructors initially administered and trained the all-volunteer 1st AIF. To them must go the credit for creating a cornerstone of the foundation of the military success enjoyed by Australia in the Great War. The Instructional Staff was restricted to training in Australia and as a consequence the 1st AIF later developed its own training regime mostly overseas but with recruit training at home. Many members of the Instructional Staff, keen for active service, volunteered and served for long periods as officers in the 1st AIF. These included Quartermaster and Honorary Major John Martin Hawkey, MC, a Boer War veteran who served with the 36th Battalion, AIF,[35] and Quartermaster and Honorary Major James William Shreeve, who fought with the Commonwealth Horse in the Boer War prior to further active service in the 1st AIF as the Adjt of 33rd Bn.[36] These were among the men who joined the AIC as senior NCOs when it was raised in 1921. They brought with them extraordinary first-hand experience of the conditions of combat in two major conflicts and ensured that the AIC built a reputation for quality instruction based on practical soldiering.

The actual size of the AIC Establishment is highly significant. In 1922 the small PMF mustered a total of some 1,600 all ranks.[37] The newly formed AIC was the second-largest permanent force organisation, with only the Royal Australian Artillery (RAA), consisting of both field and garrison artillery, boasting superior numbers.[38] However, while PMF numbers may have been relatively low, Militia numbers, both volunteer and CMF, varied considerably during the interwar period, fluctuating from as high as 124,000 (1921) to as low as 26,000 (1933).[39]

The UTS Training Program

The UTS trainees adhered to a strict program of training according to age. Junior cadets between the ages of 12 and 14 years were required to attend 90 hours of training per year until junior training was phased out in 1922. Once a cadet reached the age of 14, the training requirements were more onerous, covering four complete days, 12 half-days and 24 night drills of six hours' duration per year. This regime continued for four years until the cadet turned 18.

Adult trainees were deemed members of the Militia and bound to serve for eight years from the age of 18 to 26. For the first seven years the trainee's liability amounted to drills equivalent to 16 whole days, at least eight of which had to be served in camp. In the eighth year, the trainee was required to attend a registration or muster parade.

In addition to these scheduled training days, there were specific training requirements for particular corps. Artillery and engineer trainees, for example, were required to train 25 days annually of which 17 days had to be in camp. Naval forces were subject to the same requirements.[40]

The task confronting new AIC instructors such as 364 Staff Sergeant Major Harrold Edwin Oswald Trounson was enormous.[41] Harrold Trounson was a veteran gunner from the 1st AIF who had been wounded in France. He was also a former member of the A&I Staff who thus had long experience in instruction to bring to his new appointment. As a member of the AIC he later attended and graduated from No. 1 Special School (to qualify instructors) at Liverpool in 1920. SSM Trounson and the AIC now had to prepare to train the 72,000 UTS trainees who were to be conscripted in 1921–22.

In a race against time, the AIC had fewer than nine months to have its national training program operational. Thus, less than a year after its establishment, the Corps was facing its first great challenge.

Fig 1. *Colonel Ernest Latchford MC, at his desk 1940.*

CHAPTER ONE
NOTES

1.   Manning Clark, *A History of Australia*, Vol. VI, *The Old Dead Tree & The Young Tree Green, 1916-1935*, Melbourne University Press, 1987 (1999), p. 115.

2.   Heather Radi, '1920-1929' in *A New History of Australia*, Frank Crowley (ed), William Heinemann, Melbourne, 1974 (1980), p. 374.

3.   The size of the war debt was £700,000,000. See Stuart Macintyre, *A Concise History of Australia*, Cambridge University Press, Melbourne, 1999, p. 165.

4.   T. B. Millar, *Australia's Defence*, Appendix B, p 175.

5.   The exact date of the transition in terms from Militia to CMF remains unclear, although it appears to have occurred during World War II. See Al Palazzo, *The Australian Army*, Oxford University Press, Melbourne, 2001, p. 141.

6.   In the Federation Army a brigade, consisting of 3,000 to 5,000 men, was the largest formation.

7.   Military Order 158-1906, Commonwealth Cadet Corps, 'The following officers permanently employed in connection with Cadet Corps under State organisation are transferred to the Admin. And Inst. Staff (Officers) of the Com. Cadet Corps, on the taking over of such Cadet Corps by the Commonwealth.'

8.   John Mordike, *An Army for Nation, A history of Australian military developments 1880-1914*, Allen & Unwin, Sydney, 1992, p. 191.

9.   Thomas W. Tanner, *Compulsory Citizen Soldiers*, Alternative Publishing Co-operative Ltd., Sydney, 1980, p. 226.

10.   Ian Kuring, *Redcoats to Cams, A History of Australian Infantry 1788–2001*, Australian Military History Publications, Sydney, 2004, p. 39.

11.   Albert Palazzo, *The Australian Army, A History of its Organisation 1901-2001*, Oxford University Press, Melbourne, 2001, Table 2.4 p.29 & Table 2.5 p.30.

12.   Jeffrey Grey, *The Australian Army*, Oxford University Press, Melbourne, 2001, p. 29.

13.   Military Order 132-1911, Military Forces of the Commonwealth, Administrative & Instructional Staff (Officers), Establishment 1911-1912.

14.   Military Order 290-1911, 'Instructional Staff (W & NC Officers), with reference to MO 421/1910 & MO 69/1911 the following is the seniority of the non commissioned officers appointed to the Instructional Staff from the Special School of Instruction, Albury, July to December 1910 [lists 186 names].' Military Order 252-1911, 'Instructional Staff (W & NC Officers), the undermentioned Sergeants having qualified at the School of Instruction, Portsea are appointed to the Instructional Staff with seniority according to the order in which their names are shown [lists 30 names].' Military Order 252-1911, 'Instructional Staff (W & NC Officers), the undermentioned Sergeants having qualified at the School of Instruction, Portsea are appointed to the Instructional Staff with seniority according to the order in which their names are shown [lists 30 names].' Military Order 468-1911, 'Special School of Instruction at Albury, NSW, for the training of candidates for Appointment to the Instructional Staff (W & NCOs), 40 places allocated.' Military Order 468-1911, 'Special School of Instruction at Albury, NSW, for the training of candidates for Appointment to the Instructional Staff (W & NCOs), 40 places allocated.' See also Arthur Newton, 'The Australian Instructional Corps', The Army Journal, Vol. 33, 18 September 1912. Without Arthur Newton's publication of articles about the AIC in 1971 it is doubtful that this history could have been written.

15.   John Barratt, *Falling In, Australians and Boy Conscription 1911-1915*, Hale and Iremonger, Sydney, 1979, p. 70.

16.   Tanner, *Compulsory Citizen Soldiers*, p. 214.

17.   Barratt, *Falling In*, pp. 188–89.

18.   Alexander Witt, 39th, 37th/39th, 22nd/39th Battalions, 1933–1940, quoted in Garth Pratten, Under rather discouraging circumstances: the Citizen Military Force in Melbourne's Eastern Suburbs Between the Wars, 1921-1939, BA Hons thesis, University of Melbourne, 1995, p. 22.

19.   Military Order 37-1922, 'James Ernest Newland, VC, late Captain, Reserve of Officers, and an ex-member of the Instructional Staff (W & NCOs), is appointed Warrant Officer, Class I., 12 Mixed Brigade. Dated 31st December 1921.'

20.   M30/864 of 2 Dec 18, 'List to AAG, 3rd Military District: Instructional Staff : T/Lieut./Col McArthur, J, 9th Bn, promoted Lt/Col 1-3-18, CAC 163/18, MO 508/18 Lt.-Col John McArthur, DSO and Bar, commanded (temporarily) 31 Bn, CAG 24/19. Also Lt.-Col. T R Marsden, DSO; Staff Course (Junior) from 29-12-17 to 4-4-18 at Clare College, Cambridge.'

21.   Military Board Agenda 347/20, 'Establishments, 7 Warrant Non Commissioned Officers–Instructional Staff.'

22.   Military Board Agenda No. 253/20, Item 4 (i) 'That Regulations be approved for a new Corps to be designated the Staff Corps, and that such officers of the Permanent Forces as are to constitute it, be transferred thereto from their present units.'

23.   Australian Military Regulations, Regulation 52A, Statutory Rule 73, 14 April 1921.

24.   B.F.S Baden-Powell, & H.M.E. Brunker, , *The Army Annual & Year Book 1910*, William Clowes and Son, London, 1910, p 176.

25.   NAA: A1838/6 Report to the Minister of Defence on 'Certain Matters of Defence Policy' by the Committee chaired by Honorable G. Swinburne, Melbourne, 30 June 1919.

26.   Report on the Military Defence of Australia by a Conference of Senior Officers of the Australian Military Forces 1920, Melbourne, Albert J. Mullett, Government Printer, 6 February 1920, Item 26(i).

27. Report of the Inspector General of the Australian Military Forces, Lieutenant General Sir H.G. Chauvel, 1921, Melbourne, Albert J. Mullett, Government Printer for the state of Victoria, Item 21.

28. Neville Meaney, *Australia and World Crisis: A History of Australian Defence and Foreign Policy 1901–1923*, Vol. II, 1914–23, Sydney University Press, 2009, pp. 423–24.

29. Report on 'Certain Matters of Defence Policy', Item 17.

30. Ibid., Item 6.

31. Military Forces of the Commonwealth, General Orders 1903, No. 230, Wednesday 7 October.

32. Peter Dennis, Jeffrey Grey, Ewan Morris, and Robin Prior, *The Oxford Companion to Australian Military History*, Oxford University Press (2nd Edn), Melbourne, 2008, p. 64.

33. The legal process that created the AIC was effected by amendments to Australian Military Regulation 52, Division 3A, through Statutory Rule 73. Statutory Rule 73 was signed by the Governor-General on 8 April 1921.

34. NAA NSW SP196/3 Barcode 3224501 Latchford, Ernest William, Captain.

35. Hawkey retired in 1936 as an honorary lieutenant colonel in the 21st Light Horse Regiment (Illawarra Light Horse), where he had served as Adjutant and Quartermaster from 1921 to 1929. Notes on the career of Major John Hawkey, MC, supplied by Lockhart Museum, November 2007.

36. NAA Vic B1535 859/16/298. Shreeve survived the war and was nominated for Blacktown Council in 1934.

37. F. W. Perry, *The Commonwealth Armies: Manpower & Organisation in two World Wars*, Manchester University Press, 1988, p.160.

38. Report of the Inspector General of the Australian Military Forces, Lieutenant General Sir H. G. Chauvel, GCMB, KCB, Part 1, dated 31 May 1922, Items 49 and 50. For a description of the size and composition of the RAA at this time see Report of the Inspector General of the Australian Military Forces, 31 May 1928, Parlimentary Report No.257, 13 September 1928, item 50.

39. Millar, *Australia's Defence, Appendix B*, p. 175.

40. Military Journal, July 1913, p. 456.

41. Lieutenant Colonel H. W. O. Trounson , LSGCM (Long Service and Good Conduct Medal) MSM (Meritorious Service Medal) joined the PMF in 1911, serving with the 55th Australian Siege Battery, Royal Australian Garrison Artillery, in France. He was wounded in 1917, rehabilitated and posted to the A & I Staff in 1919 on promotion to warrant officer Class Two. As an honorary lieutenant, he joined the 13th Field Brigade at Keswick, South Australia and, in 1937 was a captain and Adjutant of the 27th Infantry Battalion. He served as Major Administration at the School of Artillery from 1940 to 1946, and in the same position at the Australian Staff College, Queenscliffe, Victoria. See, *Reveille*, Vol.79, No.6, May-June 2006, p.25.

CHAPTER TWO
THE ESTABLISHMENT AND RAISING OF THE AIC

Even within the armies of the British Empire the AIC was an unusual instructional training organisation. Comparison of the AIC with other Dominion instructional units is outlined in Appendix 1.[1] A national posting unit that lacked its own internal command and control structure, but at the same time, had its own distinctive uniform. Officially raised on Thursday 14 April 1921, the AIC was a unique corps within the Australian Army because its establishment consisted entirely of warrant officers. In army historical terms the flat structure totally composed of staff sergeant majors (some with honorary commissions) does appear unusual. However, it was not unique until 1924. As Military Orders 457-1923 and 460-1923 illustrate, the establishment of the Corps of Military Staff Clerks was also composed entirely of warrant officers (and honorary commissioned officers) until this corps was absorbed into the Commonwealth Public Service in 1923. Some were honorary officers meaning that, while they were defined as officers within the AMF/PMF and wore the rank, they were actually substantive warrant officers class I and paid as non-commissioned officers. One such honorary officer was Lieutenant Harry Shappere, the instructor in mounted drill and riding at the Royal Military College (RMC), Duntroon, the nation's premier officer-training institution.[2]

With a different role and a larger establishment from the earlier warrant and non-commissioned Instructional Staff, the AIC was a discernibly different organisation. The much larger task of the AIC involved the instruction of the entire field Army.[3] The important primary role of the AIC was to 'train the trainers' in the practical training of soldiering. Due to spread of military establishments throughout the continent the 'trainer training' task often meant AIC teams would travel throughout the military districts (states) conducting courses. The Militia officers and NCOs qualified as instructors at these courses, were then in turn able to qualify troops locally.

The 60 honorary officers who were quartermasters looked after and administered all the stores that the divisional Army required. As previously mentioned, although these commissioned quartermasters were actually warrant officers class IA, because they were defined as officers they held honorary ranks as lieutenants, captains and majors. They were addressed as 'Quartermaster and Honorary Major' or 'Quartermaster and Honorary Captain' or 'Quartermaster and Honorary Lieutenant' in what must have been a mouthful for both their subordinates and superiors alike.

The original selection process

A large wartime Army had produced an oversupply of qualified PMF warrant officers eligible for appointment as either quartermasters or instructors. The Military Board decided that appointment to both quartermaster and instructor positions would be based on competitive selection. The Board was well aware that the most difficult selection involved those warrant officers (staff sergeant major class IA) who were to receive honorary commissions to become quartermasters. It is fair to say that honorary officers were very much a bone of contention with the Military Board (who were all very senior officers qualified by examination!). At that time all officers, except quartermasters, had to qualify by examination.

Quartermasters could be—and indeed were—appointed without formal examination. At this time their competitive selection became 'based on the individual date of officer promotion in the 1ˢᵗ AIF'.

However, a competitive examination was used in the selection of the remainder of the warrant officers, who were to become instructors with the rank of staff sergeant major classes II and III.[4] Interestingly using a competitive examination, was to prove to be a far more straightforward affair than the selection of quartermasters.

Quartermaster selection

Despite the fact that the size of the Army would increase with the change to the larger divisional structure, the PMF was faced with the task of downsizing its officer cadre to reduce the current contingent to pre-war numbers. The large number of PMF soldiers who had been commissioned into the 1ˢᵗ AIF could not expect to continue serving as commissioned officers, particularly since RMC Duntroon was continuing to produce younger trained officers. In 1919 there were 284 permanent soldiers holding AIF commissions, including 230 who had been commissioned while serving overseas.[5] All 284 PMF soldiers were candidates for the 100 honorary quartermaster commissions available. In reality, there were fewer than 100 positions available, because only 60 were to be allocated to the AIC.

The Military Board totally devoted its meetings on 12 and 13 October 1921 to the granting of quartermaster commissions to members of the PMF.[6] The Board began by selecting those quartermasters to be posted to the existing quartermaster establishment positions in the various service corps.[7] The final 60 quartermasters to join the AIC were then selected based on the seniority of their appointments to 1ˢᵗ AIF commissions. In order to separate the applicants, the Military Board created three Quartermaster Lists designated A, B and C.

List A, 'Ordinary Establishment', comprised adjutant/quartermasters on AMF service and some AIC members; while List B, 'Special Establishment' and List C, 'Temporary Establishment' consisted entirely of AIC members.[8]

The 45 quartermasters who were temporarily employed as adjutants and quartermasters of Militia units or on instructional duty at Army Headquarters (AHQ) schools were allocated to List A, 'Ordinary Establishment'.[9] Some 21 positions from this list were then allotted to selected corps:

- Royal Australian Engineers, Survey Section (one)
- Royal Australian Engineers, Works Section (nine)
- Australian Army Service Corps, Remount Section (five with two vacancies)
- Australian Army Ordnance Corps, Ordnance Section (seven)

The remaining 24 positions were allocated to the AIC.

Many of these quartermasters had distinguished military careers including Captain William Walter James, MC (awarded his MC for courage under fire when serving with the 2nd Field Company, Royal Australian Engineers, 1st AIF) and Major Frederick Herbert Trask, Distinguished Conduct Medal (DCM) , a Boer War veteran who had won his award as a sergeant major with the 6th Queensland Imperial Bushmen in South Africa. Other quartermasters on active service in the Great War included Captain John Henry Roach who served with the 33rd Battalion and Captain Arthur William Drinkwater who was a member of the 7th Australian Light Horse.

List B, 'Special Establishment', was entirely allocated to the AIC and consisted of 24 quartermasters.[10] One of these List B AIC quartermasters, Major Harold Ordish, DSO, commanded the Small Arms School for four years from 1922.[11] While there is no question of Major Ordish's competency to administer the school, there is strong evidence at the time the Military Board had decided higher standards in training needed to be met. The CGS, Major General Sir Cyril Brudenell White wrote to his successor, Major General Sir Harry Chauvel, telling him of the need to upgrade the rank of the instructor where 'there was a warrant officer of the AIC in command'.[12] Brudenell White recommended to Chauvel that a staff officer trained for the work replace the warrant officer instructor. Major Horace Robertson DSO, who had just graduated from the British Staff College at Camberly, was selected to be the next senior instructor of the Small Arms School. He spent another year in England graduating with a distinguished pass at the British Small Arms School (previously the School of Musketry), Hythe (Kent), and the Machine Gun School, Netheravon (Wiltshire). It is no coincidence that both at Hythe and Netheravon that a selected fellow student, and very rare for a warrant officer, was Captain Ernest Latchford MC.

Prior to leaving England Major Robertson completed a number of other courses in range finding, anti-aircraft defence, anti-gas and tasks.[13] Arriving back in Australia, Major Robertson officially took over as Chief Instructor (CI) of the Small Arms School in January 1926.[14]

List C, 'Temporary Establishment', was also entirely allocated to the AIC and comprised 20 quartermasters including those eligible for employment on the War Disability Supernumerary List.[15] Officers with war injuries who wished to continue to serve could apply to be placed on this list and then considered for further Army employment. This list contained some celebrated names, including a VC winner and no fewer than six MC recipients.

In creating the three lists, the Military Board authorised a total of 89 PMF quartermaster positions, of which 62 were allotted to the AIC—two more than the 60 establishment positions originally allocated. However, the 20 positions in List C 'Temporary Establishment' were transitory, allocated merely as a temporary measure. As vacancies occurred, List C would be reduced and no further appointments would be made. Natural attrition would ensure that this list would eventually cease to exist.[16]

Indeed, the Military Board advised that the approved establishment as specified by the production of the three lists was simply 'a guide to the numbers presently employed ... not to be taken as authority for filling subsequent vacancies unless special circumstances were to justify such a step.'[17]

List A 'Ordinary Establishment' and List B 'Special Establishment' quartermasters were granted permanent appointments in the AIC with ordinary rates of pay and employed as Area Officers of training districts.[18] But for those quartermasters accepting a position on List C, the Military Board imposed a number of conditions. To accept a position on List C meant resigning from the PMF, being placed on the Unattached List, AMF, and having the appointment terminated when RMC graduates became available.[19]

James Edward Newland VC

Fig 2. *Studio portrait of Captain James Ernest Newland VC of the 12th Battalion.* (Australian War Memoroial A02614)

For James Edward Newland, the only PMF warrant officer awarded a VC in the Great War, his inclusion on List C 'Temporary Establishment' was not only a serious slight, it presented a very real threat to his future in the PMF. Captain Newland had five members senior to him—and thus ahead of him on the list—who would have to be offered an appointment before he could be granted a permanent quartermaster (honorary) commission. Newland's endeavours to obtain a permanent position as an honorary quartermaster provide an interesting perspective on the inflexibility of the Military Board.

James Newland, a Boer War veteran, was a remarkable man. As a temporary captain and company commander with the 12th Battalion, 3rd Brigade, 1st Australian Division, he was awarded the VC for conspicuous gallantry in holding his position west of Boursies and Lagnicourt, France, from 8 to 15 April 1917, repelling successive German attacks.[20] Of the 64 VCs awarded to 1st AIF members during the Great War, only Newland and Sergeant John Woods Whittle, also a Boer War veteran, and a member of the 12th Australian Infantry Battalion, were from the PMF.[21] The other VC recipients were either citizen soldiers serving for the duration of the war, or former members of the Militia.[22]

Returning to Australia in 1917 at the termination of his AIF service, Captain Newland was obliged to revert to his substantive rank of warrant officer class I.[23] There had been some administrative moves to retain Newland as an officer, but ultimately this did not influence the Military Board's decision.[24] Thus this professional soldier, who had led soldiers in active service in two wars, had received field promotions and been decorated with the highest award for gallantry, had to line up with those of his contemporaries who had survived the war to determine whether he was worthy of being promoted and commissioned.

The Military Board's decision, however, was based not on the respective merit of the candidates, but rather on the date of substantive commissioned rank in the 1st AIF. James Newland had been overseas with the 1st AIF and therefore had not been eligible to be included in List A 'Ordinary

Establishment' that consisted of AMF quartermasters who had remained in Australia throughout the war.

When it came to List B, 'Special Establishment', Captain Newland was too junior—his substantive rank was warrant officer class I—to make the list of first 20 qualifiers. Principally, James Newland failed to make List B 'Special Establishment' because three warrant and non-commissioned officers of the A&I Staff were substantive lieutenant colonels and 25 majors followed them. The substantive seniority of these men relegated Newland to List C, 'Temporary Establishment'.

Even in List C, there were five AIC warrant officers senior to Newland.[25] However, it was not simply the relegation to List C that upset James Newland; it was the conditions that the Military Board attached to the acceptance of such an appointment. To accept a position on List C 'Temporary Establishment' meant resigning from the PMF, being placed on the Unattached List of (Militia) Officers, AMF, and having this appointment terminated once RMC graduates became available.[26] With five Instructional Staff warrant officers ahead of him in seniority in List C and aware that there would never be vacancies in List B, James Newland realised that it would take him some years to regain a permanent honorary commission as a quartermaster based on vacancies occurring in List A.[27]

Once he became aware that he had only made List C and was informed of the conditions incurred by this appointment, James Newland appealed through the Army hierarchy, submitting a Redress of Wrongs to be upgraded to List B. After duly considering Newland as an individual applicant, the Military Board rejected his appeal on the grounds that, if he were to be promoted to List B, each of the five Instructional Staff warrant officers senior to him would then have a Redress of Wrongs case to be answered.

Undeterred by the Military Board's rejection of his appeal, James Newland appealed once more through the Military Board, this time directly to the Minister for Defence. By now, news of the treatment of Warrant Officer Newland, VC, by the Military Board had leaked and was causing some embarrassment to the government. The Minister carefully considered James Newland's case and, after some deliberation, upheld the decision of the Military Board because it would involve supersession of the five members senior to Warrant Officer Newland.

However, in a rare display of perspicacity and flexibility, the Minister ultimately relented, explaining that he considered James Newland to be a soldier of sufficient merit to remain in the permanent service as an honorary officer. Using his ministerial discretion, the Minister had Newland gazetted as a temporary quartermaster and captain, a position that was confirmed some 12 months later.[28]

Had James Newland's case been accepted *prima facie* by the Military Board, the economic consequences would have involved the upgrading of five other warrant officers who would then have had to be paid at a higher rate for the remainder of their careers. The fact that the case had to be ultimately resolved through ministerial intervention, resulting in a single upgraded pay, lends support to an argument that economic circumstances often had a part to play in important military decisions.

Selection of instructors

In a similar situation to quartermasters, the Military Board was faced with an oversupply of well-qualified warrant officers keen to become instructors. Instigating a competitive selection process, the Board invited applications from the 1st AIF, members of the AMF (Militia) and civilians with war experience, including empire service.[29] The age requirement spanned 18 to 40, and candidates over 38 years of age could qualify for selection if they had a strong military background. Selected candidates were then invited to attend special schools to qualify as an instructor. Qualification as an instructor was based on an examination involving subjects forming part of the Army certificate of education along with practical subjects involving drill and weapons.[30] The Military Board prescribed detailed examination rules, including the possible and pass marks for each subject, and the numbers of officers required to examine each quota of candidates.[31]

Once selected to attend schools of instruction, students were enlisted in the PMF as temporary sergeants. This appointment was later revised to staff sergeant major class III. Students were paid 70 shillings (£3 10s) per week.[32] Married students with a family received an allowance of ten shillings per week for a wife and three shillings and sixpence per week for each child under 16 years of age.[33] It was a level of remuneration that was far from satisfactory, particularly as the basic wage for manual labour throughout the Commonwealth at that time varied from £3 17s 6d per week to £4.

Copying the previous system used in 1911, the selection of candidates for promotion to warrant officer and posting to the A&I Staff began with attendance at the No. 1 School of Instruction at Liverpool in NSW from 22 August 1919 to 20 November 1919. This first school boasted some 260 students. The second (No. 2) School of Instruction, also attended by 260 students, was held from 8 January 1920 to 7 April 1920.[34] The results of the two courses were combined and the 379 successful candidates joined the AIC when the A&I Staff was disbanded. Successful candidates were placed in order of merit (by examination score) and this subsequently became the seniority listing.[35] To complete the final AIC Establishment number of 540 instructors, the 379 successful candidates were joined by 161 current Instructional Staff instructors.

Among the senior Instructional Staff who were to join the AIC were NCOs who had been instructors in the Federation Army and members of the 1st AIF including Staff Sergeant Major Alfred Robert Etheredge. Alfred Etheredge had originally been commissioned as a lieutenant in the 48th Kooyong Regiment. Enlisted as an acting staff sergeant major in the Instructional Staff on 20 October 1915, Etheredge had served through the Great War as a warrant officer training troops in Australia. He was a colleague of Staff Sergeant Major Ernest Latchford when he graduated from No. 2 School of Instruction at Liverpool in 1920 as a staff sergeant major class III. Along with Ernest Latchford, Alfred Etheredge became an original founding member of the AIC in 1921.

Six months after the AIC was established, Alfred Etheredge was promoted to PMF warrant officer class II and, in 1927, promoted warrant officer class I. Etheredge served with a number of units in the 3rd Division as regimental quartermaster sergeant (RQMS) and as regimental sergeant major (RSM) including the 24th Infantry Battalion (The Kooyong Regiment) and 39th Infantry Battalion (The Hawthorne-Kew Regiment), AMF. In 1938 he was appointed temporary quartermaster and honorary lieutenant with the 39th Infantry Battalion and it was in this appointment that he again went to war.[36]

The selection of the AIC quartermasters in 1920 and the completion of the 1919 and 1920 Special Schools allowed the full complement of 600 members to be appointed to the AIC Establishment when it became operational in April 1921. The fact that there was serious competition for all PMF positions clearly indicates that senior soldiers were keen to remain in the PMF after 1919.

There were a numbers of reasons for this. Despite the fact that it was poorly paid—so much so that it provoked comment from the Inspector General in his annual report to Federal Parliament in 1922—the Army did offer some security to family men with a fixed wage and, in many cases, the provision of housing. Additional benefits were provided by meals in the mess and medical treatment at no cost to the soldier. However, as will become evident later, there were limitations to these benefits, many of which were determined by the economic circumstances of the time and the post-war military hiatus.

Command and Control

The AIC's difficulties were not restricted to matters of pay and remuneration alone. Questions of command and control were to become major challenges to threaten the status of AIC members Army-wide. In this matter they were not alone. Also involved in these challenges were members of the Australian Staff Corps. While these matters are out of sequence in a chronologically based narrative history, they are hugely important concerning the day-to-day operations of the AIC, hence their inclusion at this point.

In July 1920 the Military Board had created the Australian Staff Corps, the body of officers responsible for the leadership and administration of the new divisional Army. The establishment of a staff corps had first been mooted in February 1910 in the Kitchener Report which had recommended that entry be restricted to graduates of the proposed Royal Military College to be established the following year at Duntroon in the area in which the nation's capital would also be founded. By 1920 the Army had sufficient numbers of RMC graduates to provide a pool of young professional officers to fill the ranks of the Staff Corps advocated in the Kitchener Report.

From their earliest days, the officers of the Australian Staff Corps and the AIC were linked by a crucial connection. All warrant officers, whether they held honorary commissions or not, and all Staff Corps officers, came under command of the divisional and brigade commanders who were Militia officers. Writing about the inter-war period, historian Richmond Cubis commented that:

The prominence of the Citizen Army, and its major role in two world wars, had the effect of casting the staff officers and instructors to be 'handmaidens ... and administrators to the true defence force.'[37]

The fact was, as Cubis added,

The Army was the Militia with a 'a small permanent staff to count the rifles, saddle the horses and gun teams, and clean the depot after the men had gone home.'[38]

The Military Board (all PMF senior generals) administered the AMF consisting of a large Militia and a small PMF. In fact the majority of senior Army divisional commanders were Militia officers because the PMF formation was absorbed into the AMF command. As a consequence, often even the senior Staff Corps officer in a formation, whatever his rank, was always under command of Militia officers.

In a further devolution all AIC warrant officers were also, often administratively under command of Staff Officers (who could be of a lower substantive rank). This unusual PMF command structure was not without its problems. The most crucial of these was the matter of command of unit subordinates within the unit structure and this hinged on the tricky status of the 'honorary' commission granted to the AIC instructors and quartermasters.

As early as 1925, the ambiguity of the AIC members' status was highlighted in a confrontation between a member of the AIC and an officer of the Staff Corps. On 16 April 1925 at the Williamstown Rifle Range in Victoria, the Brigade Major of the 10th Infantry Brigade, Quartermaster and Honorary Major William Walter Tracy, had an order on parade countermanded by a staff officer who was a captain and Adjutant of the 2nd Australian Field Artillery Brigade.[39] At the centre of what would have been a heady confrontation at the time, was the key question of seniority between the two officers.

A second case, also in 1925, concerned AIC Quartermaster and Honorary Major Frederick McLean. A senior AIC officer with a 1st AIF wartime commission as a substantive lieutenant colonel, Frederick McLean had reverted to substantive rank but had been granted a commission as an honorary quartermaster.[40] Quartermaster and Honorary Major Frederick Stephen McLean, DSO and Bar, AIC, challenged what he considered to be an unlawful command. Directed to appear as an officer at a Court of Inquiry, he was to be a member serving under the appointed president, a captain in the Staff Corps. Major McLean declined the order on the grounds that he was actually the senior officer and therefore should have been appointed president. The act of declining the appointment in writing—regarded as mutinous conduct—had to be dealt with at the highest level.

The subject of command and control had caused tension between the Staff Corps and the AIC since the formation of the corps. At the heart of this dispute was the true position of quartermasters within the Army system of administration and discipline. The Military Board was faced with two difficult questions. While they held honorary commissions, the status of quartermasters had never been clarified. Where they, in fact, actually officers? This then led to the second question: if quartermasters were officers, in what circumstances did they command?

Failing to receive a satisfactory answer from the divisional commander concerning his rank and status, Major McLean met with a number of quartermasters in a Sydney pub to discuss the situation. He then went to a firm of Sydney solicitors who wrote directly to the Secretary of Defence on his behalf, seeking clarification of Major McLean's rank and status.[41] Clouding the issue was a change of status for quartermasters in the British Army. In August 1918, an amendment to the Royal Warrant provided for the appointment and promotion of quartermasters in ordinary rank. However, since this change had subsequently been repealed, the rank of quartermaster had remained 'honorary'. It was still 'honorary' in 1925 at the time of McLean's challenge.[42]

For the Army this was a serious case given the involvement of several officers and a solicitor as well as the Minister for Defence. As a result the case generated considerable public interest. The Adjutant General, having examined the matter, concluded that 'in holding an honorary commission, a warrant officer was an officer.'[43] This was because the Adjutant-General's interpretation pointed out that 'the definition of a warrant officer specifically excluded warrant officers from actually holding an honorary commission.'[44] This interpretation provided the answer to the first question since it stated that 'quartermasters could not be warrant officers because they held honorary commissions'. Therefore, by rank, quartermasters were defined as officers.

On the second important question, that of command, the Adjutant General reiterated that, under Australian Military Regulations 29 and 30, 'Honorary rank did not provide the benefit of command.' Specific limitations imposed by the regulations provided that 'Quartermasters were not entitled to any command except [of] those specially placed under their command, an example being an assistant quartermaster.'[45] This extraordinary ruling was to have significant ramifications for members of the AIC who now potentially faced challenges to their right to command from every Staff Corps officer.[46]

The divisional commander, Major General Charles Rosenthal, now aware that Major McLean was pursuing his claim through civil action and recognising that other AIC officers were involved, launched an investigation. Five AIC quartermasters and one Royal Australian Engineers (RAE) quartermaster were paraded before Rosenthal and individually questioned. Principally, he was anxious to determine whether there was a conspiracy on the part of these officers. Given that their complaints had not been made through official Army channels, there was a risk that their actions might be considered 'mutinous conduct.'[47] However, Rosenthal eventually concluded that the men had not acted in concert and that their intention had been simply to seek a civil legal opinion that could then be used to approach the Military Board.

Despite Rosenthal's finding, each officer was given a warning concerning his conduct that was entered on his record of service. The only exception was Major McLean, who had instigated the case, and who was to be singled out for further treatment. Having refused a direct order, although he actually complied when further directed, he was required by the Adjutant General to show cause as to why his commission should not be cancelled and his service in the PMF terminated.[48]

This appears to be drastic retribution for a single indiscretion. That the Military Board could contemplate such action suggests a possibility of bias by senior officers against warrant officers even after they had been appointed quartermasters, a possibility which is examined in a later chapter. In the end, Major General Rosenthal counselled the Military Board on the mitigating circumstances that applied in this case. He noted specifically that 'war related stress had induced this officer to act in a manner which would not have occurred had he been in normal health.'[49] The case concluded with the Military Board concurring with Rosenthal's assessment and deciding not to cancel Major McLean's commission. Instead, the Board advised Major McLean that he had 'incurred their grave displeasure and they expected him, in view of the Board's leniency, to show his appreciation by future loyal service.'[50] Less ostensibly, the same advice could be applied to the AIC whose members were clearly warned by the ruling in the McLean case to avoid confrontation with Staff Corps officers and provide 'future loyal service'.

CHAPTER TWO
NOTES

1. Comparison of the AIC with other Dominion instructional units is detailed in Appendix One which follows these Chapter Two Notes.

2. Shappere was formerly a member of the British Army's Royal Horse Artillery. A gatehouse lodge at RMC Duntroon, ACT, previously his residence, is named after him.

3. Report of the Inspector General of the Australian Military Forces, Lieutenant General Sir H.G. Chauvel, GCMG, KCB, Melbourne, 31 May 1925, Parliamentary Report No. 24, 14 July 1925, Item 89.

4. Only in the Interim Army did the rank of staff sergeant major disappear and these men become warrant officers (previously an administrative post and not a rank).

5. Military Board Agenda No.30-1920, 'Part II, Warrant and N.C.Os of the Permanent Forces now serving who held Commissions in the A.I.F.'

6. Military Board Agenda Item 378-1921, 'Quartermasters Establishment-Permanent Forces.'

7. Service corps such as Ordnance and Transport support the fighting arms (Infantry, Artillery, Armour, Signals and Engineers).

8. Since the Army did not maintain an AIC Nominal Roll, these three lists provide the only record that these professional soldiers were awarded quartermaster commissions.

9.   See Appendix 2 to this chapter for a full list of these men.

10.   Listed in Appendix 3 to this chapter.

11.   Military Order 370-1922, AMF, AIC, Small Arms School, 'A special allowance at the rate of £80 per annum whilst holding the temporary appointment of Chief Instructor of the Small Arms School (Ex. Min. 252).'

12.   NLA, MS 5172, Folder 25, White Papers, Notes for the new CGS (July 1923).

13.   Ian Kuring, *Australian Infantry Magazine*, The School of Infantry 100 years Young, August 2011, p 20.

14.   Jeffrey Grey, Australian Brass, *The Career of Lieutenant General Sir Horace Robertson*, Cambridge University Press, Melbourne, 1987, p. 9.

15.   Appendix 4 lists the men allocated to List C.

16.   Military Board Agenda No. 378-1920: List 'B' Special Establishment, Item 3.

17.   Military Board Agenda No. 30-1920: Part II, List 'B' Special Establishment: Item 3, Warrant and NCOs of the Permanent Forces now serving who held Commissions in the AIF, Item 6 (b), (1), (2) & (3).

18.   Military Board Agenda No. 378-1920: List 'A' Ordinary Establishment, Items 2 and 3.

19.   List 'B' Special Establishment: Item 3, Military Board Agenda 30-1920: Part II, Warrant and NCOs of the Permanent Forces now serving who held Commissions in the AIF, Item 6 (b), (1), (2) & (3).

20.   Lionel Wigmore and Bruce Harding, *They Dared Mightily*, Australian War Memorial, Canberra (2nd Edn, revised and condensed by Jeff Williams and Anthony Staunton), 1986, p. 102.

21.   Whittle, John Woods (1882–1946) biographical entry, *Australian Dictionary of Biography (ADB)*, National Centre of Biography, Australian National University.

22.   Wigmore and Harding, *They Dared Mightily*, pp. 130–31.

23.   Military Order 38-1922, 'Australian Instructional Corps, Appointment. James Ernest Newland, V.C., late Captain, Reserve of Officers, and an ex-

member of the Instructional Staff (W. and NCOs) is appointed Warrant Officer, Class 1., 12th Mixed Brigade, dated 31st December 1921.'

24.   Military Order 10-1922, 'Temporary Appointments as Adjutants & Quartermasters of Units of the Citizen Forces; Captain J. E. Newland, VC, Reserve of Officers, Adjutant & Quartermaster, 52nd Bn.'

25.   Military Board Agenda No. 378-1920, 'List 'C' Temporary Establishment: QMs & Hon. Capts M. Coats; L. J. Kimber (WDSL); C. Guilfoyle, MC; J. S. Tait & A. R. Blainey, MC.'

26.   Military Board Agenda No. 30-1920.

27.   Military Board Agenda No. 378-1920.

28.   'The Governor-General in Council has approved of the under mentioned ex-Warrant Officer of the Permanent Military Forces being appointed, from the Reserve of Officers, Area Officer of a Training Area and Quartermaster of a unit of the Citizen Forces, dated 1st January 1922 with salary commencing at The rate of £350 per annum.' ... 'To be Quartermaster and Honorary Captain—Captain J. E. Newland, V.C. (Ex. Min. No. 2)', Military Order 22-1922, Gazette Notices. Extracts from Commonwealth of Australia Gazette, No. 3 of 12 January 1922, Permanent Military Forces, Australian Instructional Corps.

29.   Military Order 409-1921, Item 4.

30.   Military Order 439-1921, Item 4, 'Rifle (SMLE) and Bayonet, Light Gun (Lewis and Hotchkiss), Machine Gun (Vickers) and Range Finding'.

31.   Military Board Agenda No. 225-1921, Central Training Depot, Candidates for Appointment to the Australian Instructional Corps, Item 9 Competitive Practical Examination; 'In examination centres where there are 30 or more candidates the Boards should consist of at least 4 officers.'

32.   Report of the Inspector General of the Australian Military Forces, Lieutenant General Sir H.G. Chauvel, GCMG, KCB, Part 1, dated 31 May 1922, Item 53.

33.   Military Board Agenda No. 225-1921, Central Training Depot, Candidates for Appointment to the Australian Instructional Corps, Item 17 Pay on Appointment.

34.   Arthur Newton, *The Australian Instructional Corps*, p. 34.

35. Military Order 167-1920, 'Instructional Staff (W. and N.C.O.s), 24/4/20, A609/24/447'.

36. Alfred Robert Etheredge was born on 12 June 1894. He served in the Second World War and was appointed captain (QM) in 1948 and later major (QM). Major Etheredge retired from the Interim Army in April 1951 having served 39 years and 326 days. Don Etheredge (son), letter to the author, 8 May 2003.

37. Richmond Cubis, *A History of A Battery, New South Wales Artillery (1871-1899), Royal Australian Artillery (1899-1971)*, Elizabethan Press, Sydney, 1978, p. 26.

38. Ibid., p. 167.

39. NAA, MP367/1, Item 409/3/2000, Military Board Agenda No. 188/1925, 'QM's Power of Command'.

40. Military Board Agenda No. 30-1920: Part II, Warrant & NCOs of the Permanent Forces now serving who held commissions in the AIF; Annex 2, 'Return of Warrant Officers, Non Commissioned Officers and Men, of the Permanent Military Forces who gained Commissions in the Australian Imperial Force', page 1 (of 11), 'WO Class 1, McLean, F.S., DSO & Bar, RAGA, Lt.-Col, DOB 19/2/1872'.

41. Letter to Secretary for Defence from Bradley, Son & Maughan, Solicitors, Sydney, June 1925.

42. Minute to the Secretary of Defence from the Adjutant General, File 409.3.1989, 2/9/1925, paras 7 and 8.

43. Based on a definition of the term 'officer' in the *Defence Act 1903-1912*.

44. Minute from the Secretary of the Attorney General's Department to the Secretary of Defence: Opinion; *Defence Act 1903-1912*; 'Whether Honorary Officers can exercise the powers of Commanding Officers under Section 108', dated 23/7/1914.

45. Minute from the Adjutant General to the Secretary of Defence, File 409.3.1989, dated 2/9/25, Item 5 (b).

46. The development of the Staff Corps throughout the interwar period and its occasionally stormy relationship with the AIC has been the subject of a

number of histories. Probably the best account is Chapter 3 of Jeffrey Grey's *The Australian Army*, Oxford University Press, Melbourne, 2001.

47.   Rosenthal's 'style of command had enormous appeal to his soldiers, and his promotion in May 1918 to command the 2nd Division was a popular choice.' See Dennis et al., *The Oxford Companion to Australian Military History*, p. 505 for a description of Charles Rosenthal.

48.   Letter from the Adjutant General to the Divisional Commander, 2nd Division, File 409/3/2006, dated 24 November 1925.

49.   Letter from Divisional Commander, 2nd Division, to the Adjutant General, File SC 409/3/2010, dated 4 December 1925.

50.   Letter from the Adjutant General to Divisional Commander, 2nd Division, File SC 409/3/2010, dated 22 December 1925.

APPENDIX ONE
INSTRUCTIONAL UNITS IN DOMINION ARMIES

Comparisons

- Dominions of Australia, Canada, South Africa, New Zealand (and Britain) each had citizen armies with non commissioned officer instructors.
- A citizen army staffed by a small number of full-time professional instructors (non commissioned officers) was common throughout the British Empire.
- Differences in force structure occurred because officer production determined each citizen army was organized appropriate to that country's defence and budget.

Britain

- Britain employed a small Regular Army (that could be deployed operationally outside the United Kingdom) as its first line of land defence.[1]
- The second line of land defence, a large citizen army called the 'Territorial Army', was supplied cadre staff by the British Regular Army[2]
- The British Regular Army supplied all the instructors for the Territorial Army.

- A vital difference, between the British and Australian Armies was the production of officers. Since 1741 British Regular army officers had been trained at the Royal Military Colleges, Woolwich,[3] and Sandhurst (established 1801).[4]
- Corps schools within the primary arms corps (infantry, cavalry and artillery),[5] were staffed by experienced corps and regimental officers who trained the NCOs in corps and regimental duties.
- An abundance of officers, and long established corps schools in Britain, negated any demand that may have existed for a separate Instructional Corps.

Canada

- Many similarities existed between the Canadian and Australian citizen armies.
- However, in the production of army officers, the Canadian citizen army was well in advance of Australia. The Royal Military College of Canada was established at Kingston, Ontario in 1874.[6]
- Many long-established Canadian regiments followed the British example of training their own NCOs. This continued throughout the inter-war period.
- After WWII 'An Administrative and Training Team, normally a captain and one or two senior NCOs were assigned to battalion sized (citizen) units.'[7]
- While there may well have been requirement in Canada for a separate Instructional Corps, no such unit was ever actually created in that country.

South Africa

- The South African Permanent Force (Army) created on 1 April 1913 included an Active Citizen Force and a Coast Garrison Force.[8]
- Officers for the Union Defence Force originally graduated the South

African Military School, later from the South African Military Academy established at Saldanha Bay within the University of Stellenbosch.[9]

- In 1912 the S.A.Permanent Force Instructional Corps held the first Military School graduating 29 instructors to the Permanent Force Subordinate Staff.[10]

- The South African Instructional Corps—Suid Afrika Instrucsee Divesse (SAIC-SAID) was formed on 1 February 1923.

- By 1933 the SAIC-SAID had an establishment of five officers and 75 other ranks.

- SAIC-SAID had its headquarters at the South African Military College, Vootrekkerhoogte (formerly Roberts' Heights)[11] and remained there until 1 June 1942 when it became a voluntary Active Citizens Force Corps.[12]

- Although the SAIC-SAID had a distinctive badge and shoulder titles their uniform was not discreetly different from other Union Defence Force units.

- The SAIC-SAID did not have commissioned Quartermasters.

- Although the SAIC-SAID was an instructional corps and performed instructional duties, it was different to the AIC due to no distinctive uniform, no members with Quartermaster duties and no honorary officers.

New Zealand

- The New Zealand Staff Corps (NZSC) was formed in 1911 as a corps of professional staff officers to administer the newly formed Territorial Force.[13]

- In 1911 the New Zealand Permanent Staff (NZPS) was also formed 'as a corps of 200 NCOs for the instruction of the newly formed Territorial Force.'[14]

- While the New Zealand Permanent Staff of 200 NCOs provided instruction for the New Zealand citizen army, the NZPS did not provide administrative staff to units (a duty by the NZ Staff Corps) and the NZPS had no honorary officers.

In Summary

- The AIC had its own badge and a distinctly different uniform.
- The AIC provided the Australian infantry battalions and light horse regiments with Quartermasters who were hon. majors,[15] hon. captains, or hon. lieutenants.
- Quartermaster duties were often in addition to administrative tasks that frequently included the position of adjutant.[16]
- The AIC provided Australian infantry battalions and light horse regiments with the RSM, the RQMS and usually two NCOs as instructors.[17]

APPENDIX 1
NOTES

1.   This became the British Expeditionary Force (BEF), Correlli Barnett, *Britain and her Army 1509-1970, A Military, Political and Social Survey*, Allen Lane The Penguin Press, London, 1970, p. 423

2.   Field Service Regulations, Volume II, Operations –General 1935, (Reprinted with amendments 1939), His Majesty's Stationery Office, London, 1939, Chap 1 Principles and Systems of Training, Item 8 Regular Forces, Item 15, The Territorial Army

3.   Richard Holmes, *Redcoat: The British Soldier in the age of Horse and Musket*, Harper Collins, London, 2001, p. 176

4.   Holmes, *Redcoat: The British Soldier in the age of Horse and Musket*, p. 165

5.   The arms corps of infantry, cavalry and artillery are considered 'primary' because they are classed as combat arms and directly engage the enemy

6.   Canada: About RMC (updated 2003/03/20, accessed 1/4/03) http://www.rmc.ca/about_e.html

7.   Desmond Morton, correspondence with the author, 1 April 2003: Desmond Morton, *A Military History of Canada*, McClelland and Stewart, Ontario, 1992

8.   Birth of the S A Army (1912), *A Short History of the South African Army*, (accessed 1/06/2003), http://home.wanadoo.nl/rhodesia/sadhist.htm

9. John Keegan, *World Armies*, Macmillan Publishers, London, Second edition 1983, p. 531

10. Union War histories (Civil), Box 168, File ref. Narep-Unfo: 23, S.A. Instructional Corps. History (1912-1942)

11. The South African Military College, formerly Military Schools, provided qualifying courses for non-commissioned officers

12. Major G. Tylden, *The Armed Forces of South Africa*, City of Johannesburg Africana Museum Frank Connock Publication No.2, Johannesburg, 1954. p. 8

13. Ian McGibbon (ed), *Oxford Companion to New Zealand Military History*, Oxford University Press, 2000, Auckland, p. 396

14. McGibbon, *Oxford Companion to New Zealand Military History*, p. 396

15. NAA, Series MP 367/1, Item 452/1/246 Court of Inquiry, QM & Hon. Maj. T. J. Farrow, AIC, October and November 1925

16. Australian Army Order 57-1927, Changes in Allotment of Officers of the Permanent Forces Item (2), QM. and Hon. Major C. R. Speckman, MC, 1st Cav. Div. Engineers, Adjt (temp) and QM

17. Rupert Shields, correspondence with the Author 4 May 2004, William Rupert John Shields, No.7 Course AIC (1939)

APPENDIX TWO
LIST A 'ORDINARY ESTABLISHMENT'

(45 establishment positions)

AHQ	A Branch	Maj. Frederick Herbert TRASK, DCM
		Capt. G.E. SYKES
		Capt. Charles MORRIS
	Q Branch	Capt. H.E. HEYDT
Instructional Duties		
	Light Horse	Capt. John Henry ROACH
	Infantry	Capt. W.J. MACLENNAN
		Capt. G.F.C.F. SHIPLEY
		Capt. Harry NAGHTEN
	A.S.C.	Lieut. R. BREYDON
		Lieut. Charles Aiken MAYES
		Capt. Thomas Fulton COLEMAN
	Engrs.	Capt. William Walter JAMES, MC
		Capt. E.H. COTTEE
		Capt. Alfred TOOTELL
		Lieut. Frederick William PANTLIN
		Capt. Albert Edward ROBERTS

Regimental Duty

R.A.E.	Capt. William Herbert PRATT
	Capt. Arthur William DRINKWATER
R.A.G.A.	Capt. A.H. JONES
A.A.M.C.	Capt. J.H. HEATH
	Maj. James GREEN
	Maj. Charles MORLEY
RMC	Capt. Cyril HISCOCK
	Capt. Harry SHAPPERE

Total Australian Instructional Corps Quartermasters: 24

APPENDIX THREE
LIST B 'SPECIAL ESTABLISHMENT

(24 establishment positions)

QM & Hon.Maj. Robert CHRISTIE, DSO

QM & Hon.Maj. John McARTHUR, DSO (29 Bn)

QM & Hon.Maj. Frederick Stephen McLEAN, DSO

QM & Hon.Maj. Hannibal SLOAN

QM & Hon.Maj. William Walter TRACY

QM & Hon.Maj. William INGLIS, MC (33 Bn)—W.D.S.L.

QM & Hon.Maj. Walter WELLS, MC. (36 Bn)—W.D.S.L

QM & Hon.Maj. John Keating PAUL, DSO (Fd Arty)

QM & Hon.Maj. John Maurice WELLS

QM & Hon.Maj. Harold ORDISH, DSO (MGCoy)

QM & Hon.Maj. Charles Robert Victor WRIGHT, MC.

QM & Hon.Maj. Geoffrey Nicholson EAST-ALMOND

QM & Hon.Maj. William SHARP

QM & Hon.Maj. Carl Rudolph SPECKMAN, MC. (1 Pnr Bn)

QM & Hon.Maj. Claude Cadman, DSO MC

QM & Hon.Maj. Frank M. COUCHMAN, DSO

QM & Hon.Maj. John McFarlane HARVEY, MC (56 Bn)

QM & Hon.Maj. Thomas Joseph FARROW

QM & Hon.Maj. Albert William TAYLOR, MC (11 MGCoy)

QM & Hon.Maj. Thomas Henry DARLEY, OBE

QM & Hon.Maj. Edward. St.John BEERS (AMC)

QM & Hon.Maj. John DUFFY, DSO. (13 LH)

QM & Hon.Maj. Kenneth McLENNAN, MBE

QM & Hon.Capt. Charles MILLS, OBE

Note: QM & Hon. Maj. Roy Marsden, DSO was seconded to the RAAF and is thus omitted from this list.

APPENDIX FOUR
LIST C 'TEMPORARY ESTABLISHMENT

(20 establishment positions)

QM & Hon.Capt. Marmaduke COATS

QM & Hon.Capt. Lewis Joseph KIMBER—W.D.S.L.

QM & Hon.Capt. Charles GUILFOYLE, MC

QM & Hon.Capt. John Stewart TAIT

QM & Hon.Capt. Arthur R. BLAINEY, MC

QM & Hon.Capt. James Ernest NEWLAND, VC—W.D.S.L.

QM & Hon.Capt. Henry Christian PEARCE

QM & Hon.Capt. Wesley Armstrong WHITBOURN

QM & Hon.Capt. William KENNEDY, MC

QM & Hon.Capt. Albert Edward Llantrisant MORGAN

QM & Hon.Capt. Charles Perry GRIEVE, MC

QM & Hon.Capt. Daniel Robert GLASGOW, MC

QM & Hon.Capt. Alexander FRASER, MC

QM & Hon.Capt. Ernest Simeon WILSON

QM & Hon.Capt. William Charles Gentry RUDDOCK

QM & Hon.Capt. William Martin MACKAY

QM & Hon.Capt. Soren Frank SORENSEN

QM & Hon.Capt. James William SHREEVE

QM & Hon.Capt. George ROSEVEAR, MC

QM & Hon.Capt. Robert McILROY

CHAPTER THREE
THE POST-WAR ENVIRONMENT

Optimism

Despite the political turmoil, Australia at the end of the Great War was characterised by a widespread sense of optimism. It was reflected in an address by Prime Minister Billy Hughes, who told his fellow Australians in September 1919 that 'We live in a new world ... the whole earth has been shaken to its very core. Upon the foundations of victory we will build a new temple of our choice.'[1]

This optimism was also echoed by Official Historian Charles Bean in his book, *In your hands, Australians*, in which Bean articulated his vision for a new national spirit. This was an Australian version of the worldwide hope that survivors of the war would perform peaceful deeds that would justify the years of death and destruction.[2] Despite the optimistic rhetoric, the reality was that the majority of Australians wanted a continuation of the policy of social advancement commenced in the years prior to the Great War when the whole community looked set to benefit from government spending and action. Following the Great War it was this social advancement policy that dictated government political thought and action.

Within the Australian Army, fresh from its considerable victories on foreign battlefields, the transfer of officers to the Staff Corps in 1920 and the enlistment of staff sergeant majors in the AIC in 1921 laid the foundations for the new divisional Army. However, the nation's politicians were to undermine these foundations as the peacetime government's defence policy during the 1920s was to have a massive impact on the Army and, in particular, the training task of the AIC.

Imperial Defence

'Defence on the cheap' was the battle cry of the Hughes Federal Government. Indeed, in 1921, Prime Minister Hughes pointed out that 'the cost to each Australian was 12s 4d for the Army and 12s 6d for the RAN, compared with £2 13s 9d and £1 16s 3d in the United Kingdom.'[3] To bolster Australia's defence and, at the same time, keep a tight rein on spending, the cornerstone of Australian defence policy in 1920 became its total reliance on the doctrine of Imperial Defence. This particular doctrine had been adopted at an Imperial Conference convened in London in 1904. When the Imperial Conference reconvened in London in 1921, it reaffirmed the first two principles of its pre-war doctrine. 'Maintenance of supremacy' at sea remained the first principle, while the second dictated that 'dominions should be capable of self-defence'. This second principle effectively relegated the Army once more to the secondary role of land defence of Australia.[4] The Royal Navy (RN), supplemented by the Royal Australian Navy (RAN), was the country's first line of defence.[5] It was a considerable blow to an Army that considered itself newly victorious and was to hold serious implications for the future.

As the second line of defence, the Army was also placed second in the defence force budget allocation (and often third when the RAAF became operational). This ensured an almost continual shortage of funds for all Army operations, particularly for practical soldier training, the specific role of the AIC. The constant lack of funds was to severely impact on the work, and sometimes the morale, of every member of the Corps throughout its lifetime. Just how low the levels of defence funding fell is clearly illustrated in the pattern of defence expenditure from 1920 to 1935:

Table 1. Australian Defence Expenditure 1920-1935 (expressed as £ millions)

Year	Navy	Army	Air Force	TOTAL
1920–1921	£2,756	£1,341	£140	£32,532
1921–1922	£2,692	£1,460	£278	£15,029
1922–1923	£2,124	£1,482	£179	£8,150*
1923–1924	£2,084	£1,545	£223	£9,423
1924–1925	£2,394	£1,558	£398	£6,522
1925–1926	£3,568	£1,548	£429	£6,317
1926–1927	£5,027	£1,526	£572	£7,779
1927–1928	£4,658	£1,494	£517	£7,259
1928–1929	£3,808	£1,466	£549	£6,397
1929–1930	£2,515	£1,240	£498	£4,679
1930–1931	£1,778	£1,195	£392	£3,688
1931–1932	£1,447	£995	£326	£3,052
1932–1933	£1,499	£978	£320	£3,021*
1933–1934	£1,637	£1,237	£409	£4,021
1934–1935	£2,511	£1,329	£536	£5,293

*Note the reduction in defence spending in 1922–23 and again in 1932–33.[6]

The Chanak Crisis

The doctrine of Imperial Defence was critically influenced by two important world events in 1922. The Chanak Crisis of September 1922 involved the threatened attack by Turkish soldiers on British and French troops stationed near Çanakkale (Chanak) to guard the Dardanelles neutral zone. The great powers, led by Britain and France, responded by attempting to invoke the Treaty of Sevres, signed between the Allies and the Ottoman Empire (although never ratified) to control Turkey and the major Mediterranean waterway to Russia.[7] Britain had to abandon its plans for offensive action when the majority of the dominions refused to provide the assistance promised in invoking the treaty. While the Chanak Crisis did not involve the Australian Army directly, it led military planners to again prepare for the overseas involvement of expeditionary military forces. Plan 401, drawn up to meet the Chanak Crisis, was not implemented in 1922, but was eventually employed as the basis for the rapid expansion of military forces including the raising of the 6th Division and the deployment of the AIC in 1939.[8]

The Washington Naval Conference

The second major world event involving the doctrine of Imperial Defence was the Washington Naval Conference from December 1921 to February 1922. The objective of the conference was to restrict the burgeoning sea power of Japan by imposing limits on capital shipbuilding.[9] An immediate consequence was that Britain faced the prospect of restricting the size of the RN. These constraints impacted directly on the RAN which began paying off its submarine force, closing the submarine depot and later scuttling the battle cruiser *Australia* off Sydney Heads.[10] The planning and operation of the Army had to be readjusted, as its already stringent budget was further tightened. According to Official Historian Gavin Long, 'It was decided to reduce the permanent staff of the Army to 1,600 ... maintain the seven Militia divisions at only 25% of their war strength and reduce training to six days in camp and four days at local centres per year.'[11]

Downsizing in 1922

Downsizing in 1922 as a result of the Washington Naval Conference, the Australian Government ordered both components of the Army, the PMF and the Militia, to reduce numbers.[12] As mentioned it also imposed restrictions on Militia training.[13] Fortuitously, recruiting for the citizen Army had been well below expectation and this made the reductions less painful. The Army had a wartime set of establishment numbers and positions (war establishment) and a much reduced version for peacetime. Thus, on paper, the AMF war establishment boasted seven Militia divisions (around 180,000 men) but was actually reduced to a projected strength of 30,000.[14] Within the PMF it was the Staff Corps and the AIC that bore the brunt of the losses. From the Staff Corps, 72 regular officers from a total of 300—some 24%—were compulsorily retired.[15] One of the officers retrenched was Alex B. ('Bandy') MacDonald who had graduated from RMC Duntroon in 1920. After a spell in the wool industry he was invited to rejoin the Staff Corps and, in 1938, Major MacDonald was appointed to command the Darwin Mobile Force (DMF).[16]

The effect of the redundancies on these long-serving officers is difficult to imagine. One Duntroon graduate compulsory retired, George Wootten—later Major General Sir George Wootten, KBE—decided to make the best of his plight and studied law, later becoming a country solicitor. His family, living on a property in the tiny country town of West Wyalong in western NSW, struggled to make ends meet, even once he was qualified and practising. He often received chickens and rabbits as payment for his services and, like so many others; home-grown vegetables supplemented the family diet. Called to the colours when war erupted again,

George Wootten became a distinguished 2nd AIF commander. The redundancies were so far-reaching that even the sons of Lieutenant General Sir Harry Chauvel, the Inspector General, left Australia, seeking a military career in the Indian Army.[17]

The PMF was reduced by 467 (100 officers and 367 other ranks) including, most damagingly, 188 warrant officers. The Staff Corps losses were followed on 30 June 1922 by cuts to the AIC which lost 169 from an establishment of 600—28% of the Corps.[18] There was an immediate and significant casualty as 'training courses for instructors went into abeyance until 1935.'[19] The prospects for the large number of AIC members thrown out of work in 1922 were dismal. Many were Boer and Great War veterans and, while they did receive some compensation, this took the form of superannuation that they could not access until retirement.[20] Some of the staff sergeant majors had trades, many employed by the Army as electrical and mechanical engineers, while others in Ordnance Corps and the Pioneer companies had building qualifications. However, even qualified tradesmen had to rely on finding a suitable vacancy.

One of the 169 staff sergeant majors made redundant was Ernest Henrys who was born in Bourke, western NSW, on 13 October 1899. Henrys enlisted as a 17-year-old and went to France with the 33rd Infantry Battalion. He survived the war and was selected to attend No. 2 School at Liverpool in 1920. He graduated with a solid score of 776 (the highest score was 805 and the lowest 646) and was posted to the 2nd Military District (2 MD) as a staff sergeant major class II (warrant officer class II).[21]

Having successfully graduated and been posted by the Army, Henrys must have assumed that his future was secure. However, by 1922 he was unemployed and returned to western NSW where he trapped rabbits and worked as a plumber until 1927 when he re-enlisted in the PMF.[22] He remained a professional soldier for the rest of his working life. After service in World War II he gained a quartermaster commission and, on 11 October 1954, retired as a major.

While the redundancies were disappointing for those Staff Officers and AIC members personally affected, there was some good news in amongst the gloom. In 1922 the Federal Government agreed to extend the Public Service Superannuation scheme to cover the full-time military services. Soldiers who were made redundant thus received limited financial compensation in recognition of previous service. While the redundant officers did not benefit immediately, they could glean some comfort from the prospect of a small nest-egg on retirement.

Arthur John Coghill

However, the loss of experienced serving members was only one of a number of problems that afflicted the AIC in 1922 and 1923. Many of these problems would have remained largely hidden and certainly un-addressed were it not for a singularly determined individual named Arthur Coghill. In 1925 Major Coghill, a Boer War veteran who had served in South Africa with the 6th Commonwealth Light Horse, used public foray to highlight a number of problems affecting members of the AIC.[23]

Coghill had retired from the Army in 1922 and, almost immediately, prepared a series of petitions that he submitted to the Minister for Defence on behalf of serving AIC officers and NCOs. In one submission entitled 'Suggestions for the elimination of Disabilities and the General Improvement of the Australian Instructional Corps', Coghill listed 19 areas that he recommended be addressed to improve conditions for members of the Corps.[24] The items listed included: pay; the high cost of living; pensions; the standard of personnel; the training of personnel; prospects for promotion; barrack square duties; quartermaster commissions; shortage of instructors; transfers out of the AIC; and the provision of quarters.

As a direct result of Major Coghill's representations, the Military Board investigated each of the 19 suggestions for improvement. Although generally sympathetic to Coghill's cause, the Board eventually recommended to the Minister for Defence that no changes be made. The Board's reasons ranged from financial constraints, such as the prohibitive expense of increases in pay and a separate superannuation scheme, to refusal to change the status quo in some sensitive areas such as honorary commissions.[25] The Military Board submitted its final report on Coghill's list to the Minister in September 1925.[26] To Major Coghill's chagrin, cabinet secrecy meant that the answers provided to the Minister by the Military Board would not be made public.

When the Minister replied to Major Coghill, his answer was framed in the terms used by the Military Board. He told Coghill that 'these matters are being looked into'. Like Coghill, the AIC members he represented interpreted this reply as a rejection of their claims by the Military Board. Whether this was the case or not, the AIC members instigated further action through Major Coghill who expressed his views in another pamphlet entitled 'The Coghill Recognition Fund'.

A copy of this pamphlet soon came to the attention of the Adjutant General who was a member of the Military Board.[27] The pamphlet recorded that, 'at a meeting of over 100 members of the AIC in Melbourne in February 1925, £218 had been raised and presented to Major Coghill for successful labours on behalf of AIC members.' The AIC and its vociferous champion were not going to simply disappear and it was clear that the Minister's platitudes had done nothing to quell their disquiet.

Since, at that time, a warrant officer earned as little as £5 a week, £218 represented around a year's wages—a small fortune to those concerned. The Military Board now regarded Major Coghill as the figurehead of a rogue organisation comprised of AIC quartermasters and warrant officers: 'There is a combined movement among the AIC to seek personal advantages to conditions of service through means expressly forbidden and most prejudicial to discipline.' This last phrase 'prejudicial to discipline' was commonly used in military law and signalled the Board's new tactic—to use military law to resolve the situation. Countering the claims of the pamphlet, the Board's submission to the Minister argued that 'the matter [is] subject to outside influences on service conditions and prejudicial to discipline.'[28]

Recognising that the Minister was unlikely to dismiss any argument that was couched in such terms, the Military Board bolstered its case, further claiming that 'If this matter [is] not dealt with as an issue of discipline, it may lead to a growth of organised propaganda with paid agitators and a species of unionism disastrous to [the] discipline of the permanent forces.'[29] Indeed, there is every reason to believe—and evidence from the Military Board proceedings supports the contention—that discontent was widespread within the AIC at that time. In an Army rooted in British Military Law, however, unauthorised meetings of soldiers clearly spelt sedition.[30] It is some indication of the sorry state of the Army at the time that a meeting attended by more than 100 honorary officers and warrant officers (16% of the AIC) was liable to provoke charges of sedition and incitement to mutiny.

Claims of sedition aside, at the heart of the matter lay the woeful state of the Army's funding. While AIC members had legitimate claims recognised by their superiors, the Military Board was in such an economic straightjacket that it could do little or nothing to improve existing working conditions and was not prepared to consider changes of any other nature.[31] Having reviewed the contents of the pamphlet, the Board considered taking action against Major Coghill, whose name was on the list of retired officers. Coghill had clearly anticipated this action and wisely retired overseas beyond the reach of the Board.

Major Coghill's representations to the Minister produced two significant outcomes. Coghill was informed in writing that his grievances had been considered: 'Such matters as are mentioned by him [Coghill] have already received the consideration of Ministers and the Military Board in framing the organisation of the Military Forces.' But there were no promises of measures to address the issues that he had raised. The second, far less desirable outcome was that the Adjutant General issued a General Order circulated throughout the Army. This made it clear to all members of the Army that there would be severe disciplinary consequences should they choose to infringe regulations, particularly for those who used 'outside influence to obtain changes in the conditions of service.'

The training model

The structure of the new divisional Army was the product of a compromise between the government—keen for a politically and economically acceptable force—and the military's need for a force with sufficient numbers to mount a credible defence. In upgrading the post-war training system, the Military Board established a Central Training Depot (CTD) at Liverpool, NSW. With a new national training corps and new national training depot, the restructured divisional Army inherited a training model dictated by the present and probable future operational constraints. Given the very tight (straitened) economic circumstances of the times, the upgrading of the existing scheme appeared a very practical solution to the system that the AIC was designed to operate.

AIC tasks and duties

The AIC task to 'train the trainers' in all corps throughout the Australian continent required a large organisation of considerable complexity. To fill this role, as previously stated, the Military Board created an establishment of 600 men comprising 41 quartermasters, 21 warrant officers class 1A, 164 warrant officers class 1B, and 374 warrant officers class II.[32] While the AIC's official establishment was 600, in 1922–23 its numbers fell to 559 members. At that time, 153 warrant officers were engaged in regimental duties while 406 performed general instructional duties. A number of those posted to general instruction filled appointments in individual units.[33]

Members of the AIC posted to regimental duties, joined an infantry battalion or a light horse regiment as an officer or NCO. On 24 September 1929, Quartermaster and Honorary Captain Charles Mills, OBE, was appointed Adjutant and Quartermaster of the 3rd Division Signals.[34] AIC NCOs were also appointed to the crucial position of RSM. Interestingly, Honorary Lieutenant George David Duncan (WO1A) was appointed RSM of the 24th Battalion, (The Kooyong Regiment) AMF, on 20 April 1923 rather than to an officer's position.[35]

The principal task for the AIC under the umbrella of 'general instructional duties' involved appointment as an Officiating Area Officer or Area Instructor for one of Australia's 144 training areas. A typical appointment took place in November 1923 when Warrant Officer Class II Charles Deves was appointed Officiating Area Officer, Area 3A (Granville, NSW), 2nd Divisional Area, replacing Warrant Officer Class I William Henry Barham, a Boer War veteran.[36] Officiating Area Officers held overarching responsibility for the practical training of all regimental units within the designated training area of a District Base or a Military District. Their annual reports were used by staff officers to determine the efficiency of citizen Army training.

AIC uniform and corps badge

'You could always tell an AIC man', commented a soldier who served in the interwar period, 'they had a different uniform jacket and badges.'[37] The AIC 'blues' dress was distinct from the conventional AMF

Blue Patrol Jacket uniform in its epaulettes, badge of rank and corps badges. Most distinctive were the jacket epaulettes, which were two half-inch (one centimetre) wide scarlet stripes, with a half-inch gap between them, worn on both shoulders. The crown, the badge of rank, was enclosed in an oval wreath and worn on the right sleeve only.

Fig 3. *Uniform of a Master Gunner, AIC*
Collection of the late Monty Webb, OAM, Monarch Military Museum,
Williamtown, NSW.

The distinctive AIC badge was adopted from 1930 onwards following an Army-wide competition that attracted 57 designs.[38] Major Marmaduke Coats, Adjutant of the 32nd Battalion (The Footscray Regiment), AMF, Footscray, Victoria, wrote:

> All members of the AI Corps attached to this Bn strongly recom-
> mend that the Commonwealth Rising Sun Badge be retained, as
> this badge has been that of the Corps since its inception. It is recom-
> mended ... the crown be raised on a red enamelled background. This
> was the badge worn before the war by Officers of the A and I Staff
> and WOs of the Instructional Staff.[39]

As Coats indicates, from 1921 to 1930 the AIC used the badge previously worn by the A&I Staff. This was a gold 'Rising Sun' badge with the crown set against red enamel. The distinctive uniform of the AIC saw them nicknamed 'Rosella's' for 'the distinctive red stripes on members' epaulettes.'[40]

Fig 4. *Hat badge of the Australian Instructional Corps*
Author's collection.

Operational Command and control

Soldiers are subjected to a rigorous form of discipline to enable them to conduct a variety of directed tasks in war and peace without question. The cornerstone of the administration of discipline during the life of the AIC was Australian Military Law that was embodied in a series

of Australian Military Regulations and Orders.[41] The exercise of command
and control, central to the maintenance of discipline, was delegated to
specifically appointed officers. Known as the 'Powers of Command', they
were normally directly vested in COs usually holding the rank of lieutenant
colonel. Army rules stated very clearly that the CO, in peace and war, was
responsible for the administration and discipline of the unit.[42] The operation
of 'Powers of Command' through the CO was of particular significance to
AIC members who came 'under command' of the CO when posted to a unit.
As previously mentioned, generally they were under the direct command of
the Staff Officers or the AMF/Militia brigade and battalion commanders.[43]

The organisational structure of the AIC was unusual for an Army
corps in which all its members held the same rank and where seniority was
determined by the date of appointment.

It became unique as outlined in Chapter Two when in 1922 the
Corps of Military Staff Clerks, also consisting only of warrant officers and
honorary officers,[44] was absorbed into the Commonwealth Public Service.[45]

A peacetime Army, particularly in an environment devoid of a
discernible threat, is always subject to financial pressures. The new Army
that the generals had set out to create in the 1920s had little or no priority
in the decade that followed with a government strongly committed to
social reconstruction. This was the practical political and financial climate
in which the Army had to work and it was to prove a particularly difficult
basis on which to train for another war. While this decade was to prove
problematic for all concerned, worse was to follow towards the end of the
1920s as the Great Depression reached Australia's shores.

CHAPTER THREE
NOTES

1.   William J. Hughes in *Commonwealth Parliamentary Debates*, 10 September 1919, Vol. 89, p. 12179.

2.   C.E.W. Bean, *In your hands Australians*, Cassell & Company, London (2nd edn), 1919.

3.   *Commonwealth Debates*, Vol. 93, p. 4392.

4.   Dennis et al., *The Oxford Companion to Australian Military History*, p. 307

5.   From 1923 this supremacy of the sea was often known as the 'Blue Water' strategy.

6.   Source: Joan Beaumont, *Australian Defence: Sources and Statistics*, Oxford University Press, Melbourne, 2001, Table 1.2, p. 30.

7.   Radi, '1920–1929', p. 365.

8.   Michael Evans, *From Deakin to Dibb: The Army & the making of Australian Strategy in the Twentieth Century*, Working Paper 113, Land Warfare Studies Centre, Canberra, June 2001, p. 16.

9.   Gordon Greenwood, *Australia, A Social & Political History*, Angus & Robertson, Sydney, 1955 (1978), p. 288

10.   Grey, *A Military History of Australia*, p. 125.

11.   Gavin Long, *Australia in the War of 1939-1945: Series 1 Army, To Benghazi*, Australian War Memorial, Canberra, 1952, p. 5

12.   Report of the Inspector General of the Australian Military Forces, Lieutenant General Sir H.G. Chauvel, GCMG, KCB, Part 1, dated 31 May 1922, 'Peace strength of the Army reduced from 118,000 to 30,000', Item 12.

13.   Grey, *A Military History of Australia,* p. 125

14.   Report of the Inspector General of the Australian Military Forces, Lieutenant General Sir H.G. Chauvel, GCMG, KCB, Part 1, dated 31 May 1922, Item 12.

15.   Long, *To Benghazi,* p. 5.

16.   In World War II he became SX4539 Major A.B. MacDonald.

17.   Grey, *The Australian Army,* p. 76.

18.   Military Order 288-1922, Australian Instructional Corps, Warrant Officers, Discharges, AM Regulation 358(1) xii; and Military Order 228-1922, 'Discharge owing to reduction in establishments'. See Grey, The Australian Army, p. 79.

19.   Grey, *The Australian Army,* p. 78.

20.   Ibid., p. 79.

21.   Military Order 167-1920.

22.   Major M.E. Henrys (retd), son of Ernest Henrys, interview with the author, 11 October 2011.

23.   NAA MP 367/1 Melbourne 1922 Regt. No. 45 Major Arthur John Coghill.

24.   NAA: A2653 1925, Military Board Proceedings, Vol. 2, Agenda Item 135/1923, 'Suggestions for the elimination of Disabilities and the General Improvement of the Australian Instructional Corps'.

25.   NAA: A2653 1925 Military Board Proceedings, Vol. 2, Board Minute on Agenda Item 135/1923, Item 4. 'Recommendations in connection with the High cost of Living Allowance payable to (AIC) members'. These recommendations were submitted on Agenda 70/21 (rejected by Cabinet) and on Agenda 47/23 (rejected by the Minister).

26.   A2653 1925, NAA Military Board Proceedings, Vol. 2, Agenda Item 135/1923, Improvement of Conditions in the Permanent Military Forces (including the AIC).

27.   NAA: A2653 1925, Military Board Proceedings, Vol. 2, Agenda Item 80/1925, 'Use of Outside Influence to obtain changes in conditions of service in the AIC and collective discussion of service conditions', Item 2.

28.   NAA: A2653 1925. Military Board Proceedings, Vol. 2, Agenda Item 80/1925, para 5, p. 2.

29.   Ibid.

30.   Sedition was defined as causing 'disaffection or ill-will by unlawful means' or 'engaging in conduct calculated to stir up a state of dissatisfaction'. Examples included 'maliciously false criticisms calculated to effect change by unlawful means'. See A.N. Lewis, Australian Military Law, Cox Kay & Co., Hobart, 1936, p. 97.

31.   Report of the Inspector General of the Australian Military Forces, Lieutenant General Sir H.G. Chauvel, GCMG, KCB, Melbourne, 31 May 1923, item 24.

32.   Military Order 422-1923 (29/9/23) Permanent Forces-Annual Establishments, 1923-24, (i) Australian Instructional Corps.

33.   Military Order 442-1923, Permanent Forces-Annual Establishments 1923-1924 (i) Australian Instructional Corps, (a) Summary. MO issued 29/2/23. The 153 warrant officers on regimental duty were posted to: Royal Australian Field Artillery, PMF (1), Australian Field Artillery, AMF (37), Royal Australian Garrison Artillery, PMF (33), Australian Garrison Artillery, AMF (9), Royal Australian Engineers, PMF (6), Australian Engineers—Field, AMF (17), Australian Engineers—Fortress, PMF (2), Signals, PMF (14), Australian Medical Corps, PMF (19), Australian Service Corps, PMF (13) and Australian Veterinary Corps, PMF (2). Warrant officers performing general instructional duties included those posted to headquarters staff (24), Officiating Area Officers and Area Instructors (165), Cavalry (65) and Infantry (152).

34.   Military Order 425-1923 Allotment for Duty Officers of the Permanent Forces; Appointment P.B.559/16/833.

35.   Military Order 202-1923 Australian Instructional Corps, Officiating Area Officers, Appointment, P.559/36/117.

36.   Military Order No 514-1923 Australian Instructional Corps, Officiating Area Officers, P.B. 559/15/319. 'No. 298 Warrant Officer (Class II) C. Deves, AIC, is appointed Officiating Area Officer, Area 3A (Granville), 2nd Divisional Area, vice No. 53 Warrant Officer (Class I) W.H. Barham, AIC, dated 5 November 1923'.

37.   N43917, 3rd Battalion, AMF, later NX 126952 Captain Bede Tongs, MM, 2/4 Battalion, AIF, letter to the author, 11 January 2004

38.   NAA, Series Number B1535, Symbol Number 716/2/182, AIC Badge Design, 1930.

39.   Letter from Major M. Coats, AIC, Adjutant 32nd Battalion, Footscray, Victoria, to AHQ, Ref 15/1/596 dated 26 September 1930

40.   Rob Youl, *Swan Street Sappers, 1860-1996: A History of the Engineer Training Depot, Swan Street, Melbourne and of Sappers in Victoria,* HQ Logistic Support Force Engineers, Melbourne, 1995, p. 13..

41.   Replaced by the *Defence Force Discipline Act (DFDA)* in 1982.

42.   Australian Military Orders & Regulations, 53–63.

43.   Military Forces of the Commonwealth, General Orders 1903, No.230, Wednesday 7 October, Instructional Staff, Warrant Officers and Non Commissioned Officers: (d) 'Warrant Officers & Non Commissioned Officers of the Instructional Staff are under the command of the Commanding Officers of those Regiments & Corps to which they are attached."

44.   Military Order 457-1923; Military Staff Clerks (1) Promotion to Warrant Officers (Class I).

45.   Military Order 460-1923, 'AMF, Appointments, Corps of Military Staff Clerks: To be Honorary Lieutenants & Captains'.

CHAPTER FOUR
AIC OPERATING CONDITIONS
1921–1931: TRAINING THE ARMY

Phases of training

Over the period of two decades from 1919 to 1939, Army training was reshaped in three distinct phases. The initial phase, commenced in 1920, recruited the instructors and brought the Universal Trainees into the divisional Army. The middle phase, initiated by the Scullin Government in 1929, suspended the UTS and converted the AMF/Militia to an all-volunteer force. During both these phases while new instructors were appointed individually no new training courses for instructors took place. Effectively both a change of government and the onset of the Great Depression halted any further progress for some years. The final phase commenced in 1935 when the Lyons Government began rebuilding the Army in preparation for war. During this third and final phase the Army initiated a series of special courses in which the AIC resumed compulsory instructor training for all warrant officers posted or inducted into the Corps.

AMF administrative command

During the interwar period, AIC members posted as quartermasters and instructors served all over Australia within the administrative command of the AMF in both fixed locations and mobile formations. Fixed locations included Military Districts, District Bases and schools. There were seven Military Districts:

1st Military District (1 MD) Queensland

2nd Military District (2 MD) NSW and the Australian Capital Territory

3rd Military District (3 MD) Victoria

4thMilitary District (4 MD) South Australia

5th Military District (5 MD) West Australia

6th Military District (6 MD) Tasmania

7th Military District (7 MD) Northern Territory

Prior to 1919, the state-based Military Districts had total control of administration.[1] In 1920, however, District Bases were introduced into the Army's organisational chain. Principally responsible for supplies and logistical support for field force units, District Bases were also involved in coastal defence including the garrison of principal ports.[2]

Formations

Formations, commanded by AHQ, were essentially made up of divisions (around 17,000 men) and brigades (approximately 3000 to 5000 men). An infantry division was made up of three brigades plus support services, and a cavalry (armoured) division, three light horse brigades plus divisional troops.[3] Within the formations, the combat arms, services and branches were allocated to divisions and brigades on peacetime establishments. Practical soldier training took place in all locations and formations.

Every facet of the practical Army training system for soldiers intimately involved the AIC in 'training the trainers'. In 1921 no formal training command existed in the Army. Training was conducted as a directed activity from AHQ in Melbourne, the purview of the Army Director of Training. AIC instructors operated in all the Army Schools and each of the Army formations.

Army Schools

The five Army Schools provided the training of unit commanders and instructors.

RMC, Duntroon, Canberra

Artillery Schools of Instruction, North Head, Sydney

Physical Training School, North Head and Portsea, Victoria[4]

CTD, Liverpool

Small Arms School, Randwick, Sydney[5]

At each of these Army Schools, AIC instructors filled key postings. In 1922 at RMC Duntroon, the assistant instructors, as AIC warrant officers were known, were Warrant Officer Class I William Henry Thomas and 122 Warrant Officer Class I Harold Vere Chumleigh.[6] Harold Chumleigh was appointed RSM to the Corps of Staff Cadets at RMC Duntroon in 1914, a position he held until 1928. An old soldier, Chumleigh had served with the British Army in South Africa (12th Royal Lancers) and India. After migrating to Australia in 1909, he enlisted in the RAA. In 1911 he graduated from the 1st Special School of Instruction and was posted to RMC Duntroon as an assistant instructor specialising in drill, rifle shooting and signalling.[7]

Warrant Officer Chumleigh's influence on the RMC cadets was to be enormous, and he was fondly remembered by Duntroon graduates under the sobriquet 'the Marquis'. Chumleigh trained many officer graduates who served in the Great War and later held senior positions in World War II. Colonel J. E. Lee, DSO MC, author of *Duntroon* refers to Warrant Officer Chumleigh, 'as a first class instructor singularly devoted to his job, a loyal friend and a sympathetic adviser'. Harold Chumleigh was a colourful storyteller, accredited with an equally colourful private life. According to his biographers, 'he was in no small way responsible for the mutual understanding and respect established between the Australian Staff Corps and the AIC during the interwar years of compulsory training.'[8]

Posted to the staff of the Artillery Schools of Instruction in 1922 were 517 Honorary Lieutenant John Edward Hendry, 333 Honorary Lieutenant Arthur Leslie Roberts, MC, and 357 Honorary Lieutenant Leonard Charles Wade.[9] Both John Hendry and Leonard Wade were to have long careers in the Artillery schools, later occupying senior positions. However, following the closure of the CTD in late 1922, it was the Small Arms School at Randwick, NSW, that a great many members of the Corps came to regard as their 'home' base.

From 1922 onwards there were always several AIC members on the staff of the Small Arms School. Early staff members in 1923 were Honorary Lieutenants Reginald Francis G. Edwards,[10] Allan Stefanus Stefanson[11] and Kenneth Beale,[12] and Warrant Officer Class I James Duguid Sherim.[13] James Sherim was a distinguished member of the AIC and a King's Medal champion for competitive rifle shooting several times over.

His ability with the SMLE .303 rifle was amazing, 'He could fire 45 to 50 aimed shots in one minute.'[14] The King's Medal was a highly respected competition that involved the very best rifle shots in the Commonwealth. From its inception in 1924 until 1931, it was won successively by individual AIC members including Sherim who achieved the record score (176/200) and won the medal three times (1927, 1929 and 1931).[15]

As senior staff members, AIC quartermasters were posted to key operational roles in each of these schools. A highly placed AIC member who held senior appointments was Quartermaster and Honorary Major Harold Ordish, DSO. Major Ordish had been the CI of the Small Arms School in 1919 prior to his appointment as the Quartermaster at RMC Duntroon in 1926.[16]

Training in formations

The system for the practical training of soldiers in Australia combined the structure of the operational formations (divisions, brigades, battalions and regiments) with a training scheme that utilised district bases and training areas. The formations of the Army, the divisions and brigades, were scattered throughout the continent. In a similar manner, so too were district bases and the 144 designated official training areas. 'District Bases were responsible for supplies, logistic support of the field force [in the Military District, i.e. the state] and controlling the coastal defence establishments of the major ports.'[17] Throughout the continent AIC quartermasters and instructors were appointed and posted to all formations, districts and official training areas thus ensuring total coverage of the widely dispersed Army. As previously commented upon, teams of AIC warrant officers went to various locations in each state to carry out training on instruction. The Army's system of practical training worked well. Successful students from the Army schools and courses returned to their posted units where they in turn instructed and trained the citizen Army.

While positions within the Army Schools and regimental appointments saw AIC officers and warrant officers exert considerable influence throughout the Army, it was the appointment of its members as Area Training Officers (ATO) that placed the AIC at the top of the practical soldier training tree. The 144 official training areas that covered Australia included almost every suburb and town in the country. An AIC member holding such an appointment could wield considerable influence over practical soldier training. The ATO was an appointment reserved for warrant officers class IA and warrant officers class I who were usually honorary lieutenants or honorary captains. While there were actually 144 designated official training areas in 1923–1924, there were no fewer than 165 ATO appointments.[18] Although ATO appointments were restricted to warrant officers class I, in practice, warrant officers class II often filled the vacancies. The disparity in pay for warrant officers class II who now had the same responsibilities as a warrant officer class I may have led to some instances of dissention.[19]

Army records for the years between the world wars list numerous appointments and transfers in these positions. In Victoria, in addition to his duties as Officiating Officer, Area 39B (Kew), 155 (Warrant Officer Class I) Honorary Lieutenant J. Andrew, 3rd Division, was appointed Officiating Area Officer, Area 39A (Hawthorne), following the posting of Quartermaster and Hon. Major John McArthur, DSO.[20]

Apart from the practical soldier training, regimental appointments also brought the ordinary soldier into contact with the AIC. With the key training roles in battalions and regiments such as Adjutant/Quartermaster and RSM held by AIC members, the AIC became a familiar sight throughout the Army. This was especially true in the rural training areas where AIC members were often the only PMF soldier with whom the Militia had contact. Military Medal (MM) winner Colonel Colin McPherson recalls:

> As an AIC warrant officer I was posted to 21st Australian Light Horse Regiment (Riverina Regiment) with its HQ in Wagga Wagga. We did regular scheduled inspection visits to sub unit locations, HQ [Squadron] at Cootamundra, Stockingbingal and Sydney; 'A' [Squadron] at Narrandra, Griffith & Barellan; 'B' [Squadron] at Holbrook, Urana and Culcairn; 'C' [Squadron] at Tumbarumba, Gundagi and Tarcutta.[21]

Equipment

Despite the reforms of the divisional Army, much of its substance remained deeply embedded in the past. This was particularly true of the equipment with which the new Army trained. At the conclusion of the Great War, the 1st AIF returned to Australia with equipment for five divisions.[22] This well-used equipment was then distributed to units throughout the country.[23] Such were the economies influencing the purchase and development of defence equipment for the next 20 years that many soldiers of the 2nd AIF went to war with rifles that had returned to Australia with the 1st AIF.[24] Trevor Harper, a soldier with the 55th/53rd Australian Infantry Battalion, AIF, recalled going into the combat area of New Guinea in 1939 with a single shot .303

Lee Enfield rifle stamped 1911.[25] However, during the inter-war period the Lithgow, NSW, Small Arms Factory commenced production of rifles and it is possible Trevor Harper's rifle was fully functional despite its age.

Training and modernisation 1921–1929

With the opening of the CTD at Liverpool on 11 July 1921, Army training received a major boost. The depot's objective was to conduct a range of training courses for both recruits and instructors.[26] For the short period of its existence it was able to achieve this until it became a victim of government budget cuts. No. 1 Course was run from August 1921 until February 1922 with 70 students. Due to its high standards only 20 graduated.[27] No. 2 Course commenced in late 1920 but was abandoned when the Military Board decided to close the CTD temporarily. The CTD finally fell victim to budget cuts, closing in 1922, and as previously mentioned there were no courses conducted for instructors over the next 13 years.[28] Consequently the levels of competence of instructors appointed throughout the Army during this period varied.

The overall training plan for the new divisional Army suffered considerably because of the early closure of the CTD, although it did not altogether prevent the conduct of training to national standards.[29] The four remaining Army Schools continued to conduct training courses, many of which also trained AIC instructors in corps competencies.[30]

The demise of the CTD affected the Small Arms School because cancellation of courses meant greater competition for places at SAS. Initially, the Small Arms School only trained the AIC instructors in weapons used by the infantry and cavalry (light horse) and in minor tactics. For several years qualifying courses run at the Randwick centre concentrated on the rifle and bayonet, light gun (Lewis and Hotchkiss), the Vickers machine-gun and special weapons training.[31] This expanded from 1927 onwards when a catering course was held from 14 to 25 February.[32] Later that year the first

Australian tanks arrived and the 1st Tank Section of the Australian Tank Corps was formed.[33] With RMC Duntroon training the majority of PMF officers joining the Australian Staff Corps from 1920 onwards it was the non-commissioned instructional staff, drawn almost exclusively from the AIC, that provided the practical training for these future officers.

Although the decade 1921–1929 was characterised by lack of opportunity and long-term employment problems for RMC graduates, the period did provide limited opportunities for AIC instructors. The AIC continued to exert an influence on the training of officer cadets since, from a total instructional staff (including civilians) of fewer than 20, there were always six AIC honorary officers and warrant officers at RMC performing both administrative and instructional duties.[34] These included 283 Warrant Officer Class I C.M. Knudsen, who was appointed instructor on 4 April 1928.[35] In a more specialist role was Warrant Officer Class I George Webster, DCM, who was an engineer instructor.[36] There was also a strong AIC influence at the other two permanent schools. Both the Physical Training Schools and the Artillery Schools of Instruction had AIC members assigned as instructors and students.[37]

Apart from the graduates of No. 1 and 2 Schools in 1920, all new warrant officers appointed to the AIC from 1922 to 1935 were experienced soldiers with prior wartime PMF or Militia service. No. 979 Sergeant N.E. Hutton, RAE, was appointed staff sergeant major III (on probation), promoted to the rank of warrant officer class II (on probation) and transferred to the AIC on 1 January 1927.[38] New warrant officers usually received refresher training prior to their appointment as instructors.

The AIC task encompassed training themselves, their permanent colleagues and the officers and NCOs of the citizen Army. Considerable pressure was applied to the individual AIC members to qualify (normally prior to joining the AIC) and re-qualify in all-corps (specialist) subjects, since pay and promotion depended on qualifications.[39]

Training of the PMF[40] formed a considerable portion of the work of the Small Arms School as the schedule of courses for the year 1928–1929 suggests:[41]

Serial Letter	Course Number	Nature of Course	Dates	Duration Days
A	4	Rifle & Bayonet & Section Leading Qualifying Course	25.7.1928– 4.9.1928	42
B	4	Light Automatic & Section Leading Qualifying Course	25.7.1928– 4.9.1928	42
C	11	Vickers Machine Gun Qualifying Course	7.11.1928– 18.12.1928	42
D	5	Rifle & Bayonet & Section Leading Qualifying Course	12.3.1929– 24.4.1929	44
E	5	Light Automatic & Section Leading Qualifying Course	12.3.1929– 24.4.1929	44
F	6	Rifle & Bayonet & Section Leading Qualifying Course	1.5.1929– 12.6.1929	43
G	6	Light Automatic & Section Leading Qualifying Course	1.5.1929– 12.6.1929	43

What is clearly evident from the schedule of courses, is that with the same course held in different states, it means by inference that 'travelling or mobile teams' of AIC instructors had to go to the various locations. Thus, with each of the Army schools having AIC instructors and the 'outreach programme', it is very evident the influence of the corps throughout the Army at that time was considerable.

Early modernisation and mechanisation

Despite severe budgetary restrictions, the Australian Army had made modest efforts to modernise by introducing mechanised transport and armour in the period 1921–1929. Reliance on horses to draw the guns and transport stores was recognised as a problem late in the decade. In his 1928 Annual Report, the Inspector General pointed out that 'There [are] insufficient horses in the entire continent to undertake all the tasks required by the Army.'[42]

The Army had commenced the introduction of mechanisation and motorisation in 1927 when the medium artillery began training with eight Hathi tractors made by Thorneycroft in Britain. Concurrently, the artillery survey sections took delivery of four 20 cwt Bean vans. For motorised transport, the Army was provided with five 30 cwt Thorneycroft light lorries.[43] It was the task of the AIC instructors at the Motor Transport Wing, Australian Service Corps (ASC) and Quartermaster and Administrative School, to train Army personnel to operate these vehicles before they came into service.[44]

In 1928 cavalry (light horse regiments) commenced the transition from horses to tanks. Lieutenant E.W. Lamperd, Staff Corps, and Warrant Officer Class II F.H. Brown, AIC, had been sent to England to undertake training with the Royal Tank Corps.[45] This training was the prelude to the arrival in Australia of the four Vickers medium tanks, purchased from Britain complete with ammunition and spares, for the sum of £7,200. Based at the Small Arms School in Randwick, these armoured vehicles were crewed and maintained by the AIC until sufficient personnel had been trained to form the 1st Tank Section of the Australian Tank Corps in 1929.[46] It was no coincidence that at this time the CI of the school was Major Horace Robertson who had undergone training at the Royal Tank Corps Central School at Woolwich after his staff college year in England.[47]

All-corps diversified training

In addition to infantry, cavalry, engineer and signals training, the AIC also provided instruction for the various service corps.[48] AIC members boasted a broad variety of qualifications. No. 240 Warrant Officer Class

I S.O. Smith was a qualified meat inspector, having passed a Meat & Pure Food Inspection Course held at East Sydney Technical College in 1927.[49] Similarly, Quartermaster and Honorary Captain Daniel R. Glasgow, MC (1 MD), Quartermaster and Honorary Captain Charles P. Grieve, MC (2 MD), and Quartermaster and Honorary Major William W. Tracy (3 MD) were authorised to issue Mechanical Transport Drivers' Permits.[50] The Army band was not neglected by the Corps with the promotion of 832 Bandmaster Temporary/Warrant Officer Class II J.P. O'Toole.[51] In 1928 there were AIC instructors at the ASC and Quartermaster and Administrative School, Sturt Street, South Melbourne. The school had four wings: ASC, Motor Transport, Cooking and Catering, and Administration. The instructor of the Motor Transport Wing was 103 Honorary Lieutenant A.A. Browne while the Instructor Catering and Cooking Wing was 554 Warrant Officer Class II Thomas H. Peddle.[52]

Royal Visit 1927

At the celebrations to mark the opening of Parliament House in Canberra on 9 May 1927, the combined services staged a military parade reviewed by the Duke of York, later to become King George VI. The Army established a large camp at Red Hill, Australian Capital Territory (ACT) to accommodate all the troops.[53] The AIC provided several honorary officers in key positions to oversee the administration of the camp including the Supply Officer, Quartermaster and Honorary Captain Charles P. Grieve, MC, and the Brigade Quartermaster Sergeant, Warrant Officer Class I S.T. Fletcher.[54] Most of the senior positions in the infantry group of six companies were filled by AIC honorary officers and instructors. RSM of the infantry battalion was Warrant Officer Class I A.G. Dowsett; the Regimental Quartermaster Sergeant W.J. Stinson; and the Messing Officer Warrant Officer Class II H.J. Gubbins. In A Company the Company Quartermaster Sergeant was Warrant Officer Class II Donald F. Berman, DCM; and in B Company the Company Quartermaster Sergeant was Warrant Officer Class II A.J. Raffan. C, D, E and F companies each had AIC members as Company Quartermaster Sergeants. Warrant officer instructors were also posted to the battalions to sharpen the soldiers' drill sufficiently to impress both the Army General Staff and the future king.

AIC problems resurface

AIC members had historically proven willing to advance claims for an improvement to their conditions of service to authorities as high as the Minister for Defence. Medical claims were to rise to the forefront in the years leading up to the outbreak of World War II and they would prove no less determined to seek fair compensation where they perceived this was required. Injuries, accidents and illnesses suffered by soldiers on duty were subject to exhaustive investigative procedures instigated by the Military Board. Any reported injury, accident or illness had to be keenly investigated, statements taken, professional opinions sought where necessary, and a report compiled. Unless the incident was dealt with summarily by the CO, a report relating to an injury, accident or illness would lead to a Court of Inquiry. Once Court of Inquiry findings were promulgated, depending on the injuries sustained, a Medical Board could be assembled to determine compensation. Both Court of Inquiry findings and Medical Board recommendations were forwarded to the Military Board for confirmation.

Financial judgments on medical conditions at the time reflect the lack of funds available to the Army in the interwar period. One soldier, 1707 Warrant Officer Class II L.B. McHenry, suffered articular rheumatism owing to overseas war service. Found to be medically unfit in 1931 and discharged on medical grounds, he was denied transfer to the War Disability Supernumerary List because there were no clerical jobs available in 5 MD, possibly due to financial constraints.[55]

The case of 657 Warrant Officer Class II R.J. Kent was handled with a similar lack of sympathy. After travelling several hours in the rain as a member of the escort for the visiting Prince of Wales in June 1920, Kent claimed that he had contracted influenza and pleurisy. Following two operations, medical officers recommended that he be sent to a warmer climate for two months' convalescence, but this did not occur.[56] Posted to RMC Duntroon as RQMS and assistant instructor in artillery, Warrant Officer Kent contracted tuberculosis (TB).[57] After due consideration, the Military Board decided that 'there was no evidence that the TB infection was acquired on service' and no compensation was paid.[58]

In another case, 141 Warrant Officer Class I R.T. Jones was injured in a motorcycle accident in 1913 while performing his military duties and, in April 1930, was found to be medically unfit.[59] Assessed as being 35% permanently disabled (55% disability for civil employment), he was paid £383 5s 0d. in a lump sum compensation.[60] Warrant Officer Jones disputed the Medical Board findings, arguing that, 'since he had been an engine driver before his 20 years service in the Army, his present medical condition prevented him from returning to his previous civilian occupation.' Despite his arguments, the Military Board remained adamant, the Director General of Medical Services commenting that it was 'very liberal ... as compensation for a sprained ankle received over 17 years ago.'[61]

The outcome of another case demonstrates the way the Military Board dealt with medical injuries inflicted while the soldier was on duty. While on a bivouac near Newcastle, NSW, with the 2/41st Battalion, AMF, on 7/8 March 1931, 232 Warrant Officer Class I William Gill suffered an injury to his shin that was later aggravated by minor knocks on the Vickers machine-gun during his instructional duties.[62] The injury developed into an indolent ulcer that resulted in his admission to the Prince of Wales Hospital in Sydney later that year. Despite the injury, Warrant Officer Gill continued 'light duties' and wore slacks (rather than leggings) at a bivouac of the

35th/33rd Battalion, AMF, in November 1931. He remained on duty for the next 10 days before reporting sick and being sent to hospital. The Court of Inquiry found that his accident took place while he was on duty and therefore his claim for payment was sustained. Evidence to support Warrant Officer Gill's claim was presented by three witnesses, with the Court taking from 3 to 12 March 1932 to hear witnesses, formulate its decision and issue its findings.

Despite an increase in the defence budget under the Lyons Government, the Military Board continued to operate under tight fiscal arrangements and worked hard to avoid unnecessary expenditure. While recruiting, arming and training the armed forces may have been a priority, conditions of service were far lower down the list, particularly in terms of settling the medical claims of military members, as members of the AIC had already discovered. That the fiscal climate had not improved was highlighted in 1938 by the cases of two warrant officers who contracted appendicitis and sought reimbursement for the fees of the attending surgeon.

Stationed at Clare, South Australia, in 1938, 538 Warrant Officer Class II R.W. Sparrow was diagnosed as suffering acute appendicitis.[63] Raymond Woodall Sparrow had joined the 1st AIF aged 16 and served in France and Belgium with the 43rd Battalion. In 1918 he joined the PMF as a warrant officer instructor and was appointed RSM of the 9th Light Horse Regiment. He was a champion rifle shot of the Army in 1925 and in 1936 was an assistant instructor at RMC Duntroon before transfer to South Australia.

Warrant Officer Sparrow was immediately admitted to Clare Hospital and his appendix removed some three hours later. Commenting on his medical condition, a medical practitioner, Dr Sangster, later reported that 'it would have been very risky to have delayed the operation for any length at all.'[64] The operating doctor submitted a claim of £21 to the Army for performing the operation. However the Army declined to pay the operating fee on the grounds that 'Military Financial Regulations and Instructions,

Paras. 234-238 provide only for payment of hospital maintenance fees and do not provide for reimbursement of fees charged by medical practitioners for operations.'[65]

The Army's refusal to pay Dr Sangster's invoice and the subsequent rejection of Raymond Sparrow's claim some two years later, provide some indication of the tight financial restrictions imposed by the Treasury which were observed to the letter. This strict application of financial regulations obviously benefited the Army, but it did so without any regard for the damage to morale of PMF soldiers at a time when there was increasing pressure to train new Militia recruits. The size of the Army had increased exponentially from 29,262 in 1935 to 42,895 by 1938.[66] To his credit, Warrant Officer Sparrow overlooked the Board's callousness and continued to serve in the Army throughout World War II and beyond.[67]

An overwhelming sense of duty to his posted Militia unit saw 2610 Warrant Officer Class II Sydney Alfred Moore LeServe proceed to camp despite being ill (sub-acute appendicitis) in March 1939.[68] With the 15th Light Horse Regiment struggling to cope with a significant increase in numbers due to the looming possibility of war, Warrant Officer LeServe persuaded the Regimental Medical Officer (RMO) to allow him to attend camp at Grafton, NSW, on light duties. Unfortunately, his condition deteriorated and he developed acute appendicitis. Sydney LeServe was transported back to Lismore where his appendix was removed at the Lismore Base Hospital. Had he given priority to his health rather than to his posted unit, Warrant Officer LeServe would have proceeded on sick leave and missed the camp. At the point at which he became seriously unwell, Sydney LeServe would have been transported to the Prince of Wales Hospital at Randwick in Sydney.

LeServe sought reimbursement for the surgeon's fee and his claim was submitted to the Military Board. The Board's decision appears to have been determined solely on the basis of financial considerations. Warrant Officer

LeServe's commanding general wrote an explanatory note to the Military
Board to provide substance to LeServe's claim, arguing that,

> Had he proceeded from Lismore to Sydney for treatment at the
> Prince of Wales Hospital at departmental expense, he would have
> avoided the local professional fees of £17/17/00 [but] would also
> have incurred to the department the following fares and travel-
> ling allowances: fares £5/19/9 + travelling allowance 16/2d, total
> £6/15/11. The [hospital administration] claim for £5/4/00 (being
> £1/1/11 less) from Lismore Hospital has been paid by the DFO
> [Departmental Finance Officer] [because it] does not exceed
> the amount the department would have been charged at a public
> hospital.[69]

Warrant Officer LeServe sent his surgeon's invoice (for £17 17s 0d)
to the Army for payment but the Military Board refused to pay for his
operation. In a submission from the Major General Commanding the 1st
Cavalry Division to the Military Board he advised that the Deputy Director
General Medical Services was of the opinion that the 'illness [was] deemed
as not contracted on duty'.[70] After refusing to seek Ministerial authority for
payment, based on the advice of the Finance Member, the Military Board
subsequently ruled that 'the cost of operations involving the administration
of anaesthetic cannot be admitted as a charge against public funds.'[71]

On the maximum wage of £5 18s 2d per week,[72] this conscientious
warrant officer who opted to attend a camp with his soldiers instead of going
on sick leave, must have regarded the payment of such a large sum (£17 17s 0d
would have been the equivalent of several months' wages), as financially
crippling.[73] However, despite this appalling treatment, LeServe continued
his Army service, enlisting in the 2nd AIF where he was commissioned as a
lieutenant in the 2nd/17th Australian Infantry Battalion which served in the
Western Desert, enduring the Siege of Tobruk and battles against Rommel's
Afrika Korps including El Alamein. The battalion returned to Australia
with the 9th Division before embarking for New Guinea and later British

North Borneo in the campaigns against the Japanese. Following World War II LeServe was promoted captain and continued to serve in the Royal Australian Infantry Corps until his retirement.

The common thread running through the earlier medical histories of Warrant Officers McHenry, Jones, Kent and Gill, and the more recent cases of Warrant Officers Sparrow and LeServe is their unremitting devotion to duty, despite the injuries that each suffered and their callous treatment by the Military Board. These were experienced, battle-hardened soldiers who, despite being paid the same wages as manual labourers, continued to serve with loyalty and devotion to duty despite the apparently heartless attitude of their employer.

The Corps in 1929

In the eight years from 1921 to 1929, the AIC emerged from the shadows of the A&I Staff to stamp its own brand of practical training on the citizen Army. The fledgling organisation, which had weathered the great purge of 1922, had become a strong, self-confident corps successfully discharging its task of providing practical training of the new divisional Army. As the waves of Universal Trainees joined the AMF each year, the size of the Army had significantly increased. Despite its corresponding lack of growth, the AIC had kept pace with the increasing training needs of the burgeoning citizen Army.

This came to an abrupt halt in 1929 when the political balance of power shifted away from the conservative parties and the Australian Labor Party (ALP) swept into government. It was the policy of the new ALP Government, led by James Scullin, to have an Army based totally on volunteers rather than conscripts. Through a simple government administrative decision in 1930, the operating conditions of the AIC were drastically changed for almost the whole of the next decade.

CHAPTER FOUR
NOTES

1.   Dennis et al., *The Oxford Companion to Australian Military History*, p. 395.

2.   Grey, *Australian Brass*, p. 50.

3.   Dennis et al, *The Oxford Companion to Australian Military History*, p. 187.

4.   MBI G61 Preliminary Courses of Instruction 1927–1928 were conducted at Portsea.

5.   Report of the Inspector General of the Australian Military Forces, Lieutenant General Sir H.G. Chauvel GCMG, KCB, dated 31 May 1921,Item 45, the Royal Military College, and Item 46, Schools of Instruction and Training Depots.

6.   Military Order 2-1923: AIC Transfers.

7.   Military Order 52-1911, Special School of Instruction For The Training of Candidates for Appointment to the Instructional Staff (W & NCOs) Defence Act, Section 21B.

8.   J.P. Fielding and J.H. Thyer, 'Chumleigh, Harold Vere (1880-1970)', *ADB*. http:/adp.anu.edu.au/biography/chumleigh-harold-vere-5592/text9505, accessed 21 October 2011

9.   Military Order 482-1922: Master Gunners Course 30 October 1922 to 2 December 1922.

10.   Military Order 90-1923 : AIC Promotions.

11.   Military Order 426-1923: AIC Transfers.

12.   Military Order 443-1923: AIC Transfers.

13.   Military Order 225-1923: AIC Promotions.

14.   Newton, *The Australian Instructional Corps,* Australian Infantry Magazine, October 2013-April 2014, pp 56-67

15.   Military Order 334 of 1924 incorporated provisions of the UK Army Order 174 of 1923 for the award of the King's Medal. From 1923 to 1988, through amended Military and Australian Army Orders, the Australian awards were made under British Army rules.

16.   Military Order 520-1926: Award of the Meritorious Service Medal. The MSM was awarded for 22 years efficient, faithful, valuable and meritorious service in the PMF. To be eligible the recipient must previously have been awarded the LSGCM (Long Service and Good Conduct Medal).

17.   Grey, *Australian Brass,* p. 50.

18.   They were posted in the following numbers: 1 MD, 20; 2 MD, 63; 3 MD, 45; 4 MD, 17; 5 MD, 12; 6 MD, 8; to a total of 165

19.   Military Order 18-1922; Australian Instructional Corps, Appointments as Area Officiating Officers: Training Area 31A Charters Towers, 11th Mixed Bde, WO II G.C. Ashton vice WO II T. Howard, MM, dated 5/11/22. (A 'Mixed' Brigade consisted of both Infantry Battalions and Light Horse Regiments).

20.   Australian Army Order 107-1925.

21.   Colonel C.W. McPherson, MM, interview with the author, 25 November 2002.

22.   Grey, *The Australian Army,* p74.

23.   Grey, *A Military History of Australia*, p. 134.

24.   Long, *To Benghazi*, p. 40.

25.   N247472, later NX196764 Private Trevor Harper, 55th/ 53rd Battalion, AIF, interview with the author, 2 February 2005.

26.   Newton, T*he Australian Instructional Corps*, p. 36

27.   Ibid., p. 38.

28.   Ibid., p. 39.

29.   Report of the Inspector General of the Australian Military Forces, Lieutenant General Sir H.G. Chauvel, GCMG, KCB, Part 1, dated 31 May 1922, Item 58, the Central Training Depot.

30.   Military Order 86-1922, 'Central School of Physical Training; 1/22 & 2/22 Preliminary Courses of Instruction in Physical Training & Correlated Subjects; Qualifying AIC members included T/QM & Hon Capt William Martin McKay & WO II F.E. Stammer, MM.'

31.   Military Order 236-1923, Small Arms School, Courses for Permanent Forces for the Year 1923-24.

32.   Australian Army Order 155-1927.

33.   Paul Handel, *Dust, Sand & Jungle, A History of Australian Armour During Training & Operations,* RAAC Memorial & Tank Museum, Puckapunyal, Victoria, 2003, p. 4.

34.   Military Order 422-1922; Permanent Forces—Annual Establishments 1923-1924; (i) Australian Instructional Corps, (b) Detail; 2nd Military District, Royal Military College. There were six staff sergeants major 2nd or 3rd Class and one RQMS.

35.   Australian Army Order 179-1928.

36.   Australian Army Order 397-1928.

37.   Military Order 422-1922; Permanent Forces—Annual Establishments 1923-1924; (i) Australian Instructional Corps, (b) Detail; 2nd Military District. At the Artillery Schools of Instruction there were two 1st Class master gunners, staff sergeants major 1st Class (IA) and one 2nd or 3rd Class master gunner, staff sergeant major Class IB or II and two battery sergeants major.

38.   Australian Army Order 42-1927

39.   Australian Army Order 240-1928: Examination Results—No.4 Army Anti-Gas School; Engineers Depot, Moore Park, NSW, Practical (Drill & Inspection) Theoretical (Written). Lists 22 AIC members and 1 RAE.

40.   The primary task of the AIC was to train officers, warrant officers and NCOs of the citizen army so that they, in turn, could train their troops. For example, in 1922 in Queensland, the AIC provided instructors at Enoggera for a local small arms course for citizen officers and senior cadet officers. Later that month a similar course was held in Victoria.

41.   Australian Army Order 161-1928.

42.   Report of the Inspector General of the Australian Military Forces, Lieutenant General Sir H.G. Chauvel, Part 1, Melbourne, 31 May 1928, Item 61(b).

43.   Ibid., 31 May 1927, Item 66.

44.   Australian Army Order 412-1928.

45.   Report of the Inspector General of the Australian Military Forces, Lieutenant General Sir H.G. Chauvel, Part 1, Melbourne, 31 May 1928, Appendix (B).

46.   Dennis et al., *The Oxford Companion to Australian Military History,* p. 50.

47.   Jeffrey Grey, *Australian Brass, The Career of Lieutenant General Sir Horace Robertson,* Cambridge Press, 1992, p 60.

48.   Australian Army Order 25-1926, 'Army Signal School, Liverpool, 10th November—15th December 1925: Part I Cable Wagon School & Part II General Signalling, 503 SSM 3rd Class (WO II) Hon. Lt. W.S. Roddick.'

49.   Australian Army Order 177-1928, 'Meat & Pure Food Inspection Course held at East Sydney Technical College 1927, 240 SSM 2nd Class (WO I) S.O. Smith, AIC.'
        Australian Army Order 241-1928: Serial EQ Army Catering Course, Randwick 16th-28th April 1928: Lists 5 AIC members & 1 RAA.

50.   Australian Army Order 111-1927, 'Mechanical Transport Drivers' Permits; Authorised to issue Mechanical Transport Drivers' Permits (A.M. Form M.T.9) Class III and II.'

51.   Australian Army Order 89-1928, 'Australian Instructional Corps; Promotion, 832 Bandmaster (T/WO II) J.P. O'Toole.'

52.   Australian Army Order 358-1928.

53.   Australian Military Forces; Infantry Group Special Order, Military Camp, Canberra, 9 May 1927; Appendix I Infantry Group HQ: RSM WO I A.G. Dowsett, RQMS W.J. Stinson, Mess Officer WO II H.J. Gubbins; A Company CQMS WO II D.F. Berman, DCM; B Company CQMS WO II A.J. Raffan.

54.   Australian Military Forces; Infantry Group Special Order, Military Camp, Canberra, 9 May 1927; Appendix II: Canberra Camp Organisation.

55.   NAA, B 1535,Item 827/14/11, L.B. McHenry.

56.   NAA, B 1535, Item 738/3/120R. J. Kent.

57.   'R.J. Kent, SSM 3rd Class (WO II), RQMS & Asst. Inst. in Arty. to Adjutant etc. Royal Military College, Victoria Barracks, Sydney', Compensation No. 657 SSM R.J. Kent, AIC, dated 23 June 1932.

58.   Ruling of the Finance Member of the Military Board, Item 4, Memo to the Military Board, Agenda Item 3-1933, dated 6 January1933.

59.   NAA, B 1535, Item 738/4/38 R.T. Jones.

60.   Department of Defence, 738/4/15; 4596, 'Claim for Compensation on account of ex No. 141 S.S.M. 2nd Class (W.O. I) R. Jones, AIC, dated 22 April 1931.'

61.   Department of Defence Minute Paper, 'F5/IM/19; D 738/4/15: Subject: Ex No.141 Staff Sergeant Major 2nd Class (Warrant Officer 1) R. Jones, AIC—Compensation.'

62.   NAA, B 1535, Item 729/3/240 W. Gill.

63.   Lieutenant Colonel Raymond Woodall Sparrow, details of service, letter to the author from Lionel R. Sparrow (son), 11 January 2003.

64.   Letter from the Solicitor General to the Secretary of the Military Board, Reference W3141, No. 48 of 1941, dated 8/7/41; Military Financial Regulations, Regulations 95, 96, 97 & 101: 'Hospital Treatment' of Members of the Permanent Military Forces: Whether Includes Surgical Operations, Opinion.

65.   NAA, A472/6, Control Symbol W3141, R.W. Sparrow, AIC, WOII, Payment of Surgical Fees, 1941.

66.   Millar, *Australia's Defence*, Appendix B; also Grey, *The Australian Army*, p. 101.

67.   In 1939 Raymond Sparrow was commissioned lieutenant and became the Adjutant of 13th Light Horse Regiment. In 1940, promoted captain, he became Adjutant and Officer Commanding the RAASC School at Geelong, Victoria. After conducting field trials with Darwin-based troops (1943–44), Captain Sparrow was appointed Deputy Assistant Quartermaster General (Maintenance) at AHQ and served with the 1st Army in New Guinea as a major. Sparrow retired from the Army in 1953 as a lieutenant colonel.

68.   NAA, B 1535, 738/3/452, WOII S.A.M. LeServe, Non Payment of Surgical Fees.

69.   Letter from Major General Commanding 1st Cavalry Division to Secretary, Military Board, Reference 429/2/1302 dated 31 July 1939, Subject: Illness No. 2610 WO II S.A.M. LeServe, AIC.

70.   NAA B1535, Control Symbol 738/3/452; 492.2.1302 Letter of 31 July 1939 from Major General Commanding 1st Cavalry Division to the Secretary of the Military Board.

71.   NAA, B1535, Control Symbol 738/3/452, S. A.M. LeServe, 1939, Letter from Military Board to Eastern Command, Reference 738/3/452 dated 5 December 1939.

72.   Military Board Instruction F84; Effect of the Financial Relief Act 1935 on the Pay of Permanent Military Forces; Warrant Officers, Australian Instructional Corps; MFR & I 72, Warrant Officers Class II, maximum £359 per annum, minimum £240 per annum.

73.   The basic wage in the six capital cities at that time averaged £3 19s 0d per week (£206 pa). See John Barrett, *We Were There: Australian Soldiers of World War II tell their stories*, Penguin Books, Melbourne, 1987, p. 104.

Chapter Five
Training the Army in the Scullin
years 1929-1932

The Scullin Labor Government comes to power, 1929

Years of change and financial famine for the Australian Army characterize the period of the Scullin Government from 1929 to 1932. The change from a largely conscript Army to a voluntary Army massively reduced numbers, particularly as thousands of conscripted soldiers took their discharge. The government's goal of a considerable reduction in expenditure was achieved despite the huge recruiting drive that subsequently followed to source volunteers. No sooner had the dust settled when the Great Depression reached Australia cutting all government wages. The cuts to wages were followed by yet another sizable reduction in the numbers of the PMF.

Compulsory part-time military service had been a rite of passage for young Australian men from 1911 onwards. That service ceased immediately on 12 October 1929 when the Scullin Labor Government assumed power.[1] It was a legacy of the bitter conscription debates of 1916 and 1917 which had produced an ALP defence policy that now opposed any form of call-up, whether for home defence or overseas service. From 1920 onwards federal ALP politicians had vehemently opposed the manner (involving conscription) in which the new divisional Army was to be raised, and 'the Ministers who brought forward the modest defence plans of 1920 and 1921 were described by some Labor members as militarists and war mongers.'[2]

Since one of the first executive acts of the new government had been to suspend the UTS for men and youths, the Military members of the Council of Defence and the Military Board had then agreed to 12 specifications which would shape future Australian military forces:

1. The nucleus of the approved organisation should be maintained, but with a reduced strength of 35,000 Citizen Forces (to be called Militia in future) and 7,000 Senior Cadets.

2. Voluntary Regimental Cadet Detachments of 20 per cent strength of the parent unit should be raised.

3. A period of annual training of sixteen days, divided into eight days' camp and eight days' home training, should be allowed.

4. The same rates of pay should remain in force, except that all privates should be paid 4 shillings per day, including recruits who previously received 3 shillings per day.

5. Liberal allowance should be made for skill-at-arms and other military competitions in addition to the pay of specialists of all units.

6. Provision should be made for more attractive and better fitting uniforms, with regimental badges, buttons, etc, to aid in the development of *esprit de corps.*

7. A gradual provision should be made of modern equipment to keep in progress with scientific and mechanical developments.

8. The existing strengths of administrative and instructional staffs should be maintained.

9. All establishments and institutions should be continued on whatever numbers may be found with experience to be necessary for the maintenance of the efficiency of the new force.

10. A modified battalion organisation and staffs to administer recruiting organisations and promote local Citizens' Committees should be maintained.

11. The required organisation for some form of Army reserve should be inaugurated to replace the unit non-effective establishment.

12. Enlistment of Militia and Cadets should commence in January 1930, with provision for home training of four days in the period January–June 1930.[3]

As a result of the changes introduced by the Council of Defence and Military Board, the strength of the AMF/Militia dropped from 47,564 (of whom 40,650 were compulsory trainees) in 1929[4] to 25,785 (of whom 1,669 were PMF) in 1930.[5]

Training 1929–1932

The Army training program was structured to transform civilians into trained soldiers in four years. The four year programme was the cornerstone of the UTS of the AMF/Militia throughout the decade from 1921 to 1929. Naturally, the training program for AIC instructors had been structured around this four-year cycle. From 1929 onwards this formula for training was still used, but the fluctuations in conscripted soldiers who were now being demobilized and new volunteer soldiers being enlisted completely disrupted the previous stability of the program.

The release of thousands of Universal Trainees by the Scullin Government significantly altered the training duties of the AIC. Quartermasters and their staff struggled with the collection of gear and equipment previously issued to the trainees while, at the same time, attempting to deal with recruiting which had commenced on a grand scale. While the discharge/demobilisation schedule was getting into full swing, the new much shorter training day allotments, eight days in camp and eight days' home training, severely restricted the amount that could be taught to new recruits within that time. Throughout this time the loss of quartermasters and instructors through redundancies seriously challenged the ability of the Corps to adequately train the PMF and the AMF/Militia.

Despite all the difficulties facing the AIC, the extent of AMF/Militia training and instruction achieved in this period was enormous. Instead of dealing with an annual intake of approximately 15,000 young men, the intake dropped to fewer than 2,000. However, the cancellation of the UTS produced a different work situation for the quartermasters of the corps. Having prepared to receive the 1930 intake, with intakes from the previous three years already inducted, the immediate cessation of the UTS now saw the AIC quartermasters of the PMF struggle to discharge thousands of young men.

In spite of the assurances of Item 8 of the Scheme of Volunteer Training for the Army, 1930, which stipulated that 'existing strengths of administrative and instructional staffs should be maintained', the AIC was significantly affected by the changes introduced by the Scullin Government. The burden of overseeing a large number of discharges in 1929–30 and the practical training of new recruits in a smaller Army fell directly on the warrant officers of the AIC. However, even a smaller Army did not result in a diminished training obligation. In fact, the commitment increased because of the need to induct and train all the new recruits, as well as supervise large numbers of discharges. While there were fewer battalions and fewer depots, the training task now had to be undertaken by a smaller Corps. In his annual report to Federal Parliament in 1930, the Inspector-General wrote:

> When this decision was known all officers, both permanent and Militia, the warrant officers of the Instructional Staff rose to the occasion in a manner deserving all praise and embarked at once on a recruiting campaign.[6]

Prior to the change of government there had been a serious effort to recruit more instructors. A Special School of Instruction was held at Queenscliff, Victoria, in 1929 to 'enable NCOs of the Permanent Forces and other approved personnel to qualify for promotion to WO Instructors, AIC.'[7]

Unfortunately, even with new instructors joining the Corps, the numbers continued to decrease as members retired and were not replaced. By 1932, the actual strength of the corps was down to 496, a loss of 104 warrant officers from the original establishment of 600:[8]

Table 2. Strength of AIC 1929–1932[9]

Year	QMs	Instructors	Total
1928	59	589	648
1929	60	580	640
1930	46	496	542

However, no sooner had the changes to the Army's structure and size been implemented when the world entered a period of economic depression—the Great Depression—following the Wall Street crash of 1929.[10]

The Great Depression—downsizing of 1922 revisited

The pursuit of social reconstruction following the Great War had come at a massive cost and, in the decade from 1919 to 1929, Australia had been living beyond its means. Despite a massive post-war debt (£700 million), the conservative Australian politicians had borrowed heavily from London banks: 'Commonwealth and States, now co-ordinating their borrowing, returned to the City of London in the 1920s and borrowed £230 million with a further private inflow of £140 million.'[11] The Great Depression hit Australia when the London banks, desperate to remain afloat, called in their loans. The Australian Government responded with massive cuts in government expenditure including on defence, which took substantial reductions. While the total defence budget for 1921/22 had been £15,029 million, by 1928/29, the defence allocation had shrunk to £6,377 million. Even the 1928/29 total defence budget, small as it was, fell further, dropping to £3,021 million in 1932/33:[12]

Table 3. Australian Defence Expenditure 1920-1931 (in £ millions)

Year	Navy	Army	Air Force	TOTAL
1920–1921	£2,756	£1,341	£140	£32,532
1921–1922	£2,692	£1,460	£278	£15,029
1922–1923	£2,124	£1,482	£179	£8,150
1923–1924	£2,084	£1,545	£223	£9,423
1924–1925	£2,394	£1,558	£398	£6,522
1925–1926	£3,568	£1,548	£429	£6,317
1926–1927	£5,027	£1,526	£572	£7,779
1927–1928	£4,658	£1,494	£517	£7,259
1928–1929	£3,808	£1,466	£549	£6,397
1929–1930	£2,515	£1,240	£498	£4,679
1930–1931	£1,778	£1,195	£392	£3,688

In an effort to further rein in expenditure, the new government directed the Military Board to reduce the size of the PMF by identifying men superfluous to requirements. The Military Board identified 247 officers and soldiers for retrenchment, of whom 65 were Staff Corps officers and 123 were warrant officers.[13]

Aware that this number of retrenchments could cost the government as much as £200,000, the Military Board proposed an alternative. Rather than imposing retrenchment, the Board proposed a system of rationing work in which 'members of the permanent forces were required to take leave without pay for periods of 14 days up to a maximum of 8 weeks in a financial year.'[14]

There was some relief in this proposal, as soldiers earning less than £221 per year were made exempt. This ruling included warrant officers appointed staff sergeant majors class III earning an annual salary of £203 per year such as 558 Warrant Officer Class II E.S.D Kaglund serving with the Australian Army Veterinary Corps at 2 District Base (NSW). Also excluded was 1479 Warrant Officer F.H. Brown, who had recently completed an instructor's course with the Royal Tank Regiment in England and was posted as a tank instructor at the Small Arms School at Randwick, NSW. However warrant officers earning over £240 per annum were forced to take the full eight weeks' leave.[15]

Among those more highly paid, and thus less fortunate in this instance, were senior staff sergeant majors such as Honorary Lieutenant 1st Class Master Gunner Leonard Charles Wade at the Artillery Schools of Instruction whose annual salary was £312 and Honorary Lieutenant William Henry Thomas, MC, serving with the Australian Engineers in the 2nd Infantry Division (NSW).[16] This financial edict also included quartermasters such as Quartermaster and Temporary Adjutant Charles Robert Victor Wright, MC, of the 43rd/48th Infantry Battalion, AMF, and Quartermaster and Temporary Adjutant Carl Rudolph Speckman, MC, RAE, of the 11th Mixed Brigade (Queensland) who had an annual salary of £300.[17] While the Military Board's proposal succeeded in saving jobs in the short term, this was not the end of the difficulties experienced by the men of the AIC.

In 1931, the Scullin Government passed the *Financial Emergency Act 1931* which reduced the salaries and wages of all public sector employees. The following year, these measures were amended further by the *Financial Emergency Act 1932*. In the Army no-one was exempt from the salary and wage reductions. Soldiers under 21 lost £4 a year while those over 21 lost £8 per annum. Loss of salary imposed on warrant officers ranged from £3 18s 3d for those on the 1st subdivision rate such as 832 Bandmaster J.P. O'Toole serving with the RAA Band at the 3rd District Base (Victoria) to £5 4s 4d for those on the 4th subdivision rate such as Honorary Major Harold Ordish,

DSO, now at RMC who had previously been CI of the Small Arms School at Randwick.[18]

Within the PMF the economic measures introduced by the government generated a great deal of anger. Many of its members believed that this was 'an adversity which the Minister would not have dared inflict upon the more vocal civilian public service.'[19] However the reduction in pay was only a temporary measure. The real cost-cutting came into effect when establishment numbers were reduced once more. The government made 34 Staff Corps officers and 55 warrant officers redundant and closed RMC Duntroon, moving the College to Victoria Barracks, Sydney. The plight of these officers and warrant officers was further exacerbated by the lack of financial compensation, despite the fact that compensation had been paid during the downsizing in 1922.[20] The manner in which the 55 redundancies for AIC warrant officers were determined was also controversial. Those retrenched comprised of men who were close to retirement (which was brought forward); those who were medically unfit; and a number who had been recently enlisted ('last in first out').

Quartermasters 1932

By the time the Scullin Government came to power the original quartermaster base of 64 had shrunk to 46. The sole surviving quartermaster from List A 'Ordinary Establishment' was Honorary Major George E. Sykes.[21] In some ways, Major Sykes was the epitome of an AIC officer. He had enormous experience and exceptionally long service, albeit without the benefit of wartime service. Alone among the 46 quartermasters serving in 1932, Major Sykes had not seen active service. Despite extensive medical service in the Army, including tending Boer War casualties repatriated to Australia and serving in the Garrison Hospital, Victoria Barracks, Sydney, in the Great War, he suffered the fate of many AIC staff, judged too valuable to risk losing on active service. George Sykes, with 30 years service in the

Australian Army Medical Corps (AAMC), was an officer on the staff of the Director General Medical Service stationed at AHQ Melbourne. Such was his experience that Sykes presented a paper entitled 'Equipment of the Australian Medical Services' to the 1st AAMC Course in Melbourne in 1923.[22] Later that year he also delivered an address 'The Australian Medical Services' at the 5th AAMC Course held at the Small Arms School, Randwick.

Of the original 24 quartermasters in List B 'Special Establishment', almost half, now all honorary majors, remained serving in the Corps and the Army. Despite distinguished war service as 1st AIF officers; the majority of these quartermasters were classed as 'temporary' adjutants because the adjutant's positions were reserved for Staff Corps officers. The anomaly was that, at the same time, these 'temporary' adjutants were actually posted to established quartermaster positions—they were effectively doing two jobs, but only being paid for one. In NSW, this was the fate of Quartermaster and Honorary Major Thomas J. Farrow, who was the Temporary Adjutant and Quartermaster of the 1st Cavalry Division signals. QM Farrow, wounded during his service with the 1st AIF, had previously been CI at the School of Army Signals. In Victoria, Quartermaster and Honorary Major John McArthur, DSO, was Temporary Adjutant and Quartermaster, 24th Battalion (The Kooyong Regiment), AMF, 3rd Division, and was similarly disadvantaged as were many others in all the Military districts.

Of the quartermasters on List C 'Temporary Establishment' who remained from the original 20, half that number (10), now all honorary majors, were still serving. Like their more senior colleagues, in spite of occupying established quartermaster positions, they were classed as 'temporary' adjutants because these establishment positions were reserved for Staff Corps officers.

In the 11 years from 1921 to 1932 the Corps had lost 18 quartermasters. Despite these losses, the AIC had retained 46 highly experienced honorary officers who were now in key positions ready for any future expansion of the Army should it become necessary.

Warrant officer postings 1932

The Scullin Government lasted until December 1931 when it was defeated in a massive landslide by Joe Lyons' United Australia Party. By the time of the Scullin Government's demise there were some 450 warrant officer instructors serving in the AIC. Some indication of the diverse range of appointments can be gauged from some examples of typical postings. [23]

In Queensland, 1 District Base (DB) was the posting of 27 Master Gunner 1st Class D. Quirke, Hon Lt RAA. Similarly, with 1st Infantry Division, 59 Warrant Officer Class 1 R. B Webber was an instructor with the AMF Australian Garrison Artillery. Also with the 1st Infantry Division 101 Warrant Officer Class 1 H. B. Masters was a signals instructor.

In NSW, at 2 D B was 568 Warrant Officer Class II E. S. D. Kaglund posted to the Aust. Army Veterinary Corps. In the 2nd Infantry Division was 86 Warrant Officer Class 1 William H. Thomas MC, Hon Lt with the AMF Australian Engineers. Also posted to 2 DB was 165 Hon Lt Alexander Christie in the Australian Army Medical Corps. Similarly at 2DB was 27 Warrant Officer Class 1 A. E. Ridley with the Australian Army Ordnance Corps. Instructing in tanks at the Small Arms School was Warrant Officer Class II F. H. Brown who had undertaken training in England with Lt. Lamperd in 1927. Finally as a cavalry instructor with the 2nd Cavalry Division was H. M. Wainwright

There were AIC members posted to each of the permanent Army schools of instruction. At the Artillery Schools of Instruction was 510 Master Gunner 1st Class Leonard C. Wade, Hon Lt Royal Australian Artillery. At the Small Arms School NSW 112 Hon Lt Ernest W. Latchford MC, while at the Royal Military College as an assistant engineer instructor was 264 Warrant Officer Class I G. Webster DCM of the Australian Engineers.

In Victoria with the 3rd Infantry Division was 68 Hon Lt G. P. Mays, AMF Australian Field Artillery. Postings to 3 DB included 562 Company Sergeant Major J. R. Locke Royal Australian Engineers PMF and 832 Bandmaster J. P. O'Toole Royal Australian Artillery PMF.

In South Australia with the 4th MD Field Troops was Warrant Officer Class 1 W. W. Jamieson with the PMF Australian Army Service Corps.

The 6th MD. Tasmania was the posting of Warrant Officer Class 1 J. Robinson with the Infantry Field Troops. These are just a few examples of the range of postings for the 450 AIC warrant officers listed in 'The Army Staff and Gradation List of the Australian Military Forces, 1st August 1932'.

The era of the Scullin Government represented by far the darkest days of the Corps given the combination of political pressures and economic circumstances. However, even the fall of the Scullin Government in 1931 did not signal the end of the AIC's problems. There were to be further difficult days prior to the Japanese invasion of China in 1937 that was to signal a dramatic change in the fortunes of the Corps.

CHAPTER FIVE
NOTES

1.   Clark, *A History of Australia,* Vol. VI, *The Old Dead Tree & The Young Tree Green*, p. 315.

2.   Long, *To Benghazi,* p. 3.

3.   Report of the Inspector-General of the Australian Military Forces, General Sir H.G. Chauvel, GCMG, KCB, Chief of the General Staff, Part 1, Melbourne, 15 April 1930, Items 11 and 13.

4.   Ibid., Item 12.

5.   Long, *To Benghazi,* p. 14.

6.   Report of the Inspector-General of the Australian Military Forces, General Sir H.G. Chauvel, GCMG, KCB, Chief of the General Staff, Part 1, Melbourne 15 April 1930, Item 14.

7.   Australian Army Orders 128-1929, Special School of Instruction, Queenscliff, 8 April to 15 June 1929.

8.   The Army Staff and Graduation List of the AMF, 1 August 1932, by authority H.J. Green, Government Printer, Melbourne, AIC Quartermasters 60–61; AIC Warrant Officers 64–72.

9.   The Army List of the AMF, Part 1, Active List & AAMC Reserve, 1 January 1928, AIC Quartermasters 61-63; AIC Warrant Officers 239-250; and Report for the Inspector General of the Australian Military Forces, by Lieutenant General Sir H. G Chauvel, GCMG, KCB, Chief of the General Staff, Part 1, Melbourne, 31 May 1929, Item 80.

10.   Macintyre, *A Concise History of Australia,* p. 175

11.   Ibid., p. 168.

12.   Beaumont, *Australian Defence: Sources & Statistics,* p. 30.

13.   Grey, *The Australian Army,* p. 87.

14.   Ibid.

15.   Ibid., p. 88.

16.   Military Board Agenda 409-1921, Item 8, Pay & Appointment.

17.   Military Board Agenda 30-1920, Part II. Warrant & NCOs of the Permanent Forces now serving who held commissions in the AIF, Item 6.

18.   Military Board Instruction F.78-1931, Application of the Financial Emergency Act to Members of the Military Forces; Item 2 (a) to (c). The 1st subdivision referred to level one on the pay scale.

19.   Long, *To Benghazi,* p. 15.

20.   Grey, *The Australian Army,* p. 88.

21.   AWM 41, 1099, War of 1914-1918, Butler Collection, Personal Narratives: Sykes, Major G.E., AIC, AHQ.

22.   'Equipment of the Australian Army Medical Services', 1st Commonwealth AAMC Course, Albert Park Drill Hall, Melbourne, 21 August to 1 September 1923.

23.   The Army Staff and Graduation List of the Australian Military Forces, 1st August 1932, Australian Instructional Corps, Warrant Officers, pp. 64–73.

CHAPTER SIX
PREPARATION FOR WAR

Defending Australia: Army training policy 1932–1939

The strategy of Imperial Defence saw the RAN tasked with defending the seas around Australia's coastline and the Army with protecting the land itself. Cabinet directives to the CGS and the Military Board confirmed that 'the strategic policy of the Army [is] to prepare for raids and not invasion.'[1] This was not a new policy. During his ministry, Prime Minister Scullin had confirmed it as the primary task at the heart of his defence policy.[2] At a cabinet meeting on 15 February 1932, the new Prime Minister, Joe Lyons, decided to continue the policy.[3] Lyons also retained the concept of the all-volunteer Army introduced by the Scullin Government as a cost-effective measure for limiting the size of the defence budget.

This strategic policy, effectively in force throughout the period 1932–1939, provided clear direction to the Army in terms of training requirements. However, preparing the Army to repel raids rather than for defence against large-scale invasion incurred considerable manpower and mobility ramifications in addition to raising important training issues. Where repelling raids required a highly mobile force, possibly a brigade of some 5,000 men with supporting firepower and service components, defence against invasion would typically require one or more divisions each of approximately 17,000 men plus supporting services. Specifically, the chosen means of defence would significantly affect the manner in which the Army trained—from its senior officers down to the ordinary soldier. Invasion necessitating a static defence would require more guns and therefore more gunners. Conversely, the mobility required to repel raids called for more infantry, cavalry and transport.

The development of a local strategic plan for the Army based on perceived external threat or threats, the changing politics in Europe and world economic problems should not have affected the mode of training. The rise of National Socialism in Germany and fascism in Italy and Spain, while regarded as globally significant, were not considered direct threats to the defence of Australia. However Japan, with its demonstrated expansionist policies in the Far East, was perceived as a potential threat to Australia and consequently this fact was enormously influential in reshaping Army planning and training from 1935 onwards.

As the situation in Europe deteriorated with Germany reoccupying the Rhineland and Italy invading Abyssinia, the British Government began to face the realization that another war was possible—perhaps inevitable. Australia, as a member of the British Empire, was also caught up in the reaction to the changing European circumstances and preparation for a future conflict also became part of the Australian Army's plans for future training.

The AIC's most significant push to ensure the practical training of soldiers occurred between 1935 and 1939 as Australia prepared for another war. Confronted with a worsening international situation from 1935 onwards the Lyons UAP Government increased budget spending on defence. While a larger defence budget provided increased funds for training, more instructors and indirectly attracted recruits to the Militia, these funds were not always spent on training. Indeed the Official War Historian, Gavin Long, notes that, as a result of the years during which the Army was starved of funds, its leaders decided to expend the newly acquired money on coastal defences at the expense of training.[4] Their rationale centred on the possibility of a Japanese invasion—which would require coastal defences along the crucial Newcastle-Port Kembla coastline—and the even more likely scenario that the crisis would pass and the funding cease. In this case, they reasoned, while the money might disappear, the 'guns and concrete would remain.'[5] Indeed, there were also rumours that the CGS, General Lavarack, ignored the raids policy and actually planned a strategy to counter an invasion instead.[6] Such a major modification of policy would have significantly altered the AIC's plans for training and preparation because a much larger force was required to oppose an invasion. This was because an invasion policy required much larger trained and coordinated forces than the smaller, more mobile force aimed at repelling raids.

AIC instructor training 1935–1939

The Japanese invasion of Manchuria in 1931 prompted the Lyons Government to implement a strong program of defence rearmament when it came to power in January 1932. The Army's fortunes, which had been in decline since 1922, were now on the rise. The total defence vote gradually rose and by 1936/37 amounted to £8 million, of which the RAN received £3.127 million. The Army received an increased amount of £2.232 million.[7] As a consequence, both the PMF and the AIC increased in size. With a larger budget the Army now began to increase its training resources, mindful that any expansion in numbers would soon overwhelm the 490 members of the AIC.[8]

Throughout most of the interwar period the peacetime Corps establishment had remained almost unchanged. The 1937 establishment total of 603 (80 quartermasters and 523 warrant officers)[9] was almost identical to the 1921 initial establishment figure of 600 (48 quartermasters and 552 warrant officers).[10] However, in the next two years leading up to

World War II, the size of the Corps increased by over 50 per cent. The year 1938 in particular marked the high point of AIC influence within the hierarchy of the Army. The number of honorary officers (quartermasters) more than doubled (an increase of 103) and the number of warrant officers increased by over 50 per cent (an increase of 251). In 1939 there was another massive increase of 323, taking the establishment total to 957 (183 quartermasters and 774 warrant officers).[11]

Clearly the threat of war forced the Army to select, examine and qualify considerably more professional soldiers while, at the same time, enlisting large numbers in the AMF/Militia. Between 1930 and 1939, the size of both the PMF and Militia increased enormously:

Table 4. Increase in Army size 1930–1939 [12]

Year	PMF	Militia Force
1930	1,669	25,785
1935	1,800	27,462
1936	2,032	34,031
1937	2,319	34,624
1938	2,795	43,000
1939	3,500	70,000

Following a recruitment drive for experienced AMF, ex-1st AIF and Imperial soldiers, the training of new Army instructors began again in earnest in 1935 at the Small Arms School in Randwick. These instructors could expect to work long hours, often on an irregular basis, given the small size of the AIC and the fact that its purview covered both the 2nd AIF and AMF/Militia. The Military Board recognised this hard reality in its Instruction A72-1931: 'It is realised that no regular hours of duty can be laid down for members of the Permanent Forces, particularly the Staff Corps and the AIC.'[13] Both the Staff Corps and the AIC were under command of Militia officers who were only working part-time for the Army, often with civil employment taking precedence. Training parades were scheduled by the COs of Militia units and the PMF officers and soldiers had little option but to fit in with these arrangements.

From February 1935 until January 1940, the Army ran nine special courses to train instructors for appointment to the AIC. A tenth course, scheduled to begin in July 1940, was cancelled. The training program for instructors commenced with No. 1 (Special) AIC Course from 12 February to 12 June 1935 and involved 24 students, from which 17 graduated.[14] Two successful students, 1846 Les Wilson and 2080 William George Clementson retired as Lt.-Col's, the latter joining the Staff Corps and awarded an OBE after being CO 17 NS Bn Western Command.[15] The following year, No. 1 AIC General Refresher Course was run at the Cavalry and Infantry Wing of the Small Arms School from 4 February to 13 June 1936.[16] One of the successful students was 425 Temporary Warrant Officer Reginald (Reg) J. E. Spence who went on to serve on the staff of the SAS until 1939.[17] Some 24 students were panelled for No. 2 (Special) AIC Course from 4 February to 13 June 1936 and, as with the first course, 21 were successful.[18] One of these successful students was 3707 Temporary Warrant Officer Class II Arthur Newton.[19] Another was Kevin Power who, as a 2nd AIF company commander with 2nd/33rd Bn, was awarded a Military Cross.[20]

After graduating from No. 2 Special Course, Arthur Newton was initially posted to the 1st/19th Battalion at Moore Park, Sydney.[21] In October 1936 he was posted to the 56th Battalion, The Riverina Regiment, commanded by Lieutenant Colonel Ken Eather (who was to be the last Australian officer promoted to major general during World War II). When a new company of the 56th Battalion was raised at Leeton, Warrant Officer Newton was appointed as their instructor. Of that time he wrote:

> I remained at Leeton for two years but was also required to in-
> struct at Temora where another company was located. This pe-
> riod was most rewarding as I was virtually my own master. No

telephones at out-centres in those days, so communication was by post or visits. The soldiers were mostly farmers and very keen. I recall one CMF sergeant driving me to Wagga and back to obtain the loan of a lewis gun before our stores arrived. As we had no secure room at that time in the pavilion in the showground which was our training depot I slept with the lewis gun under my bed for some weeks.

In the period of two years I conducted weekly parades, ran bivouacs, coached candidates for first appointment to commissioned rank, conducted NCO classes, attended camps, was seconded on two occasions as an instructor of Divisional Courses; trained a guard for a visit of the Governor of NSW and one for the then GOC 2nd Division [Major General I.G. Mackay].

After attending a medium machine gun [Vickers] and 3 inch mortar course from April to June 1938, [I] was posted an instructor to RMC Duntroon where I remained until May 1940. Technically I was the MMG and Mortar Instructor but in those days the warrant officers taught all subjects, so I soon found out that I covered the spectrum and was also designated assistant to the PT Instructor. This latter duty was no sinecure because the instructor had the tendency to suffer from sprains and other injuries and, as a result [I] often had the job on my own ... As the only gymnastics I had done was in my school days, I really had to sweat it out at night in the gym so that I could demonstrate that exercise the next day to a class.

In May 1940, Newton left RMC to enlist in the 2nd AIF:

I left RMC in May 1940 ... [and was] appointed RSM 2nd/17th Battalion then being raised at Ingleburn ... I was lucky again as other warrant officers on the staff of RMC were retained for periods of up to two years after the outbreak of war.[22]

Arthur Newton was, as he said, lucky. His experience contrasted starkly with that of Major Sykes and Major Etheredge mentioned earlier who, despite years of exemplary service, were never to experience active service overseas.

The year 1936 saw the advent of continuous training to produce AIC instructors with the running of No. 3 (Special) AIC Course.[23] For two warrant officers who graduated side by side in No. 3 Special Course, World War II was to provide vastly different outcomes. For 4502 Acting Sergeant Vincent Dowdy, who was posted to the 1st Cavalry Division, military service would see him initially join Light Horse Regiments becoming Brigade Sergeant Major, 2nd Cavalry Brigade, in 1939. The brigade remained in Australia for the duration of the war, becoming the 2nd Australian Motor Brigade in 1942. As recounted later, Dowdy volunteered for the commando's to see active service. After World War II he graduated into the Staff Corps and was later promoted brigadier. His fellow graduate, 3072 Acting Sergeant Athol Osgood, was not so fortunate and was called on to make the supreme sacrifice after a lifetime spent in the Army.

Athol Osgood left Kogarah High School in Sydney at the age of 16. Against the wishes of his family he went to Melbourne and joined the 1st AIF as a gunner. He served in France and, after being wounded and separated from his unit, he joined a group of Canadians in the defence of the French city of Verdun. It was here that 3706 Gunner A. Osgood, Ammunition Column, 6th Brigade, Field Artillery, AIF, became the only Australian soldier known to have received the commemorative medal *Soldats de Verdun* awarded by the city to honour its defenders.[24]

At the end of the Great War, Athol Osgood continued to serve in the Army as a member of the PMF. Over the next 15 years he was promoted corporal and then sergeant. Selected for promotion, Acting Sergeant A. Osgood graduated from No. 3 Special School. Like fellow graduate Acting Sergeant Vincent Dowdy, he was appointed staff sergeant major class III (on probation), promoted to warrant officer class II on 12 December 1936 and posted to the 2nd Division Infantry. As an AIC warrant officer, Athol Osgood served in a series of postings in Sydney with the 45th Battalion, The St George Regiment, AMF, serving at Arncliffe and Kogarah drill halls. In 1938 Warrant Officer Osgood was posted to Orange, NSW. Just over a year later, in September 1939, he reported to Victoria Barracks, Paddington (Sydney), where he enlisted in the 2nd AIF and was promoted to warrant officer class I before proceeding overseas with the ill-fated 8th Division.

A third successful candidate from No. 3 (Special Course) was Temporary Warrant Officer Eric Hall. He was later to become an officer in 2nd/8th Bn AIF before finishing his career as a Lt.-Col in the Ordnance Corps.[25]

Fig 5. *WOII Eric Hall*

In 1937 there was only a single course, No. 4 (Special) AIC, conducted at the Small Arms School.[26] One significant graduate of No. 4 Special Course was 3094 Temporary Warrant Officer Class II Guy Fawcett who was later to join the unique DMF, a permanent infantry company based at Darwin in the Northern Territory.[27] Another successful student was Joseph L. A Kelly later to join the staff corps after World War II as a colonel with a DSO.[28] Alone amongst the 2,000 AIC Warrant Officers Joe Kelly was actually appointed CO of a WWII AIF battalion. The following year, 1938, there were two courses: No. 5 (Special)[29] from February to June and No. 6 (Special) from July to November.[30] One of the successful candidates from No. 5 (Special) Course was 3722 Temporary Warrant Officer Class II Stanley Roy Edgecombe who was an artillery instructor prior to World War II. Another successful student was Geoffrey (Fango) Watson who was RSM at Duntroon, where he introduced the 'pace stick' after being the Senior NCO at the London Victory Parade in 1946. He was commissioned into the Armoured Corps and retired as a Major.[31]

Graduating from the latter course was 3406 Temporary Warrant Officer Class II Leslie E. Hannell. Les Hannell joined 1 Field Regiment, Australian Field Artillery, in Newcastle, NSW, in 1933 as a gunner, progressing through the ranks and becoming a sergeant. However, as he explained, 'the AIC training (in No.6 Course) was based on infantry weapons, and A & Q administration.'[32] Despite his artillery background, he found himself posted to the infantry joining the 25th Battalion, The Darling Downs Regiment, AMF, in Toowoomba, Queensland, on graduation. The battalion had companies in Dalby and Warwick where Warrant Officer Hannell later joined A Company.

Expansion of the Army saw a further platoon raised at Stanthorpe, some 223 kilometres from Brisbane, and an area developed by soldier settlers after the Great War. Travel between the companies was sometimes by car but mostly by train once a fortnight. The raising of the Stanthorpe platoon was an interesting experience as Warrant Officer Hannell explains:

> A call for recruits produced 130+ applicants. As the establishment was for a platoon [nominally 33 men] there were problems. There were no officers or NCOs just a lot of enthusiastic would be soldiers. The division into sections [nominally 10 men] was left to the men. They divided into groups of 10 usually that included a potential NCO.
>
> In spite of the problems the company commander and I were both optimistic about taking the Stanthorpe platoon to annual camp in May 1939. We travelled to camp by train leaving Stanthorpe about 1700hrs on a Saturday. The troops assembled at the depot and marched to the railway station. I swear the whole population of the district turned out with the Mayor and Town Band to see the troops off.

From the 25th Battalion, Warrant Officer Hannell was posted to RMC Duntroon (now returned to its Canberra home) in late May 1939 as an assistant instructor, and it was from Duntroon that he was able, as a PMF soldier, to enlist in the 2nd AIF in 1942.[33]

Another successful student from No. 6 (Special) Course was Temporary Warrant Officer Cyril Hall (brother of Lt.-Col. Eric Hall of No. 3 Special Course). Cyril Hall also enlisted in the 2nd AIF and after graduating from Staff College became an Officer Instructor at the School of Infantry before serving with the Second Battalion, Royal Australian Regiment in Korea.

Fig 6. *No 6 (Special) Course*

The Small Arms School conducted No. 7 (Special) AIC Course for cavalry and infantry instructors,[34] while the Schools of Artillery ran a course to qualify artillery students.[35] Among the 101 graduates of the cavalry and infantry course was 3895 Temporary Warrant Officer Class II William Rupert John Shields.[36] As a newly promoted warrant officer earning £3 18s 0d per week, Rupert Shields was able to nominate his widowed mother as a dependant and thus claim a first class rail fare of £6 11s 5d for her to join him to take up his new appointment with the 21st Light Horse Regiment, Headquarters and Car Troop, Moree, NSW.[37] Scattered throughout the NSW Riverina the 21st Light Horse had Troops at Gunnedah, Boggabri, Narrabri, Wee Waa, Burren Junction, Walgett, Collarenebri, Mungindi, Pallamallawa, Gravesend, Warialda, Bingara, Boomi and Garah.

On the eve of World War II, the CTD in Liverpool, closed since 1922, was reopened. This was the setting for No. 8 Special AIC Course commencing 1 August 1939 with 113 infantry and cavalry students who qualified in January 1940.[38] No. 8 Special Course lasted only 12 weeks, half the time previously allocated for this training in the earlier special courses. The course also contained a strong emphasis on small arms training, the great strength of the AIC, although it was noteworthy for the complete absence of instruction on 'minor tactics'. These skills, vital to NCOs on active service, had to be learned 'on the job' when war broke out. However this was no handicap to one No. 8 Special Course graduating student. 4207 Temporary Warrant Officer Class II Percy David Hazzard had been awarded a MM while serving with the 37th Bn in the first AIF and clearly had these skills.

No. 8 Special Course, with 113 students, was particularly large and the Military Board felt it necessary to advise formations of the reason. The size of the course was, the Board wrote, directly attributable to 'the temporary shortage of instructors allocated for duty to units of the Militia forces.'[39] By implication, formations could not expect such large courses to be conducted in the future, war or no war.

Despite the increasing mechanisation of the Army, horses were still crucial to military preparations for war. Instructions from the CI CTD concerning the qualification of cavalry instructors (horsed) advised that 'they were required to pass a test in riding before selection and allocation as potential cavalry instructors.'[40] This particularly applied to the cavalry students attending No.8 Special Course. The final course for instructors was No. 9 (Special) AIC Course which ran from 25 March to 27 June 1940 and was held concurrently at the Small Arms School, Randwick, and CTD, Liverpool, and from which 157 students qualified.[41] One of the graduates was 8313 Temporary Warrant Officer Class II Thomas Arthur Dawson who was posted to the 7th AIF Recruits Receiving Battalion at Tamworth before reporting to the 31st Battalion, The Kennedy Regiment, at Townsville. NP5483 Temporary Warrant Officer Class II Leslie Francis Guest instructed at training battalions, first at Broadmeadows (Newcastle) and then at Tamworth,[42] while 3865 Temporary Warrant Officer Class II Frank W. Wiseman was posted as an instructor to a horse-drawn light field ambulance unit.[43]

The onset of World War II did not compromise the high standards previously set to qualify instructors, but it did change procedures for those who had not qualified. The 30 warrant officers who failed No. 9 Special Course were not immediately discharged from the Corps. Earlier course candidates who failed had either been discharged or returned to their original units at their substantive rank. In 1940, the first 14 who failed to qualify were appointed temporary staff sergeant (weapons training instructor). The remaining 16 were retained as temporary sergeants (weapons training instructor). The fact that all 30 soldiers who had failed No. 9 Special Course were given temporary appointments within the AIC points to a serious lack of trained instructors available to the AMF/Militia and the 2nd AIF at the outbreak of the war.[44]

The final act in the AIC instructor recruitment program occurred in 1940 when places for students were advertised for No. 10 Special Course scheduled from 13 July 1940 to 24 August 1940. Although there were

80 places available, the course was not conducted, most likely due to the huge demands by units of both the 2nd AIF and the AMF for experienced NCOs.[45] In total, the highly successful program of special courses to produce AIC instructors from 1935 to 1940 graduated 583 new warrant officer instructors for the Army. The size of the output of the special courses is even more remarkable given that the entire PMF numbered only 2795 just as Australia joined Britain in declaring war in 1939.[46]

CHAPTER SIX
NOTES

1.   Australian National Library, MS 1927, 2/459, Pearce Papers, Cabinet Minute from Senator G.F. Pearce, Minister for Defence, Cabinet Approval, J.A. Lyons, 15 February 1932.

2.   Grey, *A Military History of Australia,* p. 133.

3.   Claude Neumann, Australia's Citizen Soldiers, 1919-1939: A Study of Organisation, Command, Recruiting, Training & Equipment, MA thesis, University of New South Wales at Duntroon, 1978, p. 93.

4.   Long, *To Benghazi,* p. 25.

5.   Ibid.

6.   Albert Palazzo, 'Failure to Obey: The Australian Army and the First Line Component Deception', *Australian Army Journal,* Vol. 1, No. 1 (June 2003), p. 42.

7.   Grey, *The Australian Army,* p. 101.

8.   Australian Army Order 219-1933, Permanent Forces, Annual Establishments 1933-34, Table 2 Australian Instructional Corps, Quartermasters (Total 49), Table 3 Australian Instructional Corps, Warrant Officers (Total 441).

9.   Australian Army Order 42-1937, Permanent Military Forces, Annual Establishments 1936-37, Australian Instructional Corps,Table 1 Quartermasters, Table 3 Warrant and Non Commissioned Officers.

10. Report for the Inspector General of the Australian Military Forces, Lieutenant General Sir H.G Chauvel, GCMG, KCB, Chief of the General Staff, Part 1, Melbourne, 31 May 1925, Item 89.

11. Australian Army Order 28-1938, Permanent Military Forces, Australian Instructional Corps, Table 2 Quartermasters, Table 3 Warrant and Non Commissioned Officers.

12. T.B. Millar, *Australia's Defence,* Melbourne University Press, 1969, Appendix B.

13. Military Board Instructions A.72-1931, Permanent Forces—Hours of Duty.

14. Australian Army Order 155-1935, Appointment to the Australian Instructional Corps; No. 1 Special Course of Instruction, Small Arms School, Randwick (held from 12/2/1935 to 12/6/1935); 17 students graduated.

15. Arthur James Cahill Newton, , 'The Australian Instructional Corps', *Australian Infantry Magazine*, October 2013-April 2014., pp 57-67

16. Australian Army Order 154-1936, Small Arms School, Cavalry and Infantry Wing, No. 1 AIC General Refresher Course (held from 4/2/1936 to 13/6/1936); 8 students graduated.

17. Newton, The Australian Instructional Corps, *Australian Infantry Magazine*, October 2013-April 2014, pp 56-67

18. Newton, 'The Australian Instructional Corps', p. 41.

19. Newton, Lieutenant Colonel Arthur James Cahill, MBE (3707 T/WOII, No.2 Special Course), first interview 1 October 2002.

20. Newton, , 'The Australian Instructional Corps', *Australian Infantry Magazine*, October 2013-April 2014., pp 57-67

21. Previously the 1st Battalion (City of Sydney's Own Regiment) and 19th Battalion (The South Sydney Regiment), now the 1st/ 19th Battalion, RNSWR, The Bushman's Rifles.

22. Arthur J.C. Newton, 'A Full Military Life' in *Australian Infantry Magazine,* September/October 1972, Directorate of Military Training, Canberra.

23. Australian Army Order 24-1937, Small Arms School, Cavalry & Infantry Wing, No. 3 Special Course of Instruction for Appointment to the Australian Instructional Corps; (Held from 11/8/1936 to 12/12/1936); 46 students graduated.

24. George Osgood (son), interview with the author, 22 April 2003.

25. Newton, , 'The Australian Instructional Corps', *Australian Infantry Magazine*, October 2013-April 2014., pp57-67

26. Australian Army Order 148-1937, Small Arms School, Randwick, Cavalry & Infantry Wing No. 4 Special Course of Instruction for Appointment to the Australian Instructional Corps; (held from 9/2/37 to 12/6/37); 27 students graduated.

27. Fawcett, Colonel Guy, OBE, interview 3 May 2003.

28. Newton, , 'The Australian Instructional Corps', *Australian Infantry Magazine*, October 2013-April 2014., pp57-67

29. Australian Army Order 151-1938, Small Arms School, Cavalry & Infantry Wing No. 5 Special Course of Instruction for Appointment to the Australian Instructional Corps; (held from 8/2/1938 to 11/6/1938); 26 students graduated.

30. Australian Army Order 290-1938, Small Arms School, Cavalry & Infantry Wing, No. 6 Special Course of Instruction for Appointment to the Australian Instructional Corps; (held from 4/7/1938 to 23/11/1938); 52 students graduated.

31. Newton, , 'The Australian Instructional Corps', *Australian Infantry Magazine*, October 2013-April 2014., pp57-67

32. Hannell, Colonel Leslie E, psc (Retd), letter to the author 1 February 2002.

33. Hannell was the CI of the School of Military Intelligence before retiring in 1960. Letter to the author, 1 February 2002.

34. Australian Army Order 178-1939, No. 7 Special Course of Instruction for Appointment to the Australian Instructional Corps; Cavalry and Infantry, (held at Small Arms School from 16/1/1939 to 17/6/1939); 101 students graduated.

35. Australian Army Order 179-1939, No. 7 Special Course of Instruction for Appointment to the Australian Instructional Corps; Artillery, (held at Sydney from 13/2/1939 to 22/6/1939); 16 students graduated.

36. Shields, Major William (known as Rupert)Rupert John (DOB 12 Aug 1912), PMF No.3895. Enlisted in the Militia from 16 Dec 1930 to 5 June 1938, joined PMF on 6 June 1938 and completed No.7 Special Course; NAA MP385/3, Control Symbol 27/20/673; letter to the author, 4 May 2003.

37. Military Board Proceedings, 16 November 1921, Item 409/1921.

38. NAA, MP 385/3, Symbol Number 27/20/719, No. 8 Course AIC. See also Newton, 'The Australian Instructional Corps', p. 42.

39. NAA, MP 385/3, 27/20/719, letter from Military Board to Formations (Divisions & Attachments), Reference 112/60/499, dated 20 January 1939, Subject 'Appointment of Temporary Instructors—Australian Instructional Corps'.
40. NAA, Reference 27/20/703; MP 385/3, 27/20/719, letter from the Secretary, Military Board to Formations (Divisions & Attachments), Para 2, Instructions to the CI, CTD, dated 12 July 1939.
41. NAA, MP 385/3, Item 27/20/807, No. 9 Course, No. 9 AIC (Infantry) Course, 25/3/40—27/6/40.
42. Guest, Lieutenant Colonel Frank (No. 9 Special Course, CTD, NP5483 T/WOII), interview 22 July 2003.
43. Wiseman, Lieutenant Colonel Frank W (No. 9 Special Course: 3865 WOII-T/WO1), interview 28 January 2002.
44. NAA, MP 385/3, Item 27/20/807, Temporary Staff Sergeant (Weapons Training Instructor) & Temporary Sergeants, Page 4, No. 9 Course, No. 9 AIC (Infantry) Course, 25/3/40—27/6/40.
45. NAA, MP 385/3, Item Number 27/20/808, No. 10 Course AIC.
46. Millar, *Australia's Defence*, Appendix B.

Chapter Seven
A Corps Transformed by War

Training transformation brought about by World War II

In the interwar years of 1919 to 1939, the Army had a maximum of five permanent training establishments. These comprised RMC, founded in 1911, the School of Musketry, established on 1 September 1911 (which became the Small Arms School on 3 June 1921), the Schools of Artillery, the Central School of Physical Training established in 1920, and the CTD. Although the CTD was opened in August 1921 it had closed by February 1922 due to financial constraints. The CTD was not reopened until 1 September 1939. The need for more than five Army Schools came with the advent of war in 1939. Army training became a top priority with the rapid mobilisation of the AMF/Militia and the 2nd AIF,

A number of previously specialised courses, held annually, were rapidly converted into permanent establishments.[1] By 1941, the AIC had 285 warrant officers, almost a third of its pre-war establishment, attached to 20 Army Schools and establishments. These now included the Schools of Military Engineering, Signals, AFV, an Anti-Gas School, two Officer Training Units and four NCO Schools.[2]

Demand for training continued to increase as the war progressed. Consequently, the number of training establishments increased still further, including a series of specialist schools such as the Tactics School, the Royal Australian Artillery School of Searchlights, the Army School of Mechanisation, Australian Army Ordnance Corps School, Electrical and Mechanical Engineering School, School of Tropical Medicine and several schools for the Women's Services. Between 1941 and 1944 the number of Army schools continued to increase until, by war's end, the total number of such establishments stood at 39.[3]

The rapid increase in the number of Army training establishments, from the commencement of the war, suggests that from the start of increased war readiness from 1935, there had existed at least some prior requirement. It would appear that constrained government defence budgets had prevented their establishment. Clearly the impetus for the expansion was provided by the advent of yet another world war. By the time the Australian Regular Army was created in 1947 the number of post-war training establishments had stabilised at 34.[4]

A consequence of the enormous increase in Army training was the huge demand for instructors. Initially, demand was satisfied by AIC members but, as the war progressed, the Army drew increasingly from the officers and NCOs of both the 1st and 2nd AIF as well as from the AMF/Militia. This broad-ranging search for instructional talent was also to directly impact on the AIC as the corps emerged from World War II.

Recruitment and enlistment

As soon as war broke out the AIC became directly involved in training both the home Army, the AMF/Militia, and the new volunteer Army going oversea to fight, the 2nd AIF. The opening months of World War II brought a flood of recruits to both the AIF and the AMF/Militia, placing great strain on recruitment services.

W.E. (Bill) Andrews, a Militia soldier from 1936 to 1939, was sworn in at the Homebush (Sydney) Drill Hall as a member of the 2nd/4th Australian Infantry Battalion, AIF, on 3 November 1939 by the acting RSM of the 4th/3rd Infantry Battalion, AMF, Warrant Officer Michael Flannery, AIC, a Great War veteran.[5] Bill Andrews recalled that, 'for about three weeks we were the 'day boys'. After the day's training we went home to sleep.'

The 'Day Boys' scheme was one innovation devised to overcome the resources problem. Recruits were accepted into the 2nd AIF and given uniforms. They then reported daily to their nearest AIF recruit centre, usually their local drill hall, returning home each night to sleep.[6] They remained Day Boys for about three to four weeks before reporting to their battalion for full-time enlistment. At Auburn, NSW, the Day Boys reported to Headquarters 4th Battalion (The Australian Rifles), AMF, in 1940 before many became reinforcements for the 2nd/19th Battalion, AIF.[7] Other Day Boys were allocated to different corps; Maurice Gillespie found himself joining the 2nd/6th Armoured Regiment in 1940.

In just over six months the Army raised four infantry divisions that then became the 2nd AIF and prepared these divisions for overseas service.[8] In 1941 the first 2nd AIF cavalry (armoured) division was raised. Alongside the formation of the 2nd AIF, the introduction of full-time service for the AMF/Militia under the *Defence Act* Section 40 allowed the conscription of young men for full-time home service of three months (followed by reserve service). Conscription into the AMF/Militia battalions commenced in January 1940, authorised under the *Defence Act* Section 125.[9] Subsequently, as Jim Johns of the 36th Battalion (St George's English Rifles), AMF, commented that by January 1941, conscription was extended for the duration of the war plus 12 months.[10]

Quartermaster services

The need for experienced quartermasters was enormous because all the battalions and regiments of the 2nd AIF were being raised from scratch. By August 1940, a total of 41 quartermasters had enlisted in the AIF.[11] Both Ernest Thomas Lergessner and Edmund Allchin, MM, enlisted in the AIF on 13 October 1939. Lergessner became quartermaster of the 2/1st Battalion, AIF, raised at Victoria Barracks in Sydney.[12] The 2nd/1st Battalion went to the Middle East and into action at Tobruk. Edmund Allchin was appointed quartermaster of the 2nd/10th Battalion, AIF, raised in Adelaide.[13]

Enlistments on 1 May 1940 included Herbert Downey, Arthur B.S. Collins and Joseph (Joe) L.A. Kelly. Joe Kelly initially joined the AIF as a quartermaster and honorary lieutenant, but was soon transferred to the 2nd/13th Battalion, AIF, as a platoon commander before going to the Middle East.

Training

In 1940, 21 AIC instructors who graduated from No. 9 Special Course were posted to AIF training camps at Geelong, Balcombe and Shepparton in Victoria.[14] George Johnston, later to achieve fame as the author of the wartime novel *My Brother Jack*, was a war correspondent who described the work of the AIC in Geelong and the 'character-building' training of AASC officers:

> At North Geelong, at the 'University of the AASC' I saw officers slogging through weeks of ceaseless work and study on supply and transport courses. Covered in grease, wearing gigglesuits, and grunting with their labours was a course of officers engaged in vehicle maintenance courses. Their instructors, WO's from the Australian Instructional Corps, grilled them from morning to night, and their only respect for convention was to address the grimy, sweating, grease covered workers as 'gentlemen'.[15]

Tom Dawson, a former Militia soldier who joined the AIC and graduated from No. 9 Special Course, had been an instructor with the 7th Recruits Receiving Battalion, AIF, at Tamworth, NSW, before being posted to the 31st Battalion (The Kennedy Regiment), AMF. Dawson recalls a period of initial Militia training:

> In 1940 we conducted an officers and NCOs course of three weeks in Townsville, then a 3 months camp at Miowera, North Queensland where the whole battalion [31st Australian Infantry Battalion, AMF] began from scratch.[16]

Fig 7. *SSM3 (WOII) Thomas Arthur Dawson, 1939.*

Similar training was being conducted in the AIF. According to the 2nd /4th Battalion history:

> The battalion assembled for the first time on 3 November 1939 at Ingleburn, NSW, [and] was joined on 9 November 1939 by five graduates from No. 8 Special Course, being 5973 T/WOII G.F Airey, 4206 T/WOII W.A. Gray, 4253 T/WOII G.H. Andrews,[17] 2312 T/WOII W.T. Cross and 4271 T/WOII T.I. Eltham [who were] posted as instructors.[18]

The subsequent war careers of these instructor warrant officers illustrates and demonstrates the versatility of these professional soldiers.

George Frederick Airey, MM, who served in the Great War with the East Lancashire Regiment, became WX13977 Warrant Officer Airey, MM, and was appointed RSM of the 2nd/4th Machine Gun Regiment, AIF. Arriving in Singapore as a warrant officer class I, he was taken prisoner by the Japanese and spent the rest of the war in captivity in Java. Despite volunteering to join the AIF, William Arthur Gray spent the war in Australia as an assistant instructor at the Officer Cadet Training Unit in South Australia. George Howard Andrews attended the Land Headquarters School of Japanese Weapons Special Course in 1943 having been commissioned as a lieutenant. He was later an instructor and temporary captain at the Officer Cadet Training Unit at Woodside in South Australia.

William Thomas Cross was an instructor with No. 2 Volunteer Defence Corps Battalion and later No. 4 Volunteer Defence Corps Battalion before joining the New Guinea Force Engineering School where he became a cinema projectionist. Thomas Ivanhoe Eltham was enlisted into the AIC by Major James E. Newland, VC, in Melbourne on 17 March 1939. As VX 85284 Lieutenant T.I. Eltham, he joined the 2nd/7th Australian Independent Company, later operating as a member of Z Special Force. Temporary Captain Thomas Eltham was killed in action on 21 May 1945.

Placement of AIC warrant officer instructors was widespread. The 2nd/14th Battalion (21 Brigade), was the only Victorian battalion in the 7th Division. With many of the 2nd/14th's officers and NCOs former militiamen, the divisional history noted that 'the unit also benefited from the allocation of warrant officers from the Australian Instructional Corps.'[19] Similarly, in the 17th Brigade, the 2nd/6th Battalion's historian, David Hay, writes:

In fact each battalion of the 17th Brigade had, during the early weeks at Puckapunyal, a small group of highly trained members of the Australian Instructional Corps, who left their mark on the future officers and NCOs.[20]

When the 2nd/6th Battalion, AIF, was raised at Puckapunyal in October 1939, the incoming RSM was 3069 Warrant Officer Class I Norman Howard Rowell, AIC, a graduate of No. 3 Special Course. Bob Jackson, Secretary/Treasurer of the Sergeants' Mess at the time recalls:

> Norm Rowell was a nephew of Brig Sydney Rowell [later CGS] ... he was a tremendous influence on the discipline of the battalion in the early days ... people didn't dare put a cigarette butt on the parade ground ... he was constantly pulling people into gear ... he enforced very rigid mess etiquette ... he was very strict on dress ... there was no talking shop in the mess.[21]

As a direct entry recruit into the AIC, Frederick James Coupland enjoyed a rather different career. Originally a Militia soldier following cadet training, he was enlisted in the PMF as NP8767 Sergeant Coupland, having been initially rejected on the grounds of age: 'After I had applied to enlist in the AIF I received a notification in writing that my application had been rejected due to the fact I was under the age of 19.' At the time of his PMF enlistment Frederick Coupland was aged 17 years 7 months, possibly the youngest man ever to join the AIC. Coupland's timing, however, was to stand him in good stead: 'There was a big requirement for people who had Army training, as I had, to train the large intake of recruits into the AIF.' Both his age and lack of formal AIC training indicate that, by the second quarter of 1940, there was a serious shortage of trained instructors available for AMF/Militia engineer units.[22] Coupland joined the AIC with the rank of temporary warrant officer class II on 16 May 1940. His home was close to the Engineers Depot at Haberfield which he had attended since his cadet days and his familiarity with the depot and equipment may have encouraged his enlistment in the AIC despite the likelihood that it would be some time before he was eligible for overseas service. Since this was a direct entry enlistment, Coupland was not required to sit qualifying exams, unlike most of his AIC brethren.

Fred Coupland joined 1 Field Company, RAE, at Waratah in NSW in 1940 and spent the next two years as an instructor. On 21 March 1942 Temporary Warrant Officer Class II Coupland was posted to the war establishment of 17 Field Company, RAE, AMF, at Paddington, NSW. On 18 September 1942 Fred Coupland was discharged from the PMF at the age of 21 and enlisted in the AIF under the new regimental number of NX116219. Coupland was then posted to Thursday Island before joining the Merauke Force in Dutch New Guinea in April 1943 with 17 Field Company. In January 1945 he attended the Land Headquarters School of Infantry No. 2 Course at Puckapunyal in Victoria. He was confirmed as warrant officer class II on 13 December 1944.[23]

Fig 8. *WO II Fred Coupland instructing AIF reinforcements, Centenninal Park, 1940.*

Leadership

Despite the need for experienced instructors to remain in Australia, there was also enormous demand for AIC members in the 2nd AIF. Initially, these men occupied key appointments such as senior NCOs, RSMs and platoon commanders who were usually junior officers. Demand created opportunities in the careers of Arthur Newton, Guy Fawcett and Kevan Thomas. Arthur Newton, a graduate of No. 2 (Special) Course, was appointed RSM of the 2nd/17th Battalion, AIF, and was subsequently promoted and commissioned in 1940. He remained with the 2nd/17th Battalion through the Western Desert campaigns at Tobruk and El Alamein. He returned to Australia in 1943 and joined the staff of Advanced Land Headquarters before moving to the 17th Brigade for the campaign against the Japanese in the Wau-Salamaua and Aitape-Wewak campaigns.[24]

Similarly, Guy Fawcett of No. 4 (Special) Course had been the Company Sergeant Major (CSM) and the RSM of the DMF in 1938 and was commissioned into the 2nd/27th Battalion, AIF. Returning to Australia in 1943, the now Lieutenant Colonel Fawcett became CO of 1 Australian Army Weapon Training School at Mt Tamborine in Queensland before returning to active service as a company commander with the 2nd/27th Battalion, AIF, on Shaggy Ridge.[25] Fawcett achieved almost celebrity recognition when, during his time as a company commander, an important staging area in the Ramu Valley campaign, 'Guy's Post', was named after him.[26]

Kevan Thomas, a graduate of No. 4 (Special) Course, was posted to the 22nd Light Horse Regiment.[27] He was accepted for enlistment in the 2nd AIF becoming TX885 Lieutenant Kevan Thomas, 2nd/12th Battalion, AIF. His PMF promotion to warrant officer class I in May 1942 was followed by promotion to captain, AIF, in September 1942. For his service in the Middle East, including Egypt, East Africa, the Western Desert, Sudan, Greece, Crete and Tobruk during the period February to July 1941,

Kevan Thomas was Mentioned in Dispatches (MID). Returning to Australia in 1943, Thomas embarked on further training before departing once again for active service, this time in New Guinea where he would command D Company, 2nd/12th Battalion, AIF, and be awarded the MC for his part in the capture of Prothero II. Named Prothero II this was one of two well-defended knolls on the northern end of Shaggy Ridge. Thomas' citation reads:

> Under fire he directed attacks ... with disregard for his own safety ... [when] one of his [section commanders] was wounded ... [Thomas] personally crawled forward and brought back his NCO.[28]

Captain Joe Kelly sailed with the 2nd/13th Battalion, AIF, to the Middle East having been appointed adjutant of the battalion. He was later appointed as a Staff Captain on Headquarters 20 Brigade before moving to Headquarters 9 Division. When the CO of the 2nd/13th Battalion, AIF, was injured at Tobruk, Joe Kelly took command and, as the acting CO, led the 2nd/13th for the remainder of the battle. Kelly returned to Australia as a major and Second-in-Command of the 2nd/13th Battalion.[29]

Vince Dowdy transferred to the 2nd AIF in 1940 and was promoted captain on joining the 7th Australian Division Cavalry Regiment, with further promotion to major in 1942. Volunteering for Commandos in 1944, Vince Dowdy went to New Guinea. After service with the 3rd New Guinea Infantry Battalion, Major Dowdy was appointed CI of the New Guinea Training School in 1945 and later joined the Interim Army.

Rupert Shields, a graduate of No. 7 Special Course who had enlisted in the 2nd AIF on 22 July 1942, served as a lieutenant with the 2nd/7th Commando Squadron in New Guinea, and then as a captain at the New Guinea Training School. Shields' final World War II posting was as a company commander with the 3rd New Guinea Infantry Battalion.

Geoffrey James Watson (known throughout the Army as 'Fango') was a graduate of No. 5 Special Course.[30] 'Fango' Watson was appointed RSM of the 2nd/7th Armoured Regiment, AIF. He later transferred to the infantry and saw active service as RSM of the 2nd/4th Infantry Battalion, AIF.

At the beginning of World War II, the commissioning of warrant officers such as Newton, Fawcett, Thomas, Kelly, Dowdy, and Shields was not unusual. As a consequence of the huge deficit of officers from 1940 onwards, a large number of AIC members received commissions in the 2nd AIF and the AMF/Militia in 1941.[31] Regrettably for RSM Norman Rowell of the 2nd/6th Battalion, AIF, having been promoted lieutenant he, like a large number of his battalion, went into German prisoner of war camps after surrendering in Greece. Rowell was held at Oflag VII B, Eichstatt.[32]

Despite the fact that their skills were in great demand in Australia, a considerable number of the AIC's warrant officers managed to enlist in the AIF. Colin McPherson found the process relatively easy: 'If your CO [AMF] became AIF and he wanted you [the AIC cadre] you got a guernsey [into the AIF].[33] For others, the process was not quite so straightforward. Master Gunner Bob Whiston, an AIC warrant officer with the 1st Anti-Aircraft Brigade at Georges Heights (Sydney), received a personal visit from Brigadier John Whitelaw, Commander Coastal Artillery. Brigadier Whitelaw informed Whiston that 'the government had decided not to allow any more AIC WOs to be posted overseas or commissioned.' This was a decision ultimately based on cost. So much money had been spent on training AIC instructors that it was considered crucial to the war effort that they continue in this role in Australia. Whitelaw stressed to Whiston that good instructors were necessary, 'particularly to train men for warrant rank'.

Bob Whiston regarded this as a personal blow. He told his wife that he could not stay in the permanent forces without personal war service, declaring indignantly, 'imagine a senior warrant officer not having overseas ribbons! I would have to leave the Army.'[34]

Fortunately, in 1944, following commissioning and promotion, Captain Whiston was posted to an Ordnance unit at Torokina in Bougainville in the Solomon Islands.[35]

Fig 9. *Capt Robert Norton Whiston with his small daughter, Irene, about to leave for the Islands*

Wartime training conditions

The strain on Army resources to train riflemen was enormous and was compounded by extreme shortages of clothing and equipment. Even as late as 1941, recruits such as Peter Wright, who was eventually posted to the 55th/53rd Battalion, AMF (which became the 55th/53rd Battalion, AIF), received call-up letters which instructed them to bring their own toiletries, sandshoes, sweater, padlock, knife, fork and spoons (large and small) and sufficient food for two meals.[36]

While stories of recruits being issued with broomsticks to train instead of rifles may be apocryphal, there were certainly issues of old equipment. Private

Trevor Harper of the 55th/53rd Battalion, AMF, went into combat area of New Guinea with a single shot .303 Lee Enfield rifle made in 1911.[37] However, in the years leading up to the war the Lithgow, NSW Small Arms Factory had reconditioned thousands of rifles so while Trevor Harpur's weapon was old it was most probably in excellent condition for active service.

Training difficulties were compounded as the Infantry units of the 2nd AIF were gradually reorganised into brigades of three battalions and issued new weapons in line with the current British Army issue. The AMF/Militia, however, was still using the pre-war brigade of four battalions and stocks of existing weapons. The incompatibility of some equipment and the complete absence of other equipment were serious problems that affected all AIC practical training. As if to add insult to injury, in many cases the equipment that was available was below standard or obsolete.

If the conditions for infantry training could be described as difficult, those for artillery and armour training in 1939 were even worse. As the Australian Army entered World War II, it should have done so with equipment compatible with that of the British Army. However, nothing could have been further from the truth. In 1939, as the situation worsened in Europe, the British Army had commenced a rearmament program, modifying its divisional organisation to accommodate an influx of new weapons.[38] Australia, however, initially continued to use its Great War-era weapons, creating a serious practical training issue for AIC instructors. The arrival of new equipment served to highlight the divide between the AMF/Militia and the 2nd AIF. AMF/Militia artillery brigades were equipped with obsolete 18-pounders while the 2nd AIF artillery regiments received the new 25-pounders.[39] While the British Army had re-equipped its artillery regiments with 25-pounder guns, the Australian Army was still equipped with obsolete 18-pounders. NX43679 Gunner Noel Harrison, a 7th Division gunner who fought in Syria, the Middle East and later New Guinea with the 2nd/5th Field Regiment, RAA, describes a farcical situation:

We did drills at Ingleburn with no guns; even the Militia blokes only had experience with 18-pounders. We didn't see 25-pounders until we got to Syria and then everyone had to train really hard before we went into action.[40]

The British re-organisation and the introduction of new weapons also caused problems for the 2nd AIF when it arrived in the Middle East. The 6th Division infantry brigades had yet to be reorganised and thus consisted of four battalions while the British infantry brigades sported the new three-battalion format. This disparity caused headaches for British General Archibald Wavell in his attempts to integrate the different sized British and Australian formations. There was also an immediate training liability in early 1940 when the new weapons were introduced and each 2nd AIF infantry battalion received 17 Bren guns, six anti-tank rifles and four 2-inch mortars.[41] Fortunately NCOs who had been members of the advance guard of the 6th Division sent to Palestine in December 1939 were available to instruct troops in the use of these weapons.[42] One of the AIC warrant officers, who as VX15680, was involved with this training, was Warrant Officer Class I Leslie Fred Smith, RSM 2nd/12th Field Regiment, RAA. Fred Smith was later made a Member of the Order of the British Empire (MBE) for his wartime service in the South West Pacific.

The extraordinary difficulties of supplying weapons and equipment were offset to some extent by resourceful 2nd AIF soldiers who used captured Italian artillery pieces to supplement the deficiencies in their own supply of weapons.[43] Batteries of captured guns, known variously as 'Mr Clarke's Guns' and the 'Bush Artillery', were manned by Australian troops from various units.[44] Captain Guy Fawcett, a company commander with the 2nd/17th Battalion, AIF, in the Western Desert, later commented: 'All our equipment came from the British. Where we were deficient we simply used captured Italian vehicles etc and used them in the fight.'[45]

At the outbreak of World War II, armour was in almost as precarious a state as artillery. In 1939 the Australian Army had a total of 17 armoured vehicles manned by Militia soldiers. Two light tank companies had five tanks each.[46] The two armoured car regiments possessed three and four vehicles respectively.[47]

The impetus for rapid change in armour came from the 2nd AIF in which the 6th, 7th and 8th divisions all had cavalry regiments on their establishments. The equipping of these units took almost two years to be properly resolved. Despite all the plans to the contrary, the 6th Division went overseas with no armoured vehicles and had to be equipped from British stocks on arrival. The cavalry regiments trained in Palestine with Bren gun carriers and indeed, the '6th Division Reconnaissance Regiment became [the] 2nd/6th Australian Divisional Cavalry Regiment'.[48] When the divisions were eventually equipped, it was with British Vickers Light Tanks Mark IIB being even older models than the few Vickers Light Tanks Mark VIA already held by the Australian Army.[49] Bad as that situation was, even worse was to follow. The two light tank squadrons raised for Malayan service had their deployment cancelled in January 1942 'because no armour was available within Australia or Malaya with which to equip them.'[50] Amidst this burgeoning debacle, the essential tasks of the AIC continued as its members strove to provide the practical training programs to prepare soldiers for war.

Modernisation

Australia's entry into World War II highlighted serious problems for the Army in terms of modernisation, both in mechanisation and motorisation. Mechanisation effectively commenced in 1928 with the first moves to replace cavalry horses with tanks. However, this proved token at best. The four Vickers medium tanks of the 1st Tank Section, Australian Tank Corps, devolved into a single operational tank staffed by regular cadre used for training and demonstration purposes.[51] Attempts to introduce light armoured car squadrons into the Army in the late 1930s foundered because the procuring of suitable vehicles, cost and conservative attitudes prevented almost all attempts to test the latest technology.[52] These difficulties were compounded by a lack of locally produced instruction manuals which, in turn, created problems for the AIC instructors faced with the practical training of soldiers.[53]

With the increased defence budgets from 1935 onwards, a Staff Corps officer, Major Ronald Hopkins, and an AIC warrant officer, Keith Avery Watts, were sent to England for tank training in 1937.[54] On their return, Warrant Officer Watts joined the staff at the Small Arms School as a tank instructor. Major Hopkins was posted to AHQ as a staff officer, a position he used to lobby the Army hierarchy to form light tank units. Aware that there were insufficient funds available for such a project, the CGS rejected the proposal commenting, 'I think Hopkins should be told that we are perfectly aware of the considerations he advances, but that the decision to defer tank provision is based on the scale of attack and the financial provision.'[55]

Indeed, lack of funding had caused critical shortages of equipment throughout the entire interwar period. As Morrison explains, 'The eventual decision to convert the Light Horse [to tanks] was only made possible by the progressive increase in vehicles and funds that became available in 1942.'[56] As a consequence when war came in 1939 the Australian Tank Corps only really existed as an organisation on paper. One important outcome, already mentioned, was that no tanks went to Singapore with the 8th Division.

The Army commenced motorisation in 1927 with the purchase of artillery gun tractors, survey vans and Thorneycroft light lorries.[57] However, this was the sole issue of motorised vehicles for many years afterwards, although when the budgetary situation improved, it allowed the Army's Three-Year Plan for 1935–1937 to include the limited purchase of motor vehicles. Fortunately by this time Ford and General Motors had established factories in Australia.[58] Even though from 1938 onwards the Army budget increased, there were always insufficient vehicles for troop transport. Bob Whiston, RQMS at the 1st Anti-Aircraft Regiment (Militia), was responsible for tentage, camp stores, guns, instruments ammunition and food. He reports going to camp in January 1939 at Narrabeen (on Sydney's north shore) with a critical transport shortage: 'The only vehicles [the unit had] were two Hathi tractors to tow the guns.'[59] Similarly, Official Historian Gavin Long wrote that 'even to move a brigade in 1939, the Army still had to use hired civilian vehicles.'[60]

During the interwar period, citizen Army training followed that of the British Army as the same equipment was used by both. British Army training manuals were not modified for use outside Europe and the use of British training manuals with little local content continued even as World War II progressed.[61] Even when new equipment was issued, it was still accompanied by British Army training manuals. It was not until September 1941 that an Army Training Memorandum was issued specifically for Australian conditions for use by the AMF/Militia.[62] It made the task of the AIC instructors, already tested by the dearth of equipment for training, all the more difficult. Fortunately, the AIC ranks boasted men who had seen service in the testing conditions of the Great War.

Leadership, bravery and conspicuous service

The depth of warfighting experience from the Great War on which the AIC could draw was remarkable. In 1939 the AIC had 153 quartermasters (67 permanent and 86 temporary appointments) of whom 112 had served in the 1st AIF. Of the 541 AIC warrant officers serving in 1939, some 181 had seen active service in the 1st AIF. Between them they had been awarded one MC, six DCMs and 10 MMs. In addition to distinguished wartime service, 32 quartermasters had been nationally recognised, awarded an MBE for conspicuous individual peacetime service.

Reinforcing the ranks of these experienced active service warrant officers were many younger men who had joined the Corps from the nine special courses held between 1935 and 1940. These men were to form the backbone of the AIC throughout the next great conflict and were already making their mark on the interwar Army. Despite the fact that Australian Staff Corps officers held all the senior PMF positions, a number of AIC honorary officers occupied influential postings.[63] In the Adjutant General's department, Quartermaster and Honorary Captain Alexander Christie, MBE, who commenced his AIC career as QP165 Warrant Officer Class II Christie, was Staff Officer Medical Services. Captain Christie served in World War II under the regimental number VX101927 and, in the Interim Army he was promoted twice and ended his service as Lieutenant Colonel Alexander Christie, MBE.

In the Quartermaster General's and Master of the Ordnance Department was Quartermaster and Honorary Lieutenant Arthur Bligh Smith Collins. Arthur Collins commenced his PMF service as 310 Warrant Officer Class II Collins, the Armament Clerk for the Director of Artillery. Quartermaster and Honorary Lieutenant George David Duncan was the quartermaster to the Director of Artillery.

The Director of Ordnance Services had two quartermasters, Temporary Quartermaster and Honorary Lieutenant Walter William Matthews and Temporary Quartermaster and Honorary Lieutenant Leslie George Worthington. George Worthington, previously 371 Warrant Officer Class II Worthington, survived the war and, in the Interim Army, became 2/233 Major Worthington. The Deputy Assistant Director of Mechanisation was Quartermaster and Honorary Major Carl Rudolph Speckman, MC, while Quartermaster and Honorary Captains A.A. Brown and J.P. Gordon were quartermasters in the Ordnance Services Department. The Quartermaster to the Director of Supplies, Transport, Movements and Quartering was Temporary Quartermaster and Honorary Lieutenant Thomas Henry Peddle.

Also promoted in late 1939 was Temporary Quartermaster and Honorary Lieutenant Vincent Dowdy who was appointed Temporary Adjutant of the 15th Light Horse Regiment.

AIC officers also held influential positions in the Army Schools. 281 WO1 A.E. 'Bert' Easter ex British Army was the riding master and later became RSM of RMC. His compatriot 318 WO1 A.T. 'Dusty' Mortimer, also ex British Army, was later to serve in New Guinea in World War II.[64] However from 1936 onwards the RMC quartermaster had been Quartermaster and Honorary Major Claude Cadman Easterbrook, DSO, MC. Brigadier Geoffrey Solomon, a staff cadet at RMC from 1938–1942, writes that, 'as cadets we had no finer example of what an officer should be, but no-one would have been more embarrassed than Claude Easterbrook to have heard it said.'[65] Indeed, Solomon was lavish in his praise for members of the AIC serving at RMC and provides some indication of the esteem in which the AIC staff were held in 1938:

> The warrant officers of the AIC in the hierarchy of the PMF ranked after the Staff Corps & the Corps of Staff Cadets. [AIC] members carried out instructive and administrative duties all over the country. They knew their own particular job but additionally their familiarity with Army procedures, their ability to make the system work by giving a push here and a pull there, and their understanding of the advantage of an occasional blind eye were of enormous help to young and inexperienced graduates of Duntroon whom they served so loyally.[66]

CHAPTER SEVEN
NOTES

1. As an example, Medical Courses for PMF and AMF were held at various locations until the School of Army Health was established, located at Healesville, Victoria.

2. NAA, D844 55/3/29 1941, Schedule 'C'.

3. Schedule Showing Allied Land Forces Schools as at 29 Feb 44, Appendix 'I', Sheets 1 & 2.

4. Major General I.C. Gordon (retd), Blamey Oration, paper presented to the Royal United Service Institution, NSW, 24 June 2003.

5. Bill Andrews in Roland Millbank, *A History of the Homebush Depot*, unpublished manuscript, Homebush, NSW, 1984, letter to the author, 21 May 1984.

6. Ibid.; Maurice Gillespie, letter to the author, 21 May 1984.

7. Ibid.; Rev (Captain) P.M. Clark, letter to the author, 21 May 1984.

8. Grey, *A Military History of Australia*, p. 148.

9. Dennis et al., *The Oxford Companion to Australian Military History*, p. 148.

10. N2863304 J. Johns, 36th Battalion, AMF, interview with the author, 12 January 2002.

11. The Australian Imperial Force, Staff, Regimental, and Graduation Lists of Officers, No. 2, 1st August 1940, By Authority: Brown, Prior, Anderson Pty. Ltd., 430 Little Burke Street, Melbourne, C1.

12. Ernest Lergessner (DOB 28/11/1906) enlisted in the RAA 29/3/1927 and qualified on No.7 Master Gunners Course in 1927.

13. Almost 20 years later, Colonel Allchin, MM, was the author of *Purple and Blue: The History of the 2/10 Battalion AIF, (The Adelaide Rifles),* The Griffin Press, Adelaide, 1958.

14. NAA, MP385/3 Item 27/20/807; letter from Headquarters Eastern Command to AHQ, Reference 27/20/807 dated 15 July 1940.

15. George Johnston, *Australia at War,* Angus & Robertson Ltd, Sydney, 1942, p. 142.

16. QP8313 Lieutenant Thomas Arthur Dawson was commissioned and served out the war with the 2nd AIF. Interview with the author 5 December 2002.

17. George Howard Andrews (DOB 1/7/1903)was VP 4253 became VX101972 and finished his service as QM (ARA).

18. P.J. Jackson, P. Cade, J. Huston and K. Moses, *White over Green, 2nd/4th Battalion AIF,* Angus & Robertson, Sydney, 1963, p. 7.

19. Mark Johnson, *The Silent 7th, An illustrated History of the 7th Australian Division 1940-1946,* Allen & Unwin, Sydney, 2005, p. 8.

20. David Hay, *Nothing Over Us, The Story of the 2nd/6th Australian Infantry Battalion,* Australian War Memorial, Canberra, 1984, p. 15.

21. Ibid., p. 13.

22. Frederick James Coupland, DOB 7/10/1921; 2642 (CMF), NP8767. NX116219; correspondence with the author, 3 August 2004.

23. Ibid.

24. Newton, 'A Full Military Life,' p. 17.

25. Colonel Guy Fawcett, OBE, correspondence with the author, 25 May 2003.

26. Phillip Bradley, *On Shaggy Ridge,* Oxford University Press, Melbourne, 2004, p. 56.

27. NAA, B2458, Item 611, Thomas, Kevan Brittan.

28. NAA, B2458, Item 611, Thomas, Kevan Brittan.

29. Online biography: http://adb.anu.edu.au/biography/kelly-joseph-lawrence-andrew-10675.

30. 4762 WOII G.J. Watson, DOB 9/1/1913.

31. Grey, *The Australian Army,* p. 122. See also AWM 182-10 A-M; and AWM 182-11 N-Z, AIC and Technical Units ledger.

32. Hay, *Nothing over Us,* Appendix 9, p. 586.

33. 5547 SSM 3rd Class later Colonel C.W. McPherson, MM, interview with the author, 19 December 2003.

34. Whiston, Another Whiston Matter, p. 140.

35.   Ibid., p. 168.

36.   'Notice to Recruits' from Captain H.S. Hamilton, Area 55 Drill Hall, Forest Lodge, NSW, to Peter Wright, dated 14 January 1942.

37.   N247472, later NX196764 Private Trevor Harper, 55/53 Battalion, AIF, interview with the author, 2 February 2005.

38.   Long, *To Benghazi*, p. 51.

39.   Ibid., pp. 52–53.

40.   NX43679 Gunner Noel Harrison, interview with the author, 14 July 2005.

41.   Ibid., p. 73.

42.   Ibid., p. 68.

43.   Grey, *The Australian Army*, p. 124.

44.   Alan H. Smith, *Battle Winners, Australian Artillery in the Western Desert, 1941–42*, Echo Books, Canberra, 2014.

45.   Colonel Guy Fawcett, OBE, interview 26 May 2003.

46.   R.N.L. Hopkins, *Australian Armour, A History of the Royal Australian Armoured Corps 1927-1972*, Australian War Memorial, Canberra, 1978, p. 22.

47.   Handel, *Dust, Sand & Jungle*, p. 14.

48.   Hopkins, *Australian Armour*, p. 33.

49.   Handel, *Dust, Sand & Jungle*, p. 15.

50.   Hopkins, *Australian Armour*, p. 33.

51.   Grey, *A Military History of Australia*, p. 135.

52.   Ibid., p. 97.

53.   'There is evidence that some British Army training manuals were modified for Australian use, an example being AMF Field Service Pocket Book 1939', Letter to the author, Ian Kuring, 17 September 2013.

54.   Dennis et al., *The Oxford Companion to Australian Military History*, p. 296. 'Major Keith Avery Watts, DOB March 1904, 1st Light Horse (NSW Lancers) after training with RTC became a Gunnery Instructor at AFV School, Balcombe and Puckapunyal. Promoted major he commanded Gunnery Wing; 1942 commanded B Sqn 2/7 Armoured Regiment and in 1943 became 2IC of 2/7. In 1944 reported to HQ 4th Armoured Bde, finally an observer, US Army Engineer Special Bde.' See Handel, *Dust, Sand & Jungle*, p. 140. NAA, B1535, Item 929/21/185, Training Abroad, No. 3 Report, 3 July—16 September 1937, Attachment to 1st (Light) Battalion, Royal Tank Corps, WO K.A. Watts.

55.   Grey, *The Australian Army*, p. 98.

56. James C. Morrison, *Mechanising an Army, Mechanisation Policy and Conversion of Light Horse 1923-1940*, Land Warfare Studies Centre, Canberra, June 2006, p. 74.

57. Report of the Inspector General of the Australian Military Forces, Lieutenant General Sir H.G. Chauvel, Part 1, Melbourne, 31 May 1927, Item 66.

58. Andrew T. Ross, 'Armed and Ready, the Industrial Development and Defence of Australia, 1900–1945', *Journal of the Australian War Memorial*, Issue 28, April, 1996, p. 95.

59. 2881 Lieutenant Colonel Robert Norton Whiston, Another Whiston Matter, unpublished manuscript, Sydney 1996, p. 125.

60. Long, *To Benghazi*, p. 20.

61. Training Regulations 1934, His Majesty's Stationery Office, London.

62. Army Training Memorandum (War), No. 2 September 1941, Victorian Railway Printing Works.

63. The Army List of the Australian Military Forces, Part 1 Active List, 1 February 1939, Departments of the Military Board, pp. 10–12.

64. Newton, *The Australian Instructional Corps,* Australian Infantry Magazine, October 2013-April 2014, pp 56-67.

65. G.D. Solomon, *A Poor sort of Memory, A personal memoir of the Royal Military College, Duntroon*, Roebuck Society Publication, Canberra, 1978, p. 123.

66. Ibid., p. 98.

Chapter Eight
Training the Darwin Mobile Force (DMF)

In 1939, as the Army yet again stood on the brink of war, its AIC instructors and quartermasters worked very hard to ensure that the men would be sufficiently trained and equipped to face whatever this next great conflict would throw at them. One specific task undertaken by the AIC, largely prior to 1939, deserves special recognition—the training of the Darwin Mobile Force (DMF). The importance of this task to the Army in World War II cannot be over emphasised. The DMF was the first regular infantry field force to be raised in Australia and the role of training its members was crucial to the successful operation of the force.[1]

DMF-AIC relationship

Under the provisions of the *Defence Act (1903)*, the establishment of permanent infantry forces as elements of the Australian Army was prohibited. However, by 1938, aware that the British Empire appeared increasingly likely to be dragged into another global war, the Australian Government sought to circumvent the rules of Section 31 of the *Defence Act* and establish Regular Army mobile forces that would defend strategic locations around the country. Since Federation the *Defence Act* had authorised permanent units of the RAA and thus, under these terms, all soldiers of the DMF were enlisted as gunners in the RAA, rather than as infantry privates.[2]

The role of the DMF encompassed four distinct tasks. It would act as a mobile force to respond to sporadic raids in the Darwin area; provide basic training for all members of the force; provide experience for members of the DMF who would then join the AIC; and supply command opportunities for RMC graduates.[3] When the force was raised, a number of AIC warrant officers joined as staff. They conducted the practical training of the soldiers, many of whom would later graduate through No. 9 AIC Special Course to become instructors themselves.

Origins of the DMF

The rationale for the creation of such a force has been the subject of some debate. While some accounts have attributed the establishment of the force to changes in the Army recommended by the Inspector General, Lieutenant General E.K. Squires, CB, DSO, MC, in his first report (known as the Squires Report) this is unlikely. The Squires Report was handed down in December 1938, some weeks after the establishment of the DMF in November 1938.[4] Indeed, Cabinet approval for the raising of the DMF occurred even earlier, in October 1938. This was a result of Cabinet having considered the deliberations of the 1937 Imperial Conference and the results of a study into the preparedness of the Army for war by the CGS, Major General J.D. Lavarack, in September 1936.[5]

History of the DMF

The DMF was raised in Liverpool Camp, NSW, on 14 November 1938 and trained there for the next three months.[6] The CO was Major Alex Bath MacDonald, a 1920 graduate of RMC Duntroon who had previously commanded the 56th Battalion (The Riverina Regiment). Major MacDonald had been made redundant in 1922 but had later been recalled to the Staff Corps. The DMF's Quartermaster was the AIC's Honorary Lieutenant Andrew Barkley Stephen, DCM, who had previously served at RMC Duntroon as a physical training instructor.[7] The DMF's RSM was also from the AIC—Warrant Officer Class I Neville Franklyn Ransom, a former RSM of RMC Duntroon.

As the first Australian permanent Army infantry unit, the DMF attracted much attention. Among the distinguished visitors was the Governor-General, Lord Gowrie.[8] The force conducted intensive training in the summer of 1938–39, one of the hottest on record. The hot Sydney weather did much to provide partial acclimatisation to the heat the troops were later to experience in Darwin. On 9 March 1939, its training program completed, the DMF held a ceremonial parade in Sydney.[9] The men of the DMF then embarked on the SS *Marella* and the SS *Montoro* for their passage to Darwin, stopping at Brisbane, where another ceremonial parade was held.[10] Arriving in Darwin, the DMF was accommodated at the abandoned site of Vestey's Meatworks, some three miles (five kilometres) out of Darwin.

Darwin was a strategically important naval base, particularly in 1938, because its location was approximately midway between Sydney and the vital British naval base of Singapore. It was the only port in Australia's 'top end' capable of refuelling and provisioning naval ships in anything resembling a defensible fleet anchorage. The Army's task was to defend the port and surrounding countryside from air, sea and land attacks.

Prior to the establishment of the DMF there had been no permanent military presence in Darwin other than the gunners, who manned several 6-inch guns relocated from Thursday Island, and a number of anti-aircraft armaments. This lack of defensive presence was largely attributed to the dearth of men of British ancestry to fill the ranks of a Darwin Militia unit.[11]

The arrival of the DMF provided the city of Darwin and its surrounding districts with a strong force of keen young men ready to tackle any number of tasks including unloading ships and guarding tactical roads and oil installations. The AIC, however, was less than impressed with the long list of tasks assigned to its young charges that promised to wreak havoc with its training plans. Bob Bucknell recalls:

> I can remember 18 of us (including myself) being sent to the oil
> storages tanks under Lt. F. Hassett [later General Sir Francis
> Hassett], Sgt Jack Smiles 2ic ('Ferocious Jack') and Len Hutton the
> cook. Our duties, as well as mortar training, were to guard the oil
> tanks from being sabotaged in the event of war, which was very close
> at that time. Jack Smiles was a good soldier but was very unpopular
> with the men; his aim was to make a good soldier out of us.[12]

'Ferocious Jack'—Sergeant Jack Smiles—was later selected to join the
AIC. As a graduate of No. 9 Special Course he became 3088 Temporary
Warrant Officer Class II J.F. Smiles.

The DMF managed to achieve only four months of genuine tropical
training from April to July 1939. The force was on exercise at Adelaide
River in August/September 1939 when Prime Minister Menzies' broadcast
to the nation alerted them to the fact that they were now at war. The troops
returned to Darwin posthaste.

Back in Darwin it was only a matter of time before officers left to
join the newly raised 2nd AIF and their replacements poured in.[13] Those
candidates selected for AIC training were then posted from the force and
were duly replaced over the next three months. The replacement process
was largely completed by December 1939. However, by August 1940, when
the DMF moved to Larrakeyah Barracks in Darwin, the size of the force
had fallen to 172 from the original 233.[14] The DMF was officially disbanded
on 20 August 1940 when the gunners, who were actually infantry soldiers,
joined the newly raised Darwin Infantry Battalion.

Discrepancies in numbers

Sources differ on the precise size of the DMF. There are variations
in numbers of both officers and other ranks, including the warrant
officers. Of particular interest is the difference between the original AIC
Establishment figure of four warrant officers[15] and a published nominal
roll listing a figure of 12 warrant officers.[16] The addition of eight warrant

officers would have made a significant difference to the very small force that was the PMF at the time, particularly since their task involved the practical training of 300 soldiers specially selected for higher duties in the lead-up to active service.

So who were these eight extra AIC warrant officers? Australian Army Order No. 1-1939 provides three AIC establishment positions: one quartermaster, one warrant officer Class I and one warrant officer Class II. The fourth AIC warrant officer Class II is listed as attached to the 'rifle company'. The quartermaster was Honorary Lieutenant Andrew B. Stephen, DCM, and the warrant officer Class I was Norman F. Ransom.[17] However, instead of just two warrant officers Class II, the nominal roll published by Swifte in 1978 and copied by Collins in 1989, lists ten. The simple explanation is that at least some, if not all, of these additional warrant officers Class II were replacements. Guy Fawcett, for example, took over as RSM from Norman Ransom as enlistments in the 2nd AIF increased. Thus the nominal roll of 1978 includes everyone who joined the DMF, not just those who were originally posted to the unit in 1938. The establishment listed one Ordnance Mechanical Engineer 4th Class, R.F. Edgecome, and two staff sergeants from the Australian Ordnance Corps, J. Gibson and N. King. The identified AIC members are G.R. Cox, Guy H. Fawcett, Jack Fox, Norman F. Garrard and L.H. Male.

It is difficult to trace the post-DMF Army careers of 4478 Warrant Officer Class II G.R. Cox and 3706 Warrant Officer Class II L.W. Male, however NP2759 Warrant Officer Class II Norman Frederick Garrard survived the war to become a commissioned Ordnance Corps officer.[18] The remaining two identified establishment DMF warrant officers each became commissioned officers. Following his initial posting to the 4th Battalion, The Australian Rifles, AMF, in 1938, Warrant Officer Guy Fawcett became an instructor in the DMF. Fawcett was later promoted Warrant Officer Class I and appointed RSM of the DMF. He was eventually commissioned and served in Syria as a Bren gun carrier platoon commander with the $2^{nd}/27^{th}$ Battalion. He returned to Australia and filled an instructor's position at the School of Infantry before his request to return to the $2^{nd}/27^{th}$ saw him given command of D Company during the Ramu Valley campaign in Papua and New Guinea.[19] He was to achieve his own brand of fame with the naming of Guy's Post, a plateau overlooking the Faria River that runs into the Ramu Valley.[20] No. 4484 (SP4484) Warrant Officer Class II Jack Fox was a graduate of No. 3 Special Course, served as SX25427 in World War II and was later promoted in the Interim Army where he retired as 4/53 Major (Quartermaster) Fox.

Of the other warrant officers on the DMF Nominal Roll, 3092 Warrant Officer Class II Sydney Ronald Leach was commissioned as a quartermaster after World War II, becoming 2/177 Lieutenant (Quartermaster) Leach, MBE. A graduate of No. 4 Special Course, 2274 Warrant Officer Class II Frederick George Alexander Pickburn also served through World War II to become 1/106 Major (Quartermaster) Pickburn in the Interim Army. Finally, a graduate of No. 1 Special Course, 1846 Warrant Officer Class II Les H. Wilson, following commissioning in the Interim Army, was promoted and retired as a lieutenant colonel.

Supernumerary?

Since neither Northern Command nor the 7th Military District existed in 1939, posting warrant officers to the DMF may have been problematic. Both Guy Fawcett and G.R. Cox are shown as posted to the 4th Division, at that time located in Victoria and South Australia. It is likely that the additional warrant officers were held supernumerary to the DMF establishment, the additional staff justified by the difficulties inherent in training troops in tropical conditions in totally unfamiliar terrain.

Special training

Soldiers seeking to qualify for warrant rank had to pass the Army Certificate of Education. Bob Whiston writes:

> Now that I was fully qualified for the rank of sergeant and with the
> Anti Aircraft Gunnery Course behind me I only had to pass the
> First Class Educational Exam to qualify for Warrant Rank.[21]

Well aware of the subject matter necessary to prepare soldiers for warrant rank, the AIC warrant officers of the DMF organised specific classes.[22] Preparation of soldiers as candidates for promotion assumed a high priority as Guy Fawcett remarks: 'I personally spent many hours undertaking extra training for DMF soldiers so that they would qualify and be able to attend No. 9 Special Course.'[23] The DMF was evidently very successful in preparing its candidates for the AIC. Lieutenant Colonel L.F. (Frank) Guest, a graduate of No. 9 (Special) Course, Central Training Depot, recalls that, 'Amongst the many candidates we had a number of DMF members who were on my course No. 9 (Special Course).'[24]

Field force training of regular troops had always been an AIC task. The DMF training program was unusual because, while attached to other units, the AIC members acted as instructors; with the DMF they actually undertook NCO duties. Thus this training program resembled an extended on-the-job course under the most testing conditions.

DMF/AIC retrospective

DMF personnel who joined the AIC, among them the 38 soldiers who completed No. 9 Special Course (10 February 1940–27 June 1940), brought with them a broad range of experiences.[25] Although there were no more Special Courses after June 1940 the demand for instructors was so high that the Army took the unusual course of appointing experienced NCOs directly into the AIC. It was by this means that an additional four DMF soldiers joined the Corps. The majority of DMF soldiers who became instructors were subsequently commissioned into the AMF/Militia and AIF. One of these men was Keith H. Trevan who initially enlisted in the RAA in 1938 before transferring to the DMF and later wrote on aspects of the history of the force. By July 1940 he was a warrant officer class II in the AIC where he conducted signals training. Commissioned in World War II, Keith Trevan retired as a major and was one of only two AIC warrant officers known to have seen active service in South Vietnam.[26] The other officer was Major (later Lieutenant Colonel) Frank Guest.[27]

Some 100 DMF soldiers were commissioned into the AIF during World War II. At the end of the war, a large number of former DMF soldiers received permanent commissions and continued serving as officers in the Interim Army and the Australian Regular Army. One such soldier was 4944 Temporary Warrant Officer Class II Bernard S. Savage. He later qualified to join the Staff Corps and retired as a substantive colonel (on retirement, by Imperial honours, Brigadier). The DMF was a handpicked force (233 candidates were selected from 3,000 volunteers) and the fact that almost half of these soldiers were later commissioned is an extraordinary testament to the quality of their initial selection and training.

Like the AIC, the DMF never saw active service as a force and thus has no unit war diary to record its story. However, through the individual soldiers who made up the DMF, it is quite clear that the force made an enormous contribution to the success of the Australian Army in World War II. In particular through the DMF role as a training and proving ground for talented individuals who went on to serve with distinction in the 2nd AIF.

Chapter Eight
Notes

1.   Robert J. Rayner, *The Army and the Defence of Darwin Fortress,* Rudder Press,
     Plumpton, NSW, 1995; June Collins, *Bandy's Boys, The Darwin Mobile Force,*
     self-published, Melbourne, 1989.
2.   Collins, *Bandy's Boys*, p. 3.
3.   Rayner, *The Army and the Defence of Darwin Fortress*, p. 5.
4.   AWM 54, 243/6/58, First Report by Lieutenant General E.K. Squires, CB,
     DSO, MC, Inspector General of the Australian Military Forces, Copy No. 32.
5.   Dennis et al., *The Oxford Companion to Australian Military History*, p. 202.
6.   George Vasenry, A Short History of the Australian Army, unpublished
     manuscript, 1984, Annex C, The Darwin Mobile Force.
7.   Keith H. Trevan, 'The Darwin Mobile Force' in *The Army Journal*, No. 275
     (April 1972), p. 6.
8.   Ibid., p. 8.
9.   L.B. (Tim) Swifte, *Darwin Mobile Force: 40th Anniversary Celebrations*, Victoria
     Barracks Commemorative Booklet, 1978, DMF Highlights.
10. Ibid.
11. Palazzo, *The Australian Army*, p. 127.
12. Collins, *Bandy's Boys,* p. 9.
13. Dennis et al., *The Oxford Companion to Australian Military History*, p. 203.
14. Rayner, *The Army and the Defence of Darwin Fortress*, p. 8. Both Collins and
     Swifte give the number as 245.
15. Australian Army Order 1-1939.

16.   Swifte, *Darwin Mobile Force: 40th Anniversary Celebrations*.

17.   The Army List of the Australian Military Forces, Part 1. Active List, 1 February 1939, Permanent Military Forces, Temporary Quartermasters, Australian Instructional Corps, page 68, lists Honorary Lieutenant A.B. Stephen, DCM, as posted to the DMF on 14.11.38.

18.   Whiston, Another Whiston Matter, p. 194.

19.   Gavin Long, *The Final Campaigns, Australia in the War of 1939-1945*, Series One, Army, Vol. 7, Australian War Memorial, Canberra, 1963.

20.   Phillip Bradley, *On Shaggy Ridge*, Oxford University Press, Melbourne, 2004, pp. 52–54.

21.   Whiston, Another Whiston Matter, p. 127.

22.   Military Order 147-1933, Subjects for the Army Certificate of Education: Arithmetic; English Part 1 Essay, Part 2 Précis; History, Geography & Map Reading.

23.   Colonel Guy Fawcett, OBE, interview with the author, 26 May 2003.

24.   Lieutenant Colonel L.F. (Frank) Guest, correspondence with the author, March 2003—May 2005; interview with the author, 2 April 2003.

25.   See Appendix 5 of the conclusion of this chapter for a list of DMF soldiers who joined the AIC.

26.   Trevan, *The Darwin Mobile Force*, p. 3.

27.   Major L.F. Guest went to Vietnam as Deputy Assistant Quartermaster General (Movements). Lieutenant Colonel L.F. Guest interview with the author, 15 January 2005.

APPENDIX FIVE
DMF SOLDIERS WHO JOINED THE AIC

Family Name	Initials	Regt. No.	Rank	AIC Special Course	Subsequent Service
Allum	R C	3858		9	
Ashdown	C R W	4904		9	
Bingham	G	3976		9	
Bosworth	G	4708		9	
Bowie	R W	3298		9?	
Buckingham	D J	2434		9	
Burgess	G K	4033		9	
Cady	A	3337		9	
Clarke	R C	5311		9	
Collins	D D	4785		9	MBE
Cran	D McK	2351		9F	
Delves	G L	4006		9F	
Dettman	L P	4629		9	
Druitt	C K	4002		9	
Elbourne	A D	4909		9	

Family Name	Initials	Regt. No.	Rank	AIC Special Course	Subsequent Service
Ellis	C C	3981		9	
Fyffe	J L	4004		9	
Gardner	M C	4911		9	MBE
Gaul	A J F	4912		9	
Greer	W	3970		9	
Hills	S E	4025		9	
Huggins	A H F	4919		9	
Kennedy	K W	4922		9	
Lawn	B E	3824		9	
Magarry	R W	2345		9	MC
Meech	L E	4756		9	
Murray	W B	4938		9	
Newman	R D	4940		9	
Orme	C J	4939		9	
Savage	B S	4944		9	MBE
Smiles	J F	3088			
Smith	G L	4008		9	
Spence	K	4950		9	
Stead	A E J	3969		9	
Stewart	A A				CSM 2/1 Bn AIF
Stone	R J	3330		9	
Sydes	F	2343		9	
Taylor	W L	4020			
Warham	R E	4957		9	
Whitehouse	R J	2807		9F	
Wilson	D	3005		9	

CHAPTER NINE
POLITICS AND SOCIAL FACTORS

A view from outside the drill hall

Although a separate entity in itself, the Army never operated in a vacuum and was always part of the constituent social fabric of the country. Social factors, including politics, played an important part in shaping the life of the Army. For its members, however, the Army followed a strict policy of demanding that servicemen remain publicly apolitical regardless of their personal views. Politics, it was considered, had 'no place in the service', and this applied equally to conservative and socialist views. However this policy would be seriously challenged when the New Guard movement came to prominence in NSW in the era of the Jack Lang Labor Government.

The populist view of the Army that predominated during the interwar years was that soldiers were 'only necessary in time of war'. This was a view publicly espoused by several prominent and vocal sections of the populace and a number of politicians. This view was to have a serious impact on the professional soldiers whose job it was to train the Army.

As representative of all levels of society, the AIC certainly boasted its share of heroes and villains. While a number of AIC warrant officers displayed outstanding bravery, as will be recounted, there were some senior NCOs who discredited the good name of the corps.

The New Guard

Financial problems caused by the Great Depression exposed deep divisions in Australian politics. Socialists such as Jack Lang, Premier of NSW from 1925 to 1927 and again from 1930 to 1932, argued for the cancellation of interest payments to overseas creditors, including the London banks, until the domestic economy had improved. Conservatives led by Joe Lyons, Prime Minister from 1932 to 1939, viewed cancelling interest payments as foolhardy and, in the case of the London banks, almost as treachery against the British Empire. Disputes over debt repayment to Britain became so bitter that it resulted in violent confrontation between workers and militant members of the middle class, most notably a group known as the New Guard.

The New Guard was organised and controlled by former Army officers. The Military Board, fearful that serving officers could become involved, was prepared to impose stringent measures to ensure that the service remained aloof from any form of politics, irrespective of whether it was left wing or right wing. While the title 'New Guard' suggests the act of guarding a set of values and the community, it was, in fact, a paramilitary organisation that embraced what many regarded as a fascist ideology.

New Guard members equated socialism with communism. If a socialist government could seriously consider cancelling the debt to the London bankers, then the New Guard was prepared to take action to prevent this. They were even prepared to overthrow the legitimately elected Lang Labor Government in NSW by violent means.[2] While there is no evidence that the Army hierarchy was anxious over the spread of communism in Australia in the early post-war period, the activities of the New Guard in the second decade between the wars certainly excited a sharp response.[2]

Publicity surrounding Colonel Eric Campbell, a World War I veteran and leader of the New Guard, the movement's disruption of communist meetings and assistance to police at worker evictions ensured that New Guard activities were well known in the senior circles of the Army.[3] Any doubt would have been removed by the infamous cutting of the ribbon by New Guard member and retired Captain Francis de Groot which stymied Labor Premier Jack Lang's bid to open the Sydney Harbour Bridge. It is possible that a number of AIC members were involved with the New Guard, but there is evidence of only one quartermaster ever actually being charged by the Army with membership of the notorious association. This case, in 1933, involved Quartermaster and Honorary Lieutenant H.H. Downey, MC.

Fig 10. *Major Herbert Hamilton Downey MC, D.A.D.O.S. Corps Troops 1 Aust. Corps, Aust. Army Ordnance Corps, Major Downey's Military Cross was awarded during the First World War.* (Australian War Memoroial 002334)

Herbert Hamilton Downey was a PMF soldier who had enlisted in 1910 as a gunner in the Permanent Artillery. He joined the 1st AIF as a

Company Sergeant Major and went to France with the 2nd Australian Siege Battery. He was awarded the MC for bravery on the Western Front.[4] In New Guard terms, Herbert Downey had an impeccable pedigree, having served in the 1st AIF alongside Eric Campbell, later to become Commander of the New Guard.[5] Downey also knew Major Scott, Campbell's New Guard deputy, and Captain Francis de Groot of Sydney Harbour Bridge ribbon-cutting fame.[6]

In Victoria, Herbert Downey had been a member of an organisation formed for the purpose of maintaining constitutional government against the attacks of communists and other disloyal elements known as the 'White Army'.[7] His membership of this organisation saw Downey charged with 'disloyal activities' by the Army. In answering the charge, Quartermaster Downey assured his accusers that the organisation was well-known to prominent serving officers and its activities perhaps even condoned. Indeed, 'General [Sir Cyril Brudenell] White presided over the Melbourne organisation and ... Major Roach was its intelligence officer.' This fact 'was known to Major Scott and Major [Blair] Wark, VC, Major Scott having informed me that he had met Major Roach.'[8]

News of Herbert Downey's membership of the Melbourne organisation reached the New Guard who approached him to establish a link between the two organisations. It was Herbert Downey's misfortune that this attempted linkage between the Melbourne organisation and the New Guard came to the attention of the Army hierarchy in February 1932. A report of his activities had been sent to his CO on 27 January 1932 and, in February, Downey was paraded before Brigadier Bede Heritage, an Australian Staff Corps officer commanding 2 District Base, and informed that his activities were viewed with concern by authorities. As Downey later wrote, 'The AA&QMG [Assistant Adjutant and Quartermaster General] sent for me and informed me that certain intelligence reports had disclosed the fact that I had been addressing New Guard Meetings. I denied this.' He did not, however, deny that he belonged to a body with similar aims: 'I, in the company of several others in 1930 concerned ourselves in the formation of a body for the purpose of maintaining Constitutional Government against the attack of Communism or other disloyal elements.'[9] Brigadier Heritage clearly regarded Downey as a good man gone astray and satisfied himself with requiring Downey to give an undertaking to discontinue all activities with organisations such as the New Guard.[10] Downey honoured his promise for the remainder of his life.

The Army's pursuit of Quartermaster Downey's case raises questions concerning the Army's intrusive scrutiny of the recreational pursuits of serving soldiers. It also raises the spectre of unfair treatment of warrant officers by the Army hierarchy given that there appears to be no evidence that the Military Board ever questioned either of the Staff Corps officers mentioned by Herbert Downey in his evidence. General Sir Cyril Brudenell White, having retired, was exempt from military law. However, Major Blair Wark, VC, at that time on the Reserve of Officers, was certainly involved in the same organisation as White and Downey and may also have had some dealings with the New Guard. However there is no evidence that Wark was questioned over his involvement or penalised for his membership of the Victorian organisation. It appears that, where personal involvement in politics was concerned, a Staff Corps officer was permitted to act with impunity while Herbert Downey, a substantive warrant officer, could not.

Despite this 'black mark' on his record, 1st Class Master Gunner Herbert Downey, MC, was awarded the Long Service and Good Conduct Medal (LSGCM), followed in 1935 by the award of the Meritorious Service Medal (MSM). Enlisting in the 2nd AIF, Herbert Downey was commissioned, promoted major and appointed Deputy Assistant Director of Ordnance Services, I Australian Corps. He was deployed to Greece and, after a total of 32 years' service, Major Herbert Downey, MC, died of wounds inflicted during an air attack at Thebes in April 1941.[11]

The social fit—the public perception of the Army

The outstanding success of the 1st AIF and the growing Anzac legend had given rise to many popular perceptions about Australia's citizen soldiers. While Australia had enlisted almost 500,000 soldiers during the Great War, fewer than 2000 of these men were PMF professionals. The success of the 1st AIF citizen force appeared to set aside the need for professional soldiers. In addition, many Australians believed that the recent Great War had been 'the war to end all wars'. John Curtin had used this term when reflecting on the war in an editorial he wrote for the *Westralian Worker* on 18 December 1925. In turn this led to the belief that public money needed for reconstruction should not be spent on defence.

Well aware that the war had been enormously costly in lives, finance and subsequent repatriation and medical costs, a considerable portion of the population was prepared to go to great lengths to ensure that there would not be another war. They threw their weight behind the peace process and the newly created international body, the League of Nations, which was considered enormously important in enhancing Australia's defensive posture.[12]

What was very clear in the 1920s, was that the government had very little money to spend on defence and kept the Army to a minimum wherever it could. The opposition Labor Party under Matthew Charlton thought that peacetime training was a waste of time. Charlton's view was that the conduct of war was changing constantly, when and if hostilities seemed impending, Australia's armies could be quickly trained and raised to modern efficiency. This supported the notion that Australia should not have a regular Army of any size.

Even within the Army itself there appeared to be a view that regular soldiers were not necessary. A Staff Corps officer writing about the Army at that time commented,

> The Army was the Militia, and Australia had no need for a bunch of jack-booted Prussian regulars.

Jack booted Prussian regulars was a transposed British view of European armies where, a mistake in drill, could bring immediate corporal punishment.[13] Richmond Cubis goes on to state,

> Regular soldiers of that time (consisted of) a small permanent staff to count the rifles, saddle the horses and gun teams, and clean the depot after the men had gone home.[14]

While this description provides a rather mundane work prospect, it does clearly articulate the some of the tasks of professional soldiers in Australia in the first decade between the wars.

In direct contrast, in the interwar period the Militia officers, who had high community social standing, were actually seen as representing the officer class in Australia. These included members of parliament such as Brigadier General Harold (Pompey) Elliott, lawyers, and engineers such as General Sir John Monash. Only a relatively few senior permanent officers had any sort of broad social profile outside the Army.

After the Great War, as life returned to normal, a perception appeared to be that,

> The Army had retreated behind the walls of its fortresses and drill halls to wait for the next war.

While this might not have been a popular observation, to some extent the permanent Army was out of view. In the middle of 1936, using newly acquired motor transport; the guns of 'A' Battery Royal Australian Artillery did a long deployment to Queensland. It was reported;

> This was the first time in more than twenty years that NSW and Queensland had seen professional soldiers.[15]

On a personal level Bob Whiston (who became an AIC Warrant Officer in 1938) in 1934 was too old to be recruited as a NSW police officer at age 25. A friend recommended that he 'try for the permanent Army.' Whiston, a countryman from near Casino in northern NSW comments,

> I didn't even know there was a permanent Army![16]

Between the wars in Australia at least one social commentator saw professional soldiers in a less than favourable light compared to citizen soldiers. Presenting the citizen soldier as representatives of the general population, Jane Ross describes regulars as 'deviant sub types' inferring that they were different from the rest of the population because of their militaristic outlook.[17]

A very anti-war view on soldiers is expressed by Geoffrey Serle who states;

> All armies are an abomination: Army life is purgatory to any civilized man.'[18]

Although these two social commentators' did not think well of the Army, such views, aired publically, must have had some negative effects on the working life of the men of the corps made up 37.5% of the permanent force.

Dominion attitudes to professional soldiers

It is a mistake to imagine that public attitudes of war weariness in Australia were unusual. Similar attitudes existed in other commonwealth nations. Writing about the period after the Boer War in *Britain and Her Army* Correlli Barnett states,

> In fact neither government nor nation was very much interested in the Army except to cheer a victory.[19]

Still later, with victory won after the Great War, Barnett states,

> Once again the Army lay outside the nation's life and thought.[20]

With the Canadian Expeditionary Force (CEF) disbanded after the war and training and exercising fallen to quite a low level, a permanent officer observed,

> In the interwar years, the military were not soldiers but there were many experts on the King's Dress Regulations.[21]

Such a comment can be taken to indicate that the Army was concerned with issues within itself and almost outside public consciousness.

Public display

Even when Australia started to re-arm, negative public attitudes to war continued. This was reflected in the decision of some cinemas in Melbourne in 1936 to refuse to screen recruiting advertisements for the Militia because 'they didn't wish to risk offending patrons.'[22]

Nothing really surpassed the efforts of the Australian government to avoid war because, in collaboration with Britain, they encouraged appeasement as the best way to preserve peace. Partridge states;

> There was no aspect of the Chamberlain policy [to appease Germany] on which it appeared that Lyons or any of his ministers had any important disagreements or reservations.[23]

Throughout the interwar period, despite radial changes of government in two decades, the concept of a citizen Army supported by a small professional force remained unchanged. Governments continued to see the Militia as the Army and therefore the PMF continued to be regarded as the 'handmaidens to the citizen Army.'[24]

Professional officers and soldiers who survived the drastic cuts of 1922, the cancellation of the UTS in 1929 and the financial cuts of 1931, were often only brought out on public display on state occasions to provide honour guards for prominent civil ceremonies. Bob Whiston recorded such an occasion:

> The official opening of the [1935] Royal Easter Show was performed by the Governor of NSW, Lord Gowrie. 1 Hvy Bde RAA provided a ceremonial guard of 3 officers and 48 Ors. Three of my squad were chosen to make up the numbers and I had the honour to be one of them. It was quite an experience to perform in front of the public. After a ceremonial parade we always bought the paper to see what we looked like and sometimes even order a copy of the photo in the paper. We would criticise anyone who showed the wrong slope on his rifle or was not swinging his arm properly.[25]

Heroes

AIC warrant officers generally reflected the middle class values of their times and their willingness to fight for 'God, king and country'.[26] The courage of these men under fire is borne out in the number of bravery decorations awarded in both world wars. The high regard in which contemporary officers and soldiers held the AIC is partly a consequence of the staggeringly large number of highly decorated officers and soldiers within its ranks as a result of active service in both world wars.

Active service awards for 1,377 known members of the AIC include one VC, 27 MCs, 11 DSOs, one *Croix de Guerre* (C de G), 10 DCMs, 22 MMs, one MM and Bar and two Mentioned in Dispatches (MID). For exceptional devotion to duty in peacetime, some 13 AIC members were made Officers of the Order of the British Empire (OBE), and 25 awarded the MBE. Almost half of these warrant officers received more than one award for both bravery and devotion to duty.

Wartime service was rife with risk, and a number of AIC members undertaking corps duties, as distinct from battalion or regimental duties, died during World War II. Deceased members of the corps are commemorated in a section of Panel 59, Hall of Remembrance, Australian War Memorial, which is dedicated to the AIC.[27]

Villains

While the bulk of AIC warrant officers were both brave and conscientious, there were also a few who discredited the good name of the corps. One married quartermaster with a distinguished Great War record purported to be a single man in order to obtain a young lady's favours. After receiving complaints from the young lady's fiancé, the Adjutant-General invoked a Court of Inquiry. Although highly critical of this officer's conduct, the Adjutant-General found that 'no military offence had been committed'.[28]

During the interwar decades permanent soldiers were progressively re-engaged for three years at a time until retirement age. One AIC warrant officer complained about unfair dismissal when he was not invited to re-engage. Investigation revealed that this member had altered travel warrants for the purpose of proceeding on, or returning from, his annual recreation leave. To alter travel warrants was, of course, a criminal offence.[29]

Another intriguing case concerns a warrant officer who was dismissed after being investigated for subversive activities. According to the evidence tendered against him in 1938, he had attended a number of meetings with Italian, Japanese and German nationals in Australia. This warrant officer was a German linguist and held in high regard by the German community in Australia. He was not offered the option of further Army service when it was time for re-engagement.[30]

Perhaps the most unfortunate case was the warrant officer who, recalled from active service, had used a woman friend to pose as his wife to claim marriage allowance. Although he was entitled to claim the allowance, the Courts Martial ruled that 'this money was for his wife and for another woman to claim this money was forgery.'[31]

Two final cases possibly reflect the results of service in the Great War. One concerned an AIC honorary lieutenant discharged after conviction for indecent exposure by a civil court.[32] The second involved an AIC warrant officer listed in Military Orders as 'struck off strength as from 16 February 1923, having been posted as a deserter on that date.'[33] The evidence suggests that these were isolated cases, and that exemplary behavior was more typical of the majority of members of the AIC.

CHAPTER NINE
NOTES

1. Macintyre, *A Concise History of Australia*, pp. 179–80.
2. Extensive research by authors such as Chris Coulthard-Clark does not produce evidence of one ex-serviceman in either federal or state parliaments who was either a communist or represented them. See C.D. Coulthard-Clark, *Soldiers in Politics, The Impact of the military on Australian Political Life & Institutions,* Allen & Unwin, Sydney, 1996.
3. Macintyre, *A Concise History of Australia,* p. 180.
4. Extract from *Commonwealth of Australia Gazette*, No. 53 of 30 June 1932, Australian Military Forces; Australian Instructional Corps, To be Quartermaster (s) & Honorary Lieutenant(s) (on probation), Master Gunner 1st Class (WO 1) (Honorary Lieutenant) Herbert Hamilton Downey, MC.
5. Clark, *A History of Australia*, Vol. VI, p. 368.
6. Robertson, '1930-1939' in Frank Crowley (ed), *A New History of Australia*, p. 431.
7. Biography-Sir Cyril Brudenell White-Australian Dictionary of Biography http://adb.anu.edu.au/biography-sir-cyril-brudenell-1032.
8. NAA, S33/1/30, Subject: New Guard Activities 1933, Letter to AA & QMG, 2 Dist Base from H.H. Downey, Lt, AIC, dated 6 February 1932.
9. Ibid.
10. Ibid.
11. http://nla.gov.au/ndp/del/article/8162199
12. Greenwood (ed), *Australia, A Social & Political History*, p. 288.

13.   Cubis, *A History of 'A' Battery, New South Wales Artillery (1871-1899)*, p. 26.

14.   Ibid.

15.   Cubis, *A History of 'A' Battery, New South Wales Artillery (1871-1899)*, p. 183.

16.   Whiston, Another Whiston Matter, p.91.

17.   Ross, *The Myth of the Digger: The Australian Soldier in Two World Wars*, p116.

18.   G. Serle, 'The digger Tradition and Australian nationalism', *Meanjim* (Issue 101(2), 1965), p.149-158.

19.   Correlli Barnett, *Britain and her Army 1509-1970, A Military, Political and Social Survey*, Allen Lane The Penguin Press, London, 1970, p. 346.

20.   Barnett, *Britain and her Army 1509-1970*, p 410.

21.   J.L. Granatstein, *Canada's Army, Waging War and Keeping the Peace*, University of Toronto Press, Toronto, Reprinted 2004, p. 148.

22.   Pratten, 'Under rather discouraging circumstances'; p 33.

23.   P H Partridge, 'Depression and War 1929-1950', Gordon Greenwood (ed), *Australia, A Social & Political History*, Angus & Robertson, Sydney, Reprinted 1978, p368.

24.   Cubis, *A History of 'A' Battery, New South Wales Artillery (1871-1899)*, p. 26.

25.   Whiston, Another Whiston Matter, p.117.

26.   Arnold D. Hunt and Robert P. Thomas, *For God, King and Country: A study of the attitudes of the Methodist and Catholic Press in South Australia*, Salisbury College of Advanced Education, Salisbury, South Australia, 1979.

27.   Appendix 6.

28.   NAA, MP367/1, Control Symbol 452/1/246, Mr. Rollins complaint against QM and Hon. Maj. T. J. Farrow, AIC, 1928.

29.   NAA, B1535, Control Symbol 751/12/101, C. H. Brown, 1931.

30.   NAA, Control Symbol 751/2/148, (Name omitted) Discharge, B1535.

31.   NAA, A471/1, Control Symbol 70929, Court-Martial—NP4974 WOII J.C. Carson, AIC, 1945.

32.   Military Board Agenda No.383-1921, (Name omitted) Cancellation of Commission.

33.   Military Order 188-1923, Australian Instructional Corps, P559/15/608, Struck Off Strength.

APPENDIX SIX
AUSTRALIAN INSTRUCTIONAL CORPS
AUSTRALIAN WAR MEMORIAL—PANEL 95

Australian Instructional Corps–Died in service, World War II

Regt. No.	Rank	Christian Names	Family Name
QP334	SSM3	William John	BURGESS
NP329	WO1	Joseph John	BUTTON
QP8307	WOII	John	CLYDE
QP703	WOII	Victor Kenneth	CREED
133	SSM2	N. W. P.	DIKE
NP9972	WOII	William Alfred Leslie	GARLAND*
	WOII	N. A.	GORDON
	WOII	H. T.	HARDY
	WOII	D.S.	HERROD
485	SSM3	F. H.	LAZARUS
643	SSM3	A. V.	McMULLAN
3688	SSM3	R. M.	MORTON
VP7540(280)	SSM2	Carl Oscar.	OLSSON
104	WO1A	W. B.	O'NEIL
NP152	WO1	James Dugid	SHERIM
NP9371	WOII	Cecil Carrington	TURNER
QP185	SSM2	George Herbert	WILLIAMS

* NP9972 WOII William Alfred Leslie GARLAND is listed on the Australian War Memorial "Roll of Honour" Webpage for the Australian Instructional Corps members who died in service in WWII. However his name does not appear on AWM Panel 95.

Fig 11. *AIC WWII War Dead; Panel 95 AWM.*

Fig 12. *Officers and Staff of the Small Arms School, Randwick, 1 May 1940*
Back row:- WO R.J.I. DeGroote, WO G.M.L. Hogarth, WO A.W. Kelsey,
WO J, Appleton.
Middle row:- WO C.C. Hall, WO W.R.J. Shields, Mr F. Baulch,
WO G.A. Johnson, WO J.H. Shannon.
Front row:- WO H.J. Swanson (S.S.M.), Capt. K.C. Allman (O.I.),
Capt. E.W. Latchford, M.B.E., M.C. (C.I.), Lt J.A.M. Walker (Adjt.),
WO H.B.F. O'Rourke,

CHAPTER TEN
THE SECOND WORLD WAR COMES TO THE AIC

Setting the scene

The AIC was an organisation spread across Australia into which members were posted.[1] It was never assembled as a unit, never held parades and never marched to war as a unit. Thus there is no war diary to describe the role and fate of the individual warrant officers who served (including on active service) in World War II. Because of this lack of documented evidence, the role, tasks and experiences of the AIC can really only be extrapolated from individual histories set against the background of armies, forces, campaigns and terrains.

Australia went to war with two armies comprising one permanent force (PMF) and one voluntary corps (2nd AIF) and fought two campaigns (Middle East and Pacific Islands) against two totally different enemies (German and Japanese) in vastly different terrains. The warrant officers of the AIC were represented in each of the armies, the force and the voluntary corps. They fought in both campaigns in the different terrains, and all the evidence suggests that they performed each and all of their tasks with a high rate of success.

When Australia declared war in 1939, it boasted two armies, the AMF/Militia and the 2nd AIF. The AMF/Militia also had as its constituent parts the PMF and, by 1943, the Volunteer Defence Corps (VDC).

From 1940 to 1942 the 2nd AIF fought in the Middle East. During this time the AMF/Militia and the PMF remained in Australia defending the homeland. Following the Japanese attack on Pearl Harbor in December 1941, the US launched campaigns in the Pacific. It was then that the PMF was absorbed into the AMF/Militia and the 2nd AIF. From 1942 onwards the 2nd AIF fought in the Pacific Islands and was joined in 1943 by three divisions of the AMF/Militia, while the remaining AMF/Militia divisions and VDC formed the mainstay of Australia's homeland defence.

The World War II Army that captured popular imagination was the all-volunteer 2nd AIF of four infantry divisions recruited to fight overseas.[2] In the early stages of the war, three divisions of the 2nd AIF (the 6th, 7th and 9th) fought in North Africa and the Middle East before being recalled to Australia in 1942. In Australia they were re-formed as Jungle Divisions and deployed to New Guinea and the Pacific Islands to fight the Japanese.[3] The fourth AIF division (the 8th Division) went to Malaya where the Australians were to become prisoners of the Japanese. During the course of the war, the 2nd AIF also recruited three Armoured Divisions.[4]

The less well known Army was the AMF/Militia. Made up of eight infantry divisions, it consisted of some volunteers, but mostly conscripts.[5] The *Defence Act* allowed the government to continue to conscript men for home defence for the duration of the war. Until the Curtin Government changed Australia's boundaries in 1943 to include Australia's overseas territories of Papua and New Guinea, all AMF/Militia active service was restricted to the mainland of Australia.

For the Australian Army, World War II falls into two distinct phases: 1940 to 1941 and 1942 to 1945. The first phase of the war took place in North Africa and the Middle East. The second phase was initiated when Japan entered the war and appeared poised to invade Australia. Different enemies and dissimilar terrain resulted in two distinctly different campaigns. The period 1940 to 1942 involved land operations in desert terrain and

European-style operations in Greece and Crete; while the period 1942 to 1945 comprised primarily jungle operations in New Guinea, Malaya and the islands of the Pacific. Importantly for the AIC, radically different training was required in each of the two phases.

In the Greece, Crete and North African campaigns the AIC warrant officers undertook five tasks comprising enlistment, quartermaster services, training, weapons development and leadership. Those campaigns fought in the Pacific Islands, Malaya and New Guinea saw a sixth task, that of training local forces, added to the list.

Prior to the war, both the PMF and the AIC had increased their numbers. While the actual corps establishment had remained unchanged throughout the interwar period, by 1939 the AIC strength stood at 937 all ranks while the PMF had increased to 3500.[6] As the training requirements of the 2nd AIF and AMF/Militia continued to increase, so did the strength of the AIC. By 1940, the AIC total had risen to 1299 (232 quartermasters and 1067 warrant officers)[7] before stabilising at 1023 (234 quartermasters and 889 warrant officers), the authorised wartime establishment of the corps in 1941.[8]

The 2nd AIF had a large number of AIC warrant officers who joined as officers and senior NCOs and saw active service in all theatres of war. In addition, after 1943, many AIC members undertook active service as officers and senior NCOs with the divisions of the AMF/Militia. By then Athol Osgood, a member of the 8th Division, had been in Changi prison, Singapore, for two years. Guy Fawcett had returned to Australia as a major, having been an infantry captain with the 6th Division in the Middle East. Herbert Downey, also with the 6th Division, as was mentioned earlier, to die in an air raid in Crete later that year. Colin McPherson, formerly a warrant officer with the Light Horse, had joined the Commandos, while Des Heap, an engineer warrant officer, had become a Tank Corps officer. Bob Whiston's active service came much later in the war.

Having been commissioned, Captain Whiston was posted to an Ordnance unit at Torokina in Bougainville in the Solomon Islands in 1944 as an Ordnance officer.[9]

Harrold Edwin Oswald Trounson joined the PMF in 1911. He served with 55 Australian Siege Battery, Royal Australian Garrison Artillery, in France in 1917 where he was wounded. Returning to Australia he joined the A & I Staff in 1919 transferring to the AIC when it was formed in 1921. He was promoted in the interwar period, serving as an honorary lieutenant with the 13th Field Brigade at Keswick in South Australia. Temporary Captain Trounson served as Adjutant of the 27th Infantry Battalion (The South Australian Scottish Regiment) in 1937 and moved to the School of Artillery in 1940 on promotion to major (administration) where he served until 1946. Having survived his appendix operation prior to World War II, Warrant Officer Class II Sydney A.M. LeServe enlisted in the 2nd AIF where he was commissioned lieutenant and posted to the 2nd/17th Battalion.

However, unlike their more fortunate colleagues, both NP9948 Warrant Officer Class IA Martin John Laffy and Alfred Etheredge were still in Australia. In fact, because of their excellent qualifications, both Laffy and Etheredge were deemed too valuable to be released for overseas service. Martin Laffy, who enlisted as a gunner in 1909 had remained in Australia during the Great War. He qualified to join the AIC in 1936 and volunteered for overseas service on the outbreak of war. To his chagrin, Laffy was to spend World War II as the District Officer and Quartermaster, NSW Fixed Defences, Newcastle.[10] Alfred Robert Etheredge, however, probably represents the best example of an AIC member prevented from undertaking active service despite volunteering on numerous occasions.

Alfred Etheredge was commissioned as a lieutenant in the 48th Kooyong Regiment, AMF, prior to the Great War. Enlisted as an acting staff sergeant major in the Instructional Staff on 20 October 1915, Alfred

Fig 13. *Hon. Capt. Martin Laffy, front row on the left, in service dress with a black armband (all the rest in their newly issued "blues" designed to aid recruiting-it was 1939). Laffy was OIC Newcastle when the Jap sub fired ...*

Etheredge served through the Great War as an Instructional Staff Warrant Officer training troops in Australia. In 1920 Etheredge graduated from No. 2 School of Instruction at Liverpool as staff sergeant major class III, becoming an original founding member of the AIC in 1921. Six months after the AIC was established, Etheredge was promoted PMF warrant officer class II and, in 1927, was promoted to warrant officer class I. Alfred Etheredge served with a number of 3rd Division units as RQMS and RSM, including the 24th (The Kooyong Regiment) and 39th Infantry Battalions (the Hawthorn-Kew Regiment), AMF.

In 1938 Temporary Quartermaster and Honorary Lieutenant Alfred Etheredge, 39th Battalion, entered World War II as a temporary captain. He served as an instructor at officer training units and schools throughout the war, finishing his Army career in the Interim Army as a major on the Military Secretary's staff. Despite volunteering in both world wars, Major Etheredge was never selected to undertake active service overseas.[11]

By 1941 a total of 210 warrant officers of the AIC had establishment postings at Army Schools and coastal defence units. This represented over one third of the AIC's total pre-war establishment.[12] In the early part of World War II, the training of artillerymen was completely reliant on the government's ability to procure the necessary guns. Unsurprisingly, shortages abounded, with only the critical anti-aircraft batteries well equipped. With the high priority accorded to anti-aircraft protection during the first two years of the war, the number of anti-aircraft batteries increased dramatically requiring a commensurate increase in trained crews. This training need was to provide significant career opportunities for Honorary Lieutenant John Edward Hendry, MBE, and Honorary Lieutenant Leonard Charles Wade, MBE. John Hendry enlisted in 1911 and trained overseas at Larkhill, England in 1927-29 becoming a 1st Class Master Gunner in 1930. After being Quartermaster and Honorary Lieutenant of 9 Heavy Battery Darwin in 1939, John Hendry would be promoted major and, in 1941, appointed CI, Land Headquarters School of Artillery (Anti-Aircraft), a position he held until 1943.[13] For his part, Honorary Lieutenant Wade was promoted major and appointed CI, Land Headquarters School of Artillery (Field Artillery), from 1941 to 1942. Following further promotion, the now Lieutenant Colonel Wade was appointed to a further term as CI from 1943 to 1944.[14] To the AIC's considerable chagrin, however, it is a matter of record that as soon as Australian Staff Corps officers became available for such coveted positions these exemplary AIC honorary officers were reposted.[15]

In training Australian soldiers in the use of armour the AIC played a significant part. The big success story was the raising and operation of the Armoured Fighting Vehicle (AFV) School. Initially located at Balcombe in Victoria it relocated to Puckapunyal some two months later.[16] All instructional staff posted to the school came from the AIC, many of them graduates of No. 9 Special Course.[17]

Only two AIC warrant officers had overseas tank training: Keith

Watts, who had gone to England with Colonel Ronald Hopkins, and Cecil Ives, an English warrant officer who had transferred to Australia.[18] Colonel Hopkins selected Keith Watts to command the Gunnery and Driving Wing of the AFV School, and Cecil Ives to command the Maintenance Wing. Within a short time Keith Watts had been promoted a major, and Cecil Ives to captain. Ives' majority would follow later.

The massive task facing the AFV School involved training all of the officers and half of the other ranks of the 1st Armoured Division. This represented a total of 270 officers and approximately 2100 other ranks who were selected from 800 NCOs and 3400 soldier applicants.[19]

New Small Arms

Throughout World War II, the AIC was intimately involved in the introduction of new small arms. This particularly applied to the Owen gun, a locally designed weapon. Following a meeting with Mr. Evelyn Owen of Wollongong at Randwick, NSW, in 1939, Lieutenant Colonel Ernest Latchford, MC, CI of the Small Arms School, became closely involved in the gun's development. Latchford acted as a technical consultant for the next two years culminating in his personal testing of the first prototype on the Long Bay Rifle Range on 29 September 1941.[20] The Owen gun subsequently entered production and its value was proven by the front-line troops who used it. The contribution of Lieutenant Colonel Latchford to the development of this important close fighting weapon was considerable. According to Andrew Ross:

> The Owen SMG ... turned out to be the best sub machine gun in the Western Allies' arsenal of armaments. However, the weapon would never have emerged if it had been left in the hands of the Army MGO [Master General of Ordnance] branch and the Chief Military Advisor's Branch.[21]

During the early years of World War II the Australian Army maintained a uniformity of weapons with Britain and had no interest in a new sub-machine-gun. For almost three years the Army (through Latchford) fought the government over production of the Owen gun. In 1945 the British finally admitted that the Owen was functionally better than any British-designed weapon in its class.[22] Latchford had won his most important battle.

Another new weapon introduced to the Australian Army—this time by the British—was the Bren gun. Lieutenant Colonel George Waring was an Ordnance Corps officer at the time these new guns were purchased, commenting that:[23]

> When the first imported Bren guns came to Australia in 1941 I was working at Moorebank, NSW, Ordnance Depot. A group of four AIC warrant officers, one of whom was Jim Gordon's (our supervisor) son-in-law, came out from the Small Arms School at Randwick and demonstrated stripping and assembly of this new weapon. These lessons proved invaluable later on when we received bulk shipments of Bren gun parts and were then able to organise them into bins convenient for easy storage and retrieval.[24]

With the end of the first phase of operations in Europe and North Africa, the Australian Government turned its attention to the burgeoning threat to its north. The fall of Singapore and the bombing of Darwin brought new perils and a heightened sense of anxiety to the home front. The 6th, 7th and later the 9th Division, returned home and, in 1943, regrouped ready to undertake what was to become the South West Pacific campaign, waged in new and difficult terrain perilously close to Australia's shores.

Chapter Ten
Notes

1.   The AIC existed as a unit 'on paper'. Members joined the AIC as a 'posting' (i.e. a transfer in Australian Army Orders).In a great many cases there was no physical movement by the member when the transfer occurred.

2.   The 6th Division was raised on 12 September 1939. See Grey, *A Military History of Australia,* p. 108. The 7th Division was raised on 28 February 1940, the 8th Division on 22 May 1940 and the 9th Division in June 1940. See Palazzo, *The Australian Army,* pp. 144, 145.

3.   The 6tth Division went to Libya, North Africa, Greece and Crete. The 7th Division went to Syria and the 9th Division became part of the Tobruk Garrison. See Grey, *A Military History of Australia,* pp. 123–24; Palazzo, *The Australian Army,* p. 183.

4.   Grey, *A Military History of Australia,* p.124.

5.   The 1st 2nd, 3rd, 4th and 5th Divisions were adopted from the 1st AIF and allocated territorially throughout Australia. The 10th, 11th and 12th were also raised territorially in 1942; for example, the 12th Division was raised in the Northern Territory. See Palazzo, *The Australian Army,* p. 174.

6.   Long, *To Benghazi,* p. 29.

7.   The Army Staff and Graduation List of the Australian Military Forces, Part 1 Active List, 1 February 1940; Permanent Military Forces, Quartermasters Australian Instructional Corps, pp. 66–72; Permanent Military Forces, Warrant Officers, Australian Instructional Corps, pp. 312–342, and NAA, D884 Item 55/3/29, Schedule 'A' Australian Instructional Corps, Annual Establishment 1940-41.

8.   AHQ 11144, Para 14 of 24 Feb (MBI 11144 of 24 Feb 41) AIC Establishment.

9.   Whiston, Another Whiston Matter, p. 168.

10.   Extracted from Record of Service in possession of Major M.K. Laffey (grandson), 19 May 2004. Both Maj Kevin Laffy and his brother Capt John Laffy spelt the family name LAFFY; later generations use the spelling LAFFEY.

11.   Alfred Robert Etheredge (DOB 12 June 1894) was appointed captain (QM) in 1948 and later Majoror (QM). Major Etheredge retired from the Interim Army in April 1951 having served 39 years and 326 days. Don Etheredge (son), letter to the author, 8 May 2003.

12.   NAA, MP 742/1248/1/15, Selected Documents, Summarised List of Postings: extracted from Warrant Officers, AIC Sergeants attached to Army Schools & Coast Defences, Department of Defence Minute Paper 252/1/695, dated 10/5/1941.

13.   Ian Burch, *History of the School of Artillery 1885-1996,* Development Wing, School of Artillery, Manly NSW, 1996, p. 73.

14.   Ibid.

15.   Wade was replaced by Lieutenant Colonel J.S. Henderson, OBE, who was appointed CI on 13 March 1944. Major Hendry was replaced by Lieutenant Colonel J.V.B. Sharp, RA. See Burch, *History of the School of Artillery 1885-1996,* pp. 71–73.

16.   Handel, *Dust, Sand & Jungle,* p. 39.

17.   Australian Army Order 22-1941, Australian Instructional Corps, Item 3 Allotments.

18.   148 WOII Keith Avery Watts, DOB 12/03/1909; also NP3271 WOII Cecil Ives, DOB 13/5/1903 who joined the AIC on 20/3/1937.

19.   Handel, *Dust, Sand & Jungle,* p. 38.

20.   Major General Kevin Latchford, AO (retd); see also A History of the Australian School of Infantry, Chapter 5, World War II, unpublished manuscript held at the Infantry Corps Library, Singleton, NSW; letter to the author, 31 July 2008.

21.   Ross, *Armed and Ready,* p. 371.

22.   AWM 54, 385/9/2, MGO Technical Library, No. 2A/1018, *Small Arms Circular* Vol. 1, No. 1, January 1945.

23.   2813 Lieutenant Colonel George Waring joined the Moorebank Ordnance

Depot as a 4th Division Commonwealth employee in 1934. During World War II he was commissioned as a lieutenant in the Ordnance Corps. After the war Colonel Waring joined the Staff Corps and served in a number of postings with the Royal Australian Army Ordnance Corps, retiring from the Regular Army in 1966. Interview with the author, 25 January 2002.

24.   The Bren Light Machine Gun (LMG) was developed during the 1930s by the Czechoslovakian Small Arms Factory at Brno and the British Small Arms Factory at Enfield from the Czech Zb series. The name BREN comes from the linking of the names Brno and Enfield. British design changes saw the use of .303 calibre rimmed ammunition (interchangeable with rifle ammunition). See Dennis et al., *The Oxford Companion to Australian Military History*, p. 118.

CHAPTER ELEVEN
WAR WITH JAPAN

Into the jungle—war with Japan 1941–1945

Despite Australian Lieutenant General Henry Gordon Bennett's claim to have introduced his troops in Malaya to jungle training, jungle warfare was, in fact, almost unknown to the Australian Army in 1941.[1] Japan's entry into World War II created serious challenges in practical training and introduced new equipment previously unknown to the Army. The new type of warfare was particularly confronting for the individual members of the AIC, both in terms of their methods of practical training and their leadership ability. While training to meet the new conditions of jungle warfare took some time to resolve, the AIC's leadership ability was quickly put to the test. As the Japanese advanced in Malaya and in Papua and New Guinea, the AIC warrant officers soon found themselves in active service roles in the front line.

In Malaya, the war found Frank Smyth and John Walker under command of Lieutenant Colonel 'Black Jack' Galleghan, CO in the 2nd/30th Battalion, AIF. The 2nd/30th was part of the 8th Division, responsible for achieving the impossible task of defending British colonial interests in Malaya and Singapore against a rampant and deadly Japanese invasion.

The Japanese lightning thrust took Commonwealth forces by surprise and the rapid Japanese advance down the peninsula was only slowed at Gemas in Malaya where the 2nd/30th Battalion mounted a deadly ambush at the bridge over the Gemencheh River. The battle which ensued lasted two days and cost the Japanese 1000 casualties for the loss of 81 Australians. This was the first point during the advance that Japanese forces had enmcountered any form of resistance.

Former AIC member NP4949 Warrant Officer Class II Frank Miles Smyth, a graduate of No. 2 Special Course and previously an instructor with the DMF, had transferred to the AIF and been appointed NX68127 Lieutenant F.M. Smyth of the 2nd/30th Battalion, AIF. The RSM of the 2nd/30th was NX66387 Warrant Officer Class I Reuben Seymour (known as John) Walker a graduate of 7 Special Course.

Despite what was a tactical victory, the Australians were soon overwhelmed by the crush of advancing Japanese forces and withdrew through Gemas to the Fort Rose Estate. From there, the 2nd/30th Battalion joined the remainder of the Commonwealth forces in a steady withdrawal back down the Malay Peninsula towards the island fortress of Singapore. As the 2nd/30th Battalion made its fighting withdrawal, patrols were sent out to ascertain enemy movements and strengths. One patrol comprised a three-man boat team including Lieutenant Smyth, which took to nearby waterways checking for Japanese infiltration. They soon made contact with a Japanese boat patrol and, in the ensuing firefight, Smyth was lost overboard. He is recorded as killed in action in the Straits of Johore on 8 February 1942.[2]

When Singapore surrendered on 15 February 1942, the 2nd/30th Battalion went into captivity in Changi prison. After two months on work parties all over Singapore as a member of F Force, John Walker was sent to Thailand by train (Train 5, Truck 15) on 14 May 1942 as a member of A Force to work on the Burma-Thailand Railway. Despite becoming seriously ill, Walker survived. Returning to Australia in October 1945, Warrant Officer John Walker discharged from the AIF and was passed as medically fit to join the Interim Army, enlisting on 1 July 1947.[3]

Australian forces in Papua and New Guinea were also to see action against the Japanese who were advancing steadily towards Port Moresby. Among the new infantry battalions raised from scratch in World War II was the 1st Papuan Infantry Battalion, raised at Port Moresby on 19 June 1940. Five AIC warrant officers went to Papua to train the soldiers of this fledgling unit. The battalion history lists Warrant Officers J. Cook, 4939 C.J. Orme, R.D. Newton, L. Coulter and 4020 W.L. Taylor as filling the positions of CSM and platoon commanders.[4] The 1st Papuan Infantry Battalion moved ahead of the 39th Battalion (The Hawthorn-Kew Regiment), AMF/Militia, and its members were the first troops to meet the Japanese advancing along the Kokoda Trail.[5]

Many accounts of the Australian Army's involvement in the fighting on the Kokoda Trail in World War II have dwelt at length on the obvious problems of the AMF/Militia divisions who were sent overseas from 1939 onwards. Prior to the commencement of actual hostilities in the area, many of the troops in Port Moresby, including the men of the 53rd Battalion (The West Sydney Regiment), AMF, spent much of their time unloading ships rather than training to wage war.[6] In charge of some of these operations was Dick Yellowley, RSM 55th/53rd Battalion, AMF/Militia, later to become the 55th/53rd Battalion, AIF (The Mice of Moresby). WOI Yellowley had joined the AIC in December 1939.[7]

Recruitment and enlistment

The war with Japan brought with it the very grave threat of the invasion of Australia. Enlistment in the 2nd AIF continued throughout the country, while at the same time large numbers of men were conscripted into the AMF/Militia. By 1943 there was a common enlistment process for both the AIF and the AMF/Militia conducted by the 1st Australian Recruit Training Battalion at Cowra, NSW. After a short period of initial training, often weeks rather than months, recruits were posted to units. The large influx of conscripts changed the overall composition of the Army and, as Ross points out, 'the digger of World War II was more likely to be a militiaman working in Australia than a frontline infantryman.'[8]

Quartermaster services

While many of the AIC's 1st AIF quartermaster veterans had been retired, others were given new jobs. QP20040 Quartermaster and Honorary Lieutenant (Temporary Captain) Robert Alexander Hunter, MM, was appointed Chief Instructor of No. 1 NCO School in the Laloki Valley, New Guinea, on 29 September 1941.[9] Later this school became a jungle warfare training base.

It was not unusual for 2nd AIF battalions to have more than one AIC warrant officer in their ranks. This was certainly the case with the 2nd/10th Battalion, AIF. Edmund Allchin was appointed quartermaster when the 2nd/10th was raised in Adelaide.[10] He was joined by SX649 Temporary Warrant Officer Class II Theodore James Schmedje. Theo Schmedje had been a Militia lieutenant with the 14th Battalion (The Prahran Regiment), AMF. He was a qualified pharmacist and the chief dispensing chemist at Wonthaggi, Victoria. Theo Schmedje graduated from No. 7 Special Course which ran from 16 January to 17 June 1939 and was commissioned in the 2nd AIF. After service in the Middle East and New Guinea, Major Schmedje was one of seven officers of the 2nd/10th Battalion, AIF, to be awarded an MC for conspicuous bravery in action.

Experienced AIC instructors also assumed key positions in the armoured regiments and, when required, led them into battle. Warrant Officer Class II Desmond A. Heap was an AIC member with service and experience as an RAE instructor. He enlisted in the 2nd AIF and transferred to armour. Des Heap became a tank commander with the 2nd/6th Australian Armoured Regiment when it went into active service in New Guinea.

Lieutenant Heap's leadership was evident on 1 January 1943 in the final attack in the battle of Buna at Giropa Point in support of the 2ⁿᵈ/12ᵗʰ Battalion, AIF, when it was reported that 'Captain Rod May and Lieutenant Des Heap ran the show from the control tank.'[11]

New technology

While much time was devoted to instructing on existing equipment, the drive for new technology was particularly evident at the Small Arms School in Randwick, NSW. War correspondent George Johnston visited the Small Arms School and reported that:

> ... in New South Wales, at the old Anzac range near Randwick Racecourse, you can see one of Australia's original Army Schools (established in 1911) now instructing soldiers in the use of the Vickers medium machine gun, in gas work, and in pistol shooting. On the veranda was a Gatling gun, grandfather of the modern machine gun, first used in the United States.[12]

Johnston also observed some new technology in action and was drawn to describe the experience:

> In another room was a museum of ancient weapons—old horse-pistols and cutlasses and blunderbusses. From a window of this room I watched students testing a new type of pill box for beach defence ... methods change, but wars continue.[13]

Neville Ransom, formerly RSM of the DMF, enlisted in the 2ⁿᵈ AIF and was commissioned. He joined a specialist team in Melbourne organising new weapons and ammunition being prepared for shipping to the Pacific Islands. Bob Whiston, a Master Gunner was, by that time, a captain and member of OS3 (Technical Stores) based at Wesley College, St Kilda Road, Melbourne, which had been taken over by the Master General of the Ordnance (MGO). He remembers one of his fellow officers:

> Capt. 'Rangie' Ransom had been the RSM of the Darwin Mobile Force before the war. He was a very good soldier who stole one of our nicest typists and made her very happy.[14]

Neville Ransom was later to go overseas, finishing the war as a major with an MID for distinguished service with the 2nd Landing Group in the Pacific Islands campaign.

In 1943 two AIC warrant officers from the Small Arms School at Bonegilla, Victoria went overseas to test fire a new weapon on behalf of the Army. On 19 September 1943 VX85018 WO1 Colin Kesterton Druitt (ex DMF & No.9 Special Course) and TX10815 WO1 Albert Arthur Whitton carried out trials of the Infantry Tank Attack Projector Mark 1 in the Sogeri Valley, New Guinea. Images of these trials, now held by the AWM, were recorded on film by Lt. George Harvey Nicholson of the Army Film Unit,[15] and Robert John Buchan.[16] A photo of this operation is illustrated on the front cover of this history.

Training local forces

Colin McPherson, who had been an AIC instructor with a light horse regiment in south-western NSW prior to World War II, took on a vastly different role following enlistment in the 2nd AIF. McPherson became a commando. While undertaking parachute training in late 1944 he joined Z Special Unit and was immediately despatched to undertake language training in Malay. After a short period in Queensland, Warrant Officer McPherson flew to Darwin then Morotai and finally to Borneo where he parachuted in to join Operation Semut 1.

Semut 1, one of the most demanding operations conducted in South-East Asia, saw a small number of commandos operating behind the Japanese lines. Apart from gathering information, a major task of the carefully selected operatives was to train local forces to carry out small-scale operations such as ambushes against the occupying Japanese.[17] Colin McPherson was awarded the MM for his role in a highly successful mission under the most adverse conditions. After the war, McPherson was commissioned in the Interim Army.

Fig 14. *Colonel Colin McPherson MM psc*

AMF and 2nd AIF training 1942–1945

Warrant Officer Athol Osgood served in the Great War and, following the end of that conflict, enlisted in the PMF where he qualified to join the AIC. After enlisting in the 2nd AIF, NX41519 Warrant Officer Class I Athol Osgood (a graduate of No. 4 Special Course) joined the staff of the 8th Division. As an experienced instructor, Athol Osgood was sent to Singapore to provide extra training to the local garrison, as the training available in Singapore and Malaya was deemed inadequate. On arrival in Singapore Osgood was posted to Headquarters Base Depot, Malaya. With the fall of Singapore on 15 February 1942, Osgood was interned in Changi prison by the Japanese along with the remainder of the 8th Division.

By coincidence, Athol's eldest son, George, who had joined the RAN at age 16½ and been torpedoed as a seaman aboard HMAS *Perth*, also arrived at Changi prison. Athol Osgood's Colonel told George Osgood that his father's decision to stay with his men, implying as a warrant officer that he had a choice, 'was a stupid decision to volunteer'. Athol Osgood became one of 1494 prisoners who made up B Force sent from Singapore to Sandakan in July 1942.[18] Athol Osgood died in the Sandakan camp of malaria and starvation on 7 March 1945 aged 43. He is commemorated on the Labuan Memorial (Panel 8) and on the obelisk to the Borneo dead at Burwood Park, Burwood, NSW.

Tom Dawson was also deeply involved in the 2nd AIF practical training prior to going on active service. He joined the staff of the newly raised AFV School at Puckapunyal to train officers and NCOs for the 1st Armoured Division. This was followed by a posting to the Army Gas School at Bonegilla. Commissioned as a lieutenant Tom Dawson joined the 2nd/9th Battalion, AIF, serving in Papua and New Guinea until the end of the war.

Artillery training 1942–45

With the bombing of mainland Australia by Japanese aircraft in early 1942, Australian artillery was quickly re-equipped. Given the massive damage to Darwin and the increasing fear of Japanese air attacks on major Australian cities, large numbers of anti-aircraft batteries were established and equipped with Swedish 40-mm Bofors guns.

Anti-aircraft batteries were located throughout Australia, most surrounding the major towns and cities. They were also located on the islands to Australia's north, notably at Port Moresby in New Guinea.[19] The schools of artillery, principally located at Sydney's North Head, provided an increased number of courses to train gunners on these new weapons which came into service as the war progressed.[20] The artillery schools employed several AIC quartermasters and a number of AIC warrant officers as assistant instructors. As in other Army schools of that era, warrant officers could only be posted as assistant instructors because establishment positions for instructor were reserved for Staff Corps officers. By 1941 there were 13 AIC warrant officer instructors and assistant instructors appointed to the artillery schools.[21] These included 3498 Warrant Officer Class II Howard Clifford Guyatt and

2826 Temporary Warrant Officer Class I Norman Neels, later to become Quartermaster 2/370 Major Norman Neels, MBE. Posted to the Anti-Tank Wing was SP4473 Warrant Officer Class II G.C. Whittle, later to become Quartermaster 4/55 Major Gordon Charles Whittle and 3680 Temporary Warrant Officer Class II Thomas Edward Guest who shared his PMF recruit intake as a gunner with Bob Whiston.

Armour training 1942–45

Australian armour training for crews, squadrons and regiments underwent considerable modification until jungle operations became a reality. Initially AHQ held the view that the jungle was tank-proof country; however, Japanese successes in Malaya soon proved this assumption incorrect. Armoured regiments of the Australian Army, organised on a tropical scale establishment, were sent into action in Buna, Sattelberg, Bougainville, Borneo and Wewak.

The AIC's contribution to successful jungle operations with tanks commenced with instruction of officers and NCOs at the AFV School. Successful operations involving tanks in the jungle dictated the doctrine taught at the school. Such doctrine stressed the reality that, while infantry could work without tanks, tanks should never operate without infantry, particularly in the dense jungle environment.[22]

Armoured operations 1942–45

Even when supported by well-equipped and well-trained infantry, tanks were not always successful. This was clearly attested in the fate of a squadron of the 2nd/6th Armoured Regiment which lost six of its 11 armoured vehicles over a 16-day continuous advance in Buna. However, the squadron did manage to inflict considerable casualties on the enemy.[23] Far greater success was achieved in Bougainville where squadrons of the 2nd/4th Armoured Regiment operated in 1944 and 1945. Hopkins writes that, 'as a result of operations in the Huon peninsula, the use of Matilda tanks in tropical jungle was highly successful especially as the enemy was unable to penetrate its armour.'[24]

Tactics for jungle operations saw the tanks fighting in pairs, threes and fours, usually travelling in line ahead on tracks. Success in this mode of operations relied on engineer and infantry support in close attendance as flank protection.[25] Tank exponent Stuart Graham claimed that the principal benefit of a tropical establishment armoured regiment, which consisted of only 360 men, was its massive firepower. Graham argued that a single armoured regiment had 'the gunpower equivalent to one-and-a-half artillery field regiments, the machine gun power of six infantry battalions, and the light machine gun power of three infantry companies.'[26] Whether this claim is substantiated or not, the fact remains that tank crew training originated at the AVF School and that AIC warrant officers spearheaded that training.

On the home front—the Volunteer Defence Corps

Responding to widespread alarm caused by the outbreak of war in 1940, the Returned Sailors', Soldiers', and Airmen's Imperial League of Australia (now known as the RSL) assisted bodies of men to organise themselves to defend Australia in an organisation known as the Volunteer Defence Corps or VDC. This was a spontaneous civilian movement, very much akin to Britain's Home Guard. In May 1941 the VDC was taken over and administered by the Army.[27] Once the VDC had been issued with weapons, guns, rifles and mortars, its members were trained—a task which fell once again to the AIC.

Organised into battalions of approximately 400 men based on districts and localities, the major concentrations of VDC battalions were in the most populated states on the eastern seaboard. NSW and Queensland each had 23 battalions while Victoria had 24. Consisting of full-time members, part-time members and reserves, the battalions were often given particular missions including the protection of airbases and industrial sites. The crucial BHP Newcastle Steelworks was guarded by three VDC battalions each working an eight-hour shift.[28]

Warrant officer instructors from the AIC were posted directly to the VDC battalions. QP8542 Temporary Warrant Officer Class II J. Burchill was posted to 20 Battalion, VDC, at the town of Murgon in Queensland, while QP8497 Temporary Warrant Officer Class II H.H. Moroney was posted to 5 Battalion, VDC, at Southport on the Queensland coast. QP8348 Temporary Warrant Officer Class II W. Wynne was posted to 21 Battalion, VDC, at the inland town of Charters Towers. QP2408 Temporary Warrant Officer Class II D. Batson was posted to 2 Battalion, VDC, in Brisbane while QP8643 Temporary Warrant Officer Class II C. Pollard was posted to 17 Battalion, VDC, at Cairns.[29]

Arming the VDC in 1941 presented an enormous challenge as there were insufficient weapons, particularly machine-guns, available for home defence. From all around Australia the RSL collected approximately 2000 German Maxim MG 08 machine-guns which had been captured by Australian soldiers in the Great War. By 1942, around 1500 modified Maxim machine-guns capable of firing .303 ammunition had been issued to the VDC and garrison battalions manning the prisoner of war and internment camps.[30] Training the VDC members in the employment of these unusual armaments was yet another task for the AIC instructors.

Although the initial core structure of a VDC unit was based around an infantry battalion, later it was expanded to encompass other defence roles. Once its total size had increased to approximately 100,000 men, some VDC units were allocated mortars and anti-tank guns. By 1943, the VDC was operating a number of anti-aircraft batteries in defence of major cities in Australia.[31] Once again, instruction in anti-aircraft weapons was provided to the VDC by the AIC warrant officers graduating through the schools of artillery.

Problems

Despite their high level of training and demonstrated enthusiasm for operations, going off to war was not without its problems for the AIC, many unique to the Corps' warrant officers. These included loss of identity and that scourge of the returned soldier, reversion to substantive rank. Once AIC warrant officers were posted to a battalion or regiment, they were required to remove their distinctive AIC badges and red shoulder epaulets from their blue patrol jackets. The badges were then replaced with those of the battalion or regiment to which they were posted.[32] This loss of corps identity meant that many 2nd AIF and AMF/Militia soldiers were totally unaware they had AIC members within their ranks. Peter Wright, President of the 55th/53rd Battalion, AIF (the 'Mice of Moresby'), formerly a Militia battalion that fought on the Kokoda Trail, commented that 'it would have been nice to meet some of the gentlemen from the AIC.'[33] Ironically, and clearly unknown to Wright, the RSM of the 55th/53rd Battalion, Warrant Officer Class II Richard (Dick) Yellowley, was a 'gentleman from the AIC.'[34] While Peter Wright, as a front-line soldier, obviously knew Dick Yellowley as his RSM, clearly he, like the rest of his mates, had no idea of Yellowley's earlier career or the fact that he was a member of the AIC.[35]

By far the greatest concern for PMF NCOs was the wholesale reduction back to permanent (substantive) rank at the end of the war. This was partly addressed by an amendment to Australian Military Regulations in 1944. This amendment, designated 148A, was designed to ensure that PMF soldiers commissioned into the 2nd AIF did not lose their PMF seniority, and applied to 'members of the Permanent Military Forces who are granted commissions during the war'. The amendment promised to 'ensure the rights of these members as regards sick and recreational leave, furlough & incremental advancements etc are maintained.'[36] Despite the passing of this legislation, a number of PMF soldiers were reduced to their substantive rank at the end of hostilities in 1945 as the post-war peacetime Army took shape.

For the surviving warrant officers of the AIC, a large number of whom had been commissioned in the 2nd AIF, it was many years before the majority achieved well-deserved promotion in the regular post-war Army.[37]

The AIC in 1945

World War II provided extraordinary opportunities for the AIC and, at the same time, represented a watershed in its history. The war and the consequent mass mobilisation of Australian forces saw the training skills of the corps put to the ultimate test. However, by late 1942, the Corps had almost ceased to exist as a separate entity because all the AIC members had either enlisted in the 2nd AIF or had been posted to AMF/Militia units.[38] It was a corps in name only.

Quartermasters had likewise continued to disappear from the ranks of the Corps. By 1943, while the demand for AMF/Militia quartermaster services continued, many of the AIC warrant officers who had served with the 1st AIF in World War I were reaching retirement age. NX101655 Quartermaster and Honorary Major Septimus William Garling, a master gunner, was retired on 21 December 1943 despite the threatened invasion of his country.[39] However, Garling could boast a share of the action in defending his homeland despite never having served overseas in the war. On Saturday 7 June 1942, Japanese midget submarines entered Sydney Harbour. Bob Whiston recalls:

> In Sydney the hunt continued for the mother ship. Hon. Major Seth Garling mounted a twin six pounder gun at water level at West Head. The foundations can still be seen in the water.[40]

While the Corps may have disappeared from the minds of many in the Army, it was still very much alive in a small Military Secretary Cell in Swanson Street, Melbourne, in 1944. Evidence of this activity is provided by Warrant Officer Class 1 Colin W. McPherson who states, 'While on leave in Melbourne from No1 School of Infantry Course I visited the office housed upstairs in a public building in Swanson Street.'[41] Run by two AIC administration warrant officers, the Military Secretary Cell kept track of the postings of approximately 1600 AIC honorary officers and men of the PMF to ensure that their entitlements were fully up to date. It is likely Colin McPherson knew and had served with these warrant officers in peacetime. The service provided by this small cell would prove particularly valuable at the end of the war as surviving AIC members joined the Interim Army.

The work of the Corps on active service concluded at the end of World War II in August 1945. The 2nd AIF was disbanded and AIC members returned to the PMF. However, owing to changed strategic circumstances, by 1946 both the AMF/Militia and the PMF (including the AIC) had become part of the new Interim Army. The Interim Army was a temporary organisational structure created by executive order prior to the introduction of legislation that would see the creation of the Australian Regular Army. The Interim Army was created in May 1946, with retrospective application to 1 October 1945.[42] It was the end of an important phase in the life of the AIC.

While a large number of AIC members were commissioned into the AMF/Militia, analysis of service records shows that approximately 200 AIC warrant officers were also commissioned as officers in the 2nd AIF while on active service. AIC warrant officers, like the officers of the Australian Staff Corps, were vital components in ensuring the Australian Army's ultimate success in World War II. Just as the Australian Staff Corps provided the higher direction of the war, the AIC conducted the practical instruction of large numbers of soldiers and also often provided experienced men as leaders capable of taking companies of men into battle. Leaders and instructors were both vital and important components in the battle to defeat a tenacious enemy.

The AIC members who served the Australian Army so well in World War II gained a well-deserved reputation as the models of value and tradition.

In addition, through leadership, they supported the ethos of the Army. Within the Army, the Corps supported and upheld the strong military culture of subordinating self to the group and the ideal of sacrifice. As an indication of the extraordinary service provided by the AIC, at the end of World War II in 1945, there were five originally appointed quartermasters from 1921 still serving in the Army.[43] 'Service presented by example' was the view of the Corps projected throughout the Army. Such examples ensured that troops trained by the AIC were also instilled with the military ethos often referred to as the 'Anzac Spirit'.

Front-line soldiers respected the AIC and their training. Captain Bede Tongs, awarded the MM as an NCO in the 2nd/4th Battalion, AIF, asserted that he owed his 'survival to the AIC instructors at Studley Park [NSW].'[44] There is every reason to believe that Bede Tongs' sentiment identifies a significant reason for Australia's success on the battlefields—the AIC.

Well over 100 years ago, Rudyard Kipling wrote that 'the backbone of the Army is the non-commissioned man.'[45] True as that was for the British Army of the time, it had shown itself to be equally true for Australia in its hour of need from 1942 to 1945. However, while the Army's need for NCOs was to continue past 1945, for the warrant officers of the AIC the changed strategic situation would herald a new set of circumstances. Three important changes were to have a significant impact on the Corps over the next few years. The first of these was the establishment of an Australian Regular Army in 1945. This was followed by the relegation (over time) of the citizen Army to a reserve role and the creation of permanent arms and services corps schools. These would negate the need for a single 'instructional corps' to conduct all-corps courses throughout the country. Finally the introduction of Quartermaster examinations eliminated the need for honorary officers. The AIC was to face these vastly changed strategic circumstances as part of the Interim Army in 1945. It would be yet another chapter in a singular history.

CHAPTER ELEVEN
NOTES

1.   John Moremon, Most Deadly Jungle Fighters?: *Australian Infantry in Malaya & Papua 1941–43*, BA Hons thesis, University of New England, 1992, pp. 33–38.

2.   Lionel Wigmore, *Official History of Australia in the War of 1939–1945*, Series I, Vol. IV, *The Japanese Thrust*, AWM, Canberra, 1957 (1968), p. 318. See also 2/30 Battalion home page at: http://www.230battalion.org.au/NominalRoll/Platoon/NRPlatoonACo.

3.   See 2/30 Battalion home page at: http://www.230battalion.org.au/NominalRoll/Platoon/NRPlatoonACo.

4.   G.M. Byrnes, *Green Shadows, A War History of the Papuan Infantry Battalion, 1 New Guinea Infantry Battalion, 2 New Guinea Infantry Battalion, 3 New Guinea Infantry Battalion, 1940-1947*, self-published, Brisbane, 1989, p. 5.

5.   Colonel Donald Ramsey, CO 2nd Battalion, Papuan Infantry Regiment, interview with the author, 3 April 2006. In 1945 the Papuan Infantry Battalion merged with the New Guinea Infantry Battalion to form the Pacific Islands Regiment.

6.   Raymond Paull, *Retreat from Kokoda,* William Heinemann Ltd, Melbourne, 1956 (1958), p. 13.

7.   Clarrie James, *ANGAU, One Man Law,* Australian Military History Publications, Sydney, 1999.

8.   Ross, *The Myth of the Digger*, p. 117.

9.   'AMF, Appointment, Promotions, Etc, List No.3, HQ Allied Land
      Forces, 11 November 1943, Part II, Permanent Military Force,
      Australian Instructional Corps.'

10.   See Allchin, *Purple and Blue.*

11.   Paul Handel, *The Vital Factor, A History of the 2nd/6th Australian Armoured
      Regiment 1941-1946*, Australian Military History Publications, Sydney,
      2005, p. 188.

12.   Johnson, *Australia at War*, p. 143.

13.   Ibid.

14.   Whiston, Another Whiston Matter, p. 159.

15.   AWM, 057114 & 057112 & 057110.

16.   AWM 057152 & 057157.

17.   Bob Long, *Z Special Unit's Secret War, Soldering with the head-hunters of
      Borneo*, B. Long Publications, Bayswater, WA, 1999 (2nd edn.), Chapter 8,
      Warrant Officer I C. W. McPherson, MM, pp. 175–266.

18.   George Osgood, interview with the author, 20 November 2003.

19.   Grey, *The Australian Army,* p. 144.

20.   Burch, *History of the School of Artillery 1885-1996*, p. 49.

21.   NAA, MP742/1 248/1/15, Appendix C: Compiled Document from
      Warrant Officers, AIC, and Sergeants attached Army Schools and
      Coastal Defences.

22.   Lieutenant Colonel Stuart Graham, 'Tanks against Japan', *Army Journal*,
      Vol. 1, No. 2 (June 1955), p. 176.

23.   Ibid., p. 172.

24.   Hopkins, *Australian Armour*, p. 137.

25.   Graham, 'Tanks against Japan', p. 173.

26.   Ibid., p. 171.

27.   Palazzo, *The Australian Army,* p. 186.

28.   See Kuring, *Redcoats to Cams*; interview with the author, 24 January
      2007.

29.   AWM 60, 253/1/62 AMF Northern Command; letter of 10 Mar 1942,
      Reference 190/AIC/42, Postings AIC.

30.   Kuring, *Redcoats to Cams*, p. 150.

31.   Ibid., p. 139.

32.   Lieutenant Colonel Arthur James Cahill Newton, MBE, interview with
      the author, 1 October 2002.

33. Peter Wright, President, 55/53 Battalion, AIF, interview with the author, 16 February 2004.

34. F.W. Budden, *That Mob—The story of the 55/53 Australian Infantry Battalion, AIF,* self-published, Sydney, 1973.

35. AMF Staff & Graduation List 1940: 'PMF, Warrant Officers, p. 331, No. 2406 SSM 3rd Class Yellowley, R, DOB 24/7/1908, 2 Div, Inf.'

36. NAA, MP742/1 248/1/15, A.M.R. '148A applies only in respect of members of the Permanent Military Forces who are granted commissions during the war and it will ensure the rights of these members as regards sick and recreational leave, furlough & incremental advancements etc are maintained.' Amendments to Australian Military Regulations, Letter from Chief Finance Officer to Secretary, Department of the Army, 5 March 1944.

37. NAA, MP742/1, Item 240/1/2785, The Minister of the Army, the Hon. Cyril Chambers approved the use of the term 'Regular Army', Military Board Minute (Meeting 27 August 1947) approved by the Minister 13 September 1947.

38. Graeme Sligo, 'The Development of the Australian Regular Army, 1944-1952' in *The Second Fifty Years, The Australian Army 1947-1997,* Peter Dennis and Jeffrey Grey (eds), Directorate of Army History, Canberra, 1997, p. 27.

39. AMF, Appointment, Promotions, Etc, List No.3, HQ Allied Land Forces, 11 November 1943, Part II, Permanent Military Force, Australian Instructional Corps, (all three retirements).

40. Midget Submarines, notes by Lieutenant Colonel R. N. Whiston RL, unpublished, December 1997, p. 4.

41. Colonel C. W. MacPherson MM psc, interview with the author, 25 November 2002.

42. See NAA, MP 742/1, Item 240/12137; Military Board Minute of 3 May 1946, addendum 2 May 1956.

43. From List B they were VX13549 Lieutenant Colonel (Temporary Colonel) Carl R. Speckman, MBE, MC; VX117154 Lieutenant Colonel (Temporary Colonel) Claude C. Easterbrook, DSO, OBE, MC; and VP7598 Lieutenant Colonel Albert W. Taylor, MBE, MC; and from List C, VP7596 Major John S. Tait and TP13 Major William C.G. Ruddock. See 'Australian Military Forces, Regimental Lists & Manning Tables of Officers on the Active List, No.3, 1st October 1945, Part 1, Permanent Military Forces, General & Special Lists.'

44. N43917, 3rd Battalion, AMF later NX 126952 Captain Bede Tongs, MM, 2/4 Bn AIF, letter to the author, 11 January 2004.

45. Rudyard Kipling, 'The 'Eathen' in *The Complete Barrack-Room Ballads of Rudyard Kipling*, (ed.) Charles Carrington, Methuen & Co, London, 1973, pp. 74–76.

Chapter Twelve
Commencement of peacetime operations and the passing of the
AIC

A regular Army emerges

In 1945 the Australian Government decided it needed a modern Army to meet the demands of future conflict. The recent Pacific War and the rise of communism had convinced the Labor Government that a regular Army was required—an Army that could be quickly mobilised to provide forward or home defence. Ultimately however, the introduction of a regular Army was to lead to the demise of the AIC. There was simply no place in a modern regular Army for a single corps that performed all the tasks of the AIC. The first suggestion of the Corps' decline came with the loss of its national instructional role followed by the demise of its central role as the reservoir of quartermasters. Then when the Small Arms School was merged with the School of Infantry and finally, the remaining quartermasters were transferred from the AIC to a corps of the Australian Regular Army (ARA). When the last Quartermaster (AIC) became a Quartermaster (ARA), the AIC was consigned to history.

It took a decade from 1945 to 1955 for these losses to become reality. On the way, a number of significant changes were to transform the manner in which the Army was to do business. This transformation also affected the careers of the AIC warrant officers who survived the war and were to participate in the last decade of the life of the Corps.

Here we go again ...

Returning to Australia at the termination of his 1st AIF service in 1917, Captain James Newland, VC, the only PMF warrant officer in two world wars to be awarded the country's highest military honour, was forced to revert to his substantive rank of warrant officer class I.[1] He was not alone; this reversion to substantive rank also occurred to almost 300 other PMF soldiers who had received commissions in the 1st AIF. The unfortunate reversion to substantive rank occurred once more in 1945 at the end of World War II. Those AIC members affected by this reversion must have been appalled. Nothing had been learned from the degrading experiences of AIC officers and warrant officers in the previous post-war period.

No. 1055 Warrant Officer Class I Sydney Jamison Greville was a specialist signals instructor who had been on staff at RMC prior to World War II. He had been accepted into the 2nd AIF and commissioned as a lieutenant, Australian Signals, on 13 January 1939. He was promoted to captain on 13 February 1940 and, by 1 September 1942, had been promoted to major. By 5 May 1943, Sydney Greville was a substantive lieutenant colonel in the 2nd AIF.[2] Despite being the Commander of Signals, 11th Australian Division (AIF), at the rank of Lieutenant Colonel in 1945 when the 2nd AIF was disbanded, Greville had to revert to his pre-war PMF substantive rank. As 3/74 Warrant Officer Class I Sydney J. Greville, he became a soldier in the Interim Army, the forerunner of the ARA.

It was not until some four years later in 1949 that Sydney Greville was actually commissioned into the ARA, and then only as a lieutenant (quartermaster).[3] The lowly rank offered to Lieutenant (Quartermaster) Greville five years after he had been a field commander on active service must have been galling, despite the fact that it was no indication of any slur on his service or conduct. This was simply a situation all AIC warrant officers had to accept in a peacetime Army.

Fig 15. *Lt. Col. S.J. Greville standing at right*

In a similar situation at the end of World War II was Major Vincent Dowdy. Joining the Interim Army, Vincent Dowdy received his third Army number to become 2/51 (later 251) after transferring to the AASC as a temporary lieutenant colonel in 1946/47. Despite wearing the rank of temporary lieutenant colonel, he reverted to his pre-war rank substantive rank of warrant officer class I.

However, regression in rank for individual corps members was only a small feature of the massive changes about to take place in the Army that would see the passing of the AIC as a corps within the next decade.

Australian Interim Forces 1945–1950

A crumbling British Empire and the threat of communism in Asia in 1945 changed the entire circumstances of strategic defence for the Australian Labor Government. To meet this challenge the government scrapped the original Federation defence policy based on a large citizen Army (of approximately 70,000 men) trained by a small permanent force (1500 men). In a brand new policy, the government commenced recruiting a significantly increased permanent force (target 34,000) that was to become the ARA.[4] Unsurprisingly, the transition to a regular force took some years. In this period the AMF was described and identified as the 'Interim Army'.[5] The Interim Army included 'all members of the Australian Military Forces serving on continuous full-time duty on 1 October 1945, and personnel who join the AMF on full-time duty after that date.'[6]

It was the Australian Interim Army that sent three regular infantry battalions—the 65th, 66th and 67th Australian Infantry Battalions—to garrison Japan as part of the British Commonwealth Occupation Force (BCOF) . Collectively, these battalions formed the 34th Australian Infantry Brigade. On 23 November 1948 these three battalions became the 1st, 2nd and 3rd Battalions of the Australian Regiment. When Royal Assent was granted on 10 March 1949, the Australian Regiment became the Royal Australian Regiment (RAR) and the three battalions then became the 1st, 2nd and 3rd Battalions of The Royal Australian Regiment. It was as regular battalions of the RAR that these troops—3 RAR embarking from Japan and 1 RAR and 2 RAR from Australia—formed K Force and departed for Korea in 1950 as the Korean War erupted.

The Korean War was to be the last occasion on which Australia raised an all-volunteer expeditionary force to fight overseas. One former AIC warrant officer who fought in Korea was 6/11 Captain Kevan Thomas, MC, MID. Kevan Thomas had qualified for a Staff Corps appointment by attending and passing No. 2 Course, ' BCOF School, Royal Military College Wing, in Japan on 28 October 1948 while a member of the Interim Army.[7] Promoted to the rank of major, he was sent to Korea as a company commander in the 2nd Battalion, The Royal Australian Regiment (2 RAR). His service in Korea would see Kevan Thomas made an Officer of the Order of the British Empire (OBE).

Fig. 16. *Major Kevan Thomas OBE MC prior to going to Korea.*

Army training 1945–1955

A dramatic change in the dynamics of Army training had occurred during World War II. The huge demand for training had seen a massive increase in both the number and type of Army Schools. It was the number and diversity of these new schools that were to shape the post-war ARA. As the Army acquired more sophisticated equipment the need for more instructors increased commensurately. Greater mechanisation and motorisation demanded a more logistics-based movement system with the necessary schools to impart these new skills. Progress to more deadly technology in new weapons was also to drive the need for other new specialist Army schools.

Indeed, new specialist corps schools were at the forefront of change. Instructors at these schools were able to teach soldiers new skills and prepare them to operate in radically different battlefields beyond even the wartime experience of the current Army. One new specialist school was the Electrical and Mechanical Engineers School at Ingleburn, NSW, which trained members of the specialist corps the Australian Electrical and Mechanical Engineers, formed in 1942.

For one infantry warrant officer, this new technical corps promised a career change. No.10704 Temporary Warrant Officer Class II Maxwell

Kenneth Robertson was a cinema projectionist at the time of his enlistment in the PMF in 1939. After completing No. 9 Special Course, Max Robertson was posted to the 6th Military District, 2nd AIF Recruit Training Camp as an instructor.[8] On 30 June 1942 he enlisted in the 2nd AIF at Bonegilla, Victoria, as TX13103. Max Robertson saw active service in New Guinea during which he was commissioned as a lieutenant. After World War II Lieutenant Robertson became Adjutant of the CMF Royal Australian Electrical & Mechanical Engineers (RAEME) Recovery Unit at Anglesea Barracks, Hobart. He later moved to the Hobart suburb of Glenorchy when the CMF unit became a General Troops Workshop, RAEME.[9]

The huge increase in Army Schools following the establishment of the Regular Army is illustrated in Table 5.

Table 5. Comparison—permanent Army schools 1920–1944[10]
The five original schools are illustrated in bold.

Permanent Army Schools: 1944	Location	Founded
Royal Military College	Duntroon, ACT	1911
Staff School (Australia)	Duntroon, ACT	
Tactical School	Beenleigh, Qld	
Armoured Fighting Vehicle School	Puckapunyal, Vic	
School of Artillery (Field + Tank Attack Wing)	Holsworthy, NSW	1885
School of Artillery (Anti Aircraft)	Randwick, NSW	
School of Searchlights, Royal Australian Artillery	Middle Head, Sydney	
School of Radiophysics	Sydney, NSW	
School of Military Engineering	Liverpool, NSW	1939
Camouflage Development & Training Centre, Royal Australian Engineers	Georges Heights, Sydney	

Permanent Army Schools: 1944	Location	Founded
School of Signals	Bonegilla, Vic	
Small Arms School	Bonegilla, Vic	1921
Officer Cadet Training Unit	Woodside, SA	
School of Mechanisation	Seymour, Vic	
Australian Army Service Corps School	North Geelong, Vic	
Australian Army Ordnance Corps School	Broadmeadows, Vic	
Electrical & Mechanical Engineers School	Ingleburn, NSW	
Australian Army Medical Corps School	Ivanhoe, Vic	
School of Tropical Medicine	Sydney, NSW	
Gas School	Cabarlah, Qld	
School of Military Intelligence	Southport, Qld	
School of Physical Training	Frankston, Vic	1920
School of Army Co-operation	Canberra, ACT	
School of Hygiene & Sanitation	Sydney University	
Army Women's Services Officers School	Melbourne, Vic	
School of Army Education	Glenfield, NSW	
School of Army Cooking & Catering	Chermside, Qld	
Provost Training School	Darley, Vic	
School of Malaria Control	Brisbane, Qld	
School of Military Law		
Land Headquarters Australia Women's Services Administration (Offrs) School	Melbourne, Vic	

Permanent Army Schools: 1944	Location	Founded
School of Army Education (Women's Services) School	Keilor, Vic	
Army Women's Services Supervisor Personnel School	Darley, Vic	
Australian Army Medical Women's Services Training School	Darley, Vic	

The massive increase in corps schools established by the ARA rendered the 'all-corps instruction' obsolete and its instructors redundant. It was to sound the death-knell for the major role of the AIC.

What happened to AIC members who became officers?

Promotion in the 2nd AIF provided unparalleled opportunities for the keen young warrant officer instructors who had been commissioned. After the war many of these warrant officer instructors were able to qualify through the various wings of RMC to join the Australian Staff Corps.

Fig 17. *Colonel Guy Fawcett OBE, 2003.*

Guy Fawcett had been CO (temporary lieutenant colonel) of 1 Australian Weapons Training School at Mount Tamborine in Queensland in 1943 before returning to active service with the 2nd/17th Battalion, AIF. After the war he qualified to join the Staff Corps serving with the 65th Battalion (which became the 1st Battalion, The Royal Australian Regiment—1 RAR) 34th Brigade, BCOF, in Japan. After more active service in Korea with 1 RAR, he became CO of 16 National Service Training Battalion and, finally, Commandant of the Infantry Centre in Singleton. Colonel Fawcett described joining the Staff Corps as 'being taken into the bosom of the elite.'[11]

Rupert Shields, a graduate of No. 7 AIC Special Course, was discharged from the 2nd AIF on 30 June 1947 and enlisted in the Interim Army on 1 July 1947.[12] After joining the Staff Corps he became an officer instructor at the School of Infantry and later Adjutant of the 5th Infantry Battalion (Victoria Scottish). Appointed to the ARA on 15 August 1952, Rupert Shields was promoted major and appointed Officer Commanding Headquarters Company, Pacific Islands Regiment, retiring from the ARA on 12 August 1959.

On 7 May 1948 Warrant Officer Class I Vincent Dowdy was commissioned lieutenant (quartermaster). On 4 July 1949 he successfully qualified to join the Australian Staff Corps and was promoted lieutenant colonel and allocated to the Royal Australian Army Service Corps (RAASC). In 1951 he was appointed CO 1st Recruit Training Battalion just as the requirement for three months' continuous National Service was introduced. Promoted to colonel, he was appointed Commander RAASC, Headquarters Southern Command in 1957.[13] In his final posting, Brigadier Vincent Dowdy, OBE, psc, retired as Director of Supplies and Transport.[14] For Vincent Dowdy, a former PMF soldier, to achieve one star rank in a professional Army, surrounded by RMC graduates, was an extraordinary achievement. It amply demonstrates the strength of character and purpose that this former AIC warrant officer committed to his life as a professional soldier.

Alfred Etheredge entered World War II as a temporary captain and instructor at Officer Training Units and Officer Training Schools. He was to finish his Army career as Major Etheredge on the staff of the Military Secretary. Despite volunteering in both World Wars, Alfred Etheredge was never selected to undertake active service overseas.[15] Like Ernest Latchford, Alfred Etheredge had been a Militia soldier prior to joining the PMF but, unlike Latchford, he was prevented from joining the 1st AIF and spent the whole war in Australia instructing troops joining the AMF/Militia and the 1st AIF. Alfred Etheredge and his fellow instructors who remained at home performed valuable and essential work. However, when it came to promotion after the war, those who had seen active service were in the best position to be selected, while those without such experience were well down the list. After World War II Etheredge was commissioned as a captain (quartermaster) in 1948 and later promoted major (quartermaster). Major Etheredge retired from the Interim Army in April 1951 having served a total of 39 years and 326 days.

Fig 18. *Lt. Alfred Etheredge with Lt.-Col. E. P. Hill MM,*
CO 39th Bn. (holding horse reins)

Quartermasters

Members of the Military Board had long been concerned that PMF warrant officers class I could be appointed to an honorary quartermaster commission without undertaking any further military examination, a situation that had continued from interwar period. Indeed, a strongly held tenet of the Military Board was that 'all officers should qualify by examination, and this should also apply to the quartermasters of the Instructional Corps.' Holding an honorary commission without passing any officer examinations, quartermasters could be promoted and could advance to the field rank of major or lieutenant colonel. Even the peacetime caveat, that AIC quartermasters could only command the quartermaster staff directly subordinate to them, was not always adhered to. No. 2/64 Major Harcourt Lenard Hartnett, for example, commanded the 25th Coast Regiment, RAA, in 1952.[16]

The anomaly regarding honorary quartermaster commissions was finally removed by the Military Board shortly after the end of World War II. Amendments to the *Defence Act* had led to the introduction of Administrative and Technical Officers' courses designed to train and qualify specialist officers including quartermasters. By 1947 an Administrative and Technical School had been established which provided a range of technical courses for officers. These were known throughout the Army as 'knife and fork' courses, an oblique reference to mess etiquette rules.[17] Completing this course and successfully passing specifically officer-level technical examinations saw experienced warrant officers and NCOs then commissioned as lieutenants.

Frank (Leslie Francis) Guest (NP5483), a graduate of No. 9 Special Course, was part of an AIC extended 'family.'[18] His father, 225 Staff Sergeant Major Class II Cecil Ernest Guest, had served in the British Army with the 17th Lancers in India and was a Boer War veteran. He had seen active service in South Africa with the Rifle Brigade. After joining the AIC, Cecil Ernest Guest was appointed Area Officer in East Maitland, NSW. Frank's brother, 3073 Staff Sergeant Major

Class III Cecil Ivor Guest, was a graduate of No. 3 Special Course and was appointed RSM of the 2nd/15th Battalion in Queensland. Cecil Guest was later commissioned as a captain in World War II.

Not all warrant officers who remained in the AIC after World War II had the opportunity to qualify and pass the examinations to join the Australian Staff Corps. Frank Guest seized the opportunity to qualify as a quartermaster, graduating from an Administrative and Technical Course run at the School of Infantry at Seymour in Victoria. In a long career as a movements officer, Major Frank Guest finally returned to active service in 1965 as the Deputy Assistant Quartermaster General, Movements, at the Australian Task Force Headquarters at Nui Dat in South Vietnam.

Within five years of the introduction of the Administrative and Technical courses, the majority of the senior AIC warrant officers had qualified for regular quartermaster commissions.[19] In 1951, 55 AIC quartermasters were transferred to other corps. These included Major (Quartermaster) 5/76 George Maxwell Lambert Hogarth who was transferred to the Royal Australian Army Ordnance Corps (RAAOC). As 4576 Staff Sergeant Major Class III Maxwell George Lambert Hogarth (his first two names now interchanged), the now George Hogarth had been a graduate of No. 1 Special Course held from 12 February to 12 June 1935.[20]

Also transferred was 3/105 (ex VP387 and VX27387) Major (Quartermaster) Charles James Wilson Farnington, MBE, DCM, to the Royal Australian Army Provost Corps. Charles Farnington had been awarded his DCM for service as a sergeant with the 5th Battalion, AIF. After joining the AIC at its establishment in 1921, his long and exceptional service was recognised when he was made an MBE in 1938.

In a similar manner to quartermasters, the warrant officer instructors were also allocated, and later transferred, to the various arms and service corps in the Interim Army. When the transfer took place, a warrant officer

(AIC) became a warrant officer (Royal Australian Infantry) or warrant officer (RAA) according to his allocated corps. The transfers of quartermasters and warrant officer instructors to other corps in the decade from 1945 to 1955 effectively led to the gradual disappearance of the AIC within the Army. The actual demise of the corps was effected in three stages, the first comprising the transfer of warrant officer instructors to other corps. Secondly, and concurrently, AIC quartermasters were being commissioned and transferred out of the Corps, and finally these actions were followed by the removal of the AIC from the Australian Army's Order of Corps Precedence List on 19 May 1955.[21] After a long and distinguished career, the AIC was no more.

School of Infantry

Not all the post-war changes affecting the corps were regarded as positive in all sections of the Army. There was a major pocket of resistance to the changes affecting the AIC instructors at the School of Infantry. This concerned the warrant officers and NCOs who ran the warrant rank qualifying courses which comprised three subjects: Subject A—Drill and Weapons Training, Subject B—Tactical/Technical Training, and Subject C—Administration.[22]

For approximately five years immediately after the end of World War II, the qualifying courses for infantry warrant officers were conducted along similar lines to earlier times when the AIC was 'training the trainers.'[23] This was because the majority of the instructors at the School of Infantry at that time had been, or were, AIC warrant officers. It was many years before these warrant officers retired and were replaced by younger men who, by then, were unable to join the AIC. During these years, the ethos engendered by AIC training remained alive and well. Importantly, the standards of AIC training, later maintained through the 'Methods of Instruction' courses, were strongly imprinted on the younger soldiers coming through the ranks.

When the first RSM of the Australian Army, Warrant Officer Class 1 Wallace (Wally) Thompson, OAM, assumed his appointment in 1983, he designed as his badge of office the Australian Coat of Arms surrounded by a laurel wreath.[24] This was to be a lasting tribute to the distinctive AIC badge of rank, the crown, worn on the lower uniform sleeve, surrounded by a laurel wreath (the rank insignia of the warrant officer class II).

Task loss becomes invisibility

The raising of a regular Army had worked strongly in favour of the retention of the services of returning AIC members. This contrasted markedly with the reductions faced by the PMF in 1922 following the end of the Great War. The new ARA had a proposed establishment strength of 34,000 men.[25] In reality, owing to recruiting problems, by June 1950 Army strength stood at a mere 14,651.[26]

Even this smaller, more realistic ARA figure represented a big increase from the 1939 pre-war PMF establishment of 3,572.[27] The huge increase in Army Schools from five in 1938 to 34 in 1944 ensured a large number of positions for experienced instructors.[28]

In 1947 the Army once again required experienced instructors, a fact immediately obvious in the transfer of 145 sergeants, all with experience of active service, to the AIC on 26 August 1947. They were then appointed staff sergeant major class III and promoted warrant officer class II.[29] Appointments from three corps, the AASC, the RAA and RAE, included VP3560 (VX513) Staff Sergeant R.E. Robinson, AASC; NP5136 (NX108458) Sergeant A.D. Watt, RAA and VP3798 (VX117072) Staff Sergeant T.R. Warren, RAE.

This trend of transfer, appointment and promotion continued in 1948 when a further 90 soldiers from the Interim Army joined the AIC.[30] Appointments from four corps, RAE, AASC, AAMC and RAA, included VP4222 (VX11926) Corporal N.E. Coker, RAE; NP3413 (NX161779)

Corporal E.J. Haynes, AASC; VP3873 (VX101943) Sergeant S. Rolfe, AAMC and NP3181 (NX165146) Bombardier Alfred (Alf) Stephen Finney, RAA. Alf Finney joined the Army as a 16-year-old Universal Trainee cadet. Following Militia service he enlisted in the PMF in 1935. During World War II he was an NCO with the 2nd Australian Mountain Battery, RAA, in New Guinea and Bougainville. Changing corps, Alf Finney became the RSM of the 15th Northern River Lancers. He was credited with saving the lives of two people on 8 March 1954 when three servicemen were drowned during an exercise involving amphibious vehicles at Stockton Bight near Newcastle. When he retired from the Army, Alf Finney continued to serve his comrades and was awarded the Medal of the Order of Australia (OAM) on 26 January 1981 'for service to the welfare of ex-service personnel'.[31]

The last transfers of Interim Army soldiers to the AIC occurred in 1949 when two RAA, one RAASC and one RAE member joined the Corps.[32] From 1950 onwards, all sergeants who qualified to become warrant officers at corps schools remained with the corps in which they had qualified. This administrative action halted any further growth of the AIC.

What if...

Yet there actually was a post-war case for the retention of the AIC. The Corps function of 'training the trainers' could have been utilised when the CMF was re-raised in 1948. The citizen force had been trained by AIC instructors since its establishment in 1921. The Corps had considerable practical experience in the role, including running courses in all states of the Commonwealth. There is some speculation that a possible post-war role for the AIC was rejected by the Military Board.

Anecdotal evidence suggests that, at a very senior level, there was opposition to the AIC having a continuing role in the post-war period. This evidence comes from a long-serving officer recruited to join the ARA on the CMF Cadre Staff in 1948. Major John de Witt recalled that, at a conference held at Victoria Barracks, Sydney, the question was asked, 'Will the AIC be raised again?' The answer, John de Witt remembers, was:

> No, there is pressure from above not to have an elite group with red tabs on their arms [referring to the distinctive two red stripes on their epaulettes worn by AIC members] running the Army again.[33]

Perhaps the reason for this attitude dates back to 1925 when the then CGS, Major General Sir Brudenell White, wrote to his successor, Major General Sir Harry Chauvel, stating that there was need to upgrade the instructional facilities (at the Small Arms School) where 'there was a warrant officer of the AIC in command'.[34]

Emerging quartermasters

The loss of the training task for the AIC warrant officers was slightly offset by the fact that the quartermaster role in the ARA had considerably expanded. With materiel for the Army now physically manufactured in Australia (as distinct from overseas), the need for specialist quartermasters in the service corps units had grown almost exponentially. Thus members of the AIC remaining with the corps after World War II were employed less in the instructional role and far more in the quartermaster role. In 1949, 139 warrant officer's class I were commissioned and promoted to lieutenant (quartermaster). These included 2/311 Roger John Ivan De Groot, the son of Captain Francis De Groot of Sydney Harbour Bridge fame; 5/76 George Maxwell Lambert Hogarth; 2/188 Arthur James Cahir Newton, MBE; 3/74 Sydney Jamison Greville; 1/46 John Thomas Wellbelove, MC; 2/370 Norman Neels, MBE; and 4/55 Gordon Charles Whittle [SP4473 and 4/55 Major (Quartermaster) Gordon Charles Whittle].

Becoming undetectable

The 1940–1941 establishment figures of 234 quartermasters

provided the peak of employment for AIC quartermasters.[35] The 200+ mark remained constant for quartermasters after World War II when the 1945 establishment was 235 (143 quartermasters plus 92 temporary quartermasters).[36] Even in 1950 the establishment still numbered 220 quartermasters.[37] While from 1945 to 1949 new warrant officers joined the Corps, the existing AIC warrant officers were not replaced as they retired or were promoted to become quartermasters.

While the AIC continued to exist as a corps from 1945 to 1955, it was to become indistinguishable within the Army itself. This gradual assimilation occurred as transferred members of the corps wore the uniform and badges of the unit to which they were posted, rather than their own corps badges and distinctive uniform jackets. This loss of identity is clearly evident in the seniority listing of the AIC in The Army List of Officers for 1 October 1950.[38] Each of these 18 quartermasters is shown allocated to another corps list, as is his unit posting within that corps list. Thus 3/142 Major A.R. Etheredge, AIC, is shown as Royal Australian Infantry and his posting as Deputy Assistant Military Secretary, AHQ.[39]

The AIC was not totally invisible, however, as two personal recollections from 1949 and 1950 illustrate. Attending lectures at Victoria Barracks, Sydney in 1949, Major General Paul Cullen (a pre-war Militia officer) recalled a number of teaching sessions delivered by one or more AIC instructors who were 'easily identifiable in their distinctive uniform and badges.'[40]

Similarly, Warrant Officer Class 1 Noel Smith, an infantryman who served in the ARA from 1956 to 1990, attended a two-week Cadet Under-Officers' Course at Queenscliff, Victoria as a high school student in January 1950. Noel Smith recalled a number of the course instructors wearing 'the gilt and blue rising sun badges with Australian Instructional Corps printed across the scroll of the badge.'[41]

Loss of home

Concurrent with the loss of tasks, the final blow to the AIC was the loss of its traditional home. The Small Arms School, originally raised as the School of Musketry on 1 September 1911, became the 'de faco' home of the AIC from 21 June 1921 for the 19 years until 1940 when it was replaced by the Medium Machine Gun School.[42]

In early 1942, the Medium Machine Gun School was relocated from Randwick to Bonegilla, Victoria. At Bonegilla, the school was absorbed into a re-established Small Arms School, with two instructional wings—the General Weapons Wing and the Medium Machine Gun Wing.[43] Once the Small Arms School had been re-established in December 1945, there were still more modifications in store for this important Army training establishment.

In March 1944 Land Headquarters established a School of Infantry at Puckapunyal, Victoria.[44] The school was subsequently renamed the Headquarters, Australian Military Forces (HQ AMF) School of Infantry. When it moved to Bonegilla in December 1945, the School of Infantry took over and absorbed the Small Arms School. Although this was actually the end of an independent Small Arms School, the Infantry Wing of the HQ AMF School of Infantry continued the tradition of the Small Arms School, running courses to train warrant officer instructors for the AIC in 1944 and 1945.[45]

In rapid succession, the HQ AMF School of Infantry became the AHQ School of Infantry and then simply the Army School of Infantry. Moving to Seymour, Victoria, in 1947, the Army School of Infantry became the School of Infantry. In 1960 the School of Infantry relocated to Bardia Barracks, Ingleburn, NSW, becoming The Infantry Centre.[46]

Vietnam—the final frontier

In 1965, a decade after the AIC was removed from the Australian Army's Order of Corps Precedence, Australia sent combat troops to the Vietnam War. As has been mentioned earlier, only two former AIC warrant officers are known to have been involved in the Vietnam War, Major Keith Trevan and Major (later Lieutenant Colonel) Frank Guest, who served in Vietnam as Deputy Assistant Quartermaster General (Movements).[47]

For the Australians the war in South Vietnam commenced 20 years after the end of World War II, making it most unlikely that, apart from Frank Guest and Keith Trevan, there were any other ex-AIC warrant officers engaged in active service in South-East Asia with the Australian Task Force from 1965 onwards. However, the caveat to these very small numbers may yet be contained in The Army List of Officers of the Australian Military Forces, 1 August 1966, on which 29 former AIC members, now majors (quartermasters) are listed.

CHAPTER TWELVE
NOTES

1.   Military Order 38-1922, 'Australian Instructional Corps, Appointment. James Ernest Newland, V.C., late Captain, Reserve of Officers, and an ex-member of the Instructional Staff (W. and NCOs) is appointed Warrant Officer, Class 1, 12th Mixed Brigade, dated 31st December 1921.'

2.   Graduation List of Officers of the Australian Military Forces, Vol. I, The Active List, 7 March 1946, '1055 Sydney Jamison Greville, DOB 1/10/1899, Lt Aust Sigs 13/10/39, Capt Aust Sigs (AIF) 13/2/40, Major Aust Sigs 1/9/42, Lt.-Col Aust Sigs 11/5/1943', p. 59.

3.   Australian Army Order 30 June 1950, 'Australian Military Forces, Permanent Military Forces, Australian Instructional Corps; To be Lieutenant(s), 1st July 1949, 3/74 WO1 Sydney Jamison Greville', p. 176.

4.   NAA, MP 742/1, Item 240/1/2785, Military Board Minute, Meeting of 27 August 1947.

5.   AWM 113, Item 10, 32, J. E. Murphy, History of the Post War Army, unpublished manuscript, 1955, 'Executive Minute of the Governor-General in Council, 1 October 1947'.

6.   NAA. MP742/1 Item 2317, Military Board Minute of 3 May 1946, based on Agendum dated 2 May 1946.

7.   NAA, B2458, Item 611, Thomas, Kevan Brittan, TX 885 (TP4757) attended and qualified at No. 2 Course (BCOF) on 22 October 1948.

8.   NAA, MP385/3, 27/20/809 No. 9 Special Course for appointment to the Australian Instructional Corps.

9. Lieutenant Colonel B. Robertson RFD (son), correspondence with the author, 21 March 2012.

10. Source: Report of the Inspector-General 1921 and Major General I.C. Gordon, AM, The Blamey Oration, RUSI of NSW, 24 June 2004.

11. Colonel Guy Fawcett, OBE, interview with the author, 26 August 2004.

12. Major William Rupert John Shields (known as Rupert), letter to the author, 4 May 2003.

13. The Corps List of Officers of the Australian Regular Army and Regular Army Special Reserve, 1 July 1958.

14. The Corps List of Officers of the Australian Regular Army and Regular Army Special Supplement, 1 September 1964. Dowdy's post-retirement career took a remarkable turn when, following the death of his wife in 1972, he was ordained a priest in the Roman Catholic Church.

15. Don Etheredge (son), letter to the author, 8 May 2003.

16. Australian Army Order 30th April 1953, 'Australian Instructional Corps (Quartermasters), 2/64 Major H.L Hartnett relinquishes command of 25th Coast Regiment, 21st January 1953, (598 BSM Harcourt Lenard Hartnett, DOB 5/7/1903).

17. Warrant Officer Class I Wallace (Wally) Thompson, OAM, interview with the author, 7 August 2005.

18. Lieutenant Colonel L.F. Guest, interview with the author, 15 January 2005.

19. Australian Army Orders issued 30 November 1951, Australian Military Forces, Australian Regular Army, Australian Instructional Corps, 'The following 55 Quartermasters are transferred to RAAMC, RAAOC, RAEME, & RAProvC: e.g. Capt (QM) 5/76 (ex 4576) George Maxwell Lambert Hogarth going to RAAOC.'

20. AWM62, 112,6A/361: Transfer details of Bombardier M.G.L. Hogarth, RAA.

21. Australian Military Regulation 68, Sub Regulation (1), amended 19 May 1955.

22. Military Board Instruction 97-1951, Subjects for Promotion to Warrant Officer.

23. WOII Ian Kuring, (author *Redcoats to Cams*) interview with the author, 18 October 2004.

24. WOI Wallace (Wally) Thompson OAM, interview with the author, 7 August 2005.

25. AWM 113, Item 10, Murphy, History of the Post War Army, p. 14.

26. Grey, *The Australian Army,* p. 170.

27. Long, *To Benghazi,* p. 29.

28. See Table 5; schedule showing Allied Land Forces Schools as at 29 Feb 1944, Appendix I, Sheets 1 & 2.

29. Australian Army Order 59-1947, Australian Instructional Corps, Promotions.

30. Australian Army Order 14-1948, Australian Instructional Corps, Promotions.

31. The mantle of service to his comrades, so strongly imbued in Alf Finney, has been passed down to his son. Stephen Finney, a Vietnam veteran who served with 17 Construction Squadron, RAE, has also been awarded the OAM 'for service to veterans through a range of ex-service organisations in Newcastle and the Hunter region.' Alfred and Stephen Finney are the only known father and son to receive this prestigious award for service to their former comrades.

32. Australian Army Order 110-1949, Australian Instructional Corps, Promotions.

33. N57705, NX146011, NP13165, 2/2278, 2/130109 and 216567, Major John de Witt, commissioned September 1951, transferred to RAAMC 1965, retired as Major, SO1 to the Director of Medical Services, 1976; interview with the author, 6 August 2005.

34. NLA, MS 5172, Folder 25, White Papers, Notes for the new CGS (July 1923)

35. Military Board letter to all Commands, Reference A.G./CMB, 11144 dated 24 February 1941, Subject AIC Annual Establishment 1940-1941.

36. Australian Military Forces, 'Regimental Lists & Manning Tables of Officers on the Active List, No. 3, 1st October 1945, Part 1, Permanent Military Forces, General & Special Lists.' In 1945 there were 143 quartermasters and 92 temporary quartermasters to a total of 235.

37. The Army List of Officers of the Australian Military Forces, Vol. 1, The Active List, 1 October 1950. In 1950 there were 220 quartermasters and no temporary quartermasters.

38. Ibid., p. 133.

39. Don Etheredge (son), interview with the author, 8 May 2003.

40. Major General Paul Cullen, AC, CBE, DSO & Bar, ED, FCA; CO 2nd/1st Battalion, AIF, later CMF member of the Military Board 1964-66, interview with the author, 28 August 2005.

41. Warrant Officer Class 1 Noel Smith, letter to the author, 4 April 2002.

42. Kuring, *Redcoats to Cams,* pp. 34, 95.

43. Ibid., p. 208.

44.   Ibid.

45.   Ibid.

46.   Ibid., p. 222. The Infantry Centre is now located in Singleton, NSW.

47.   Lieutenant Colonel L.F Guest, interview with the author, 15 January 2005.

Chapter Thirteen
An Overview

During the lifetime of the AIC from 1921 to 1955, approximately 2,000 soldiers joined and served as members of the Corps.[1] The absence of a war diary or other documented records of corps activities makes it difficult to describe the experiences of those soldiers who served with the AIC. However, one member of the Corps who set out to document the life of the AIC was Lieutenant Colonel Arthur Newton, MBE, an AIC warrant officer from 1937 to 1941.

Newton wrote a personal account of his AIC service that appeared in the *Army Journal* of August 1971. This appears to be the only documented description of service in the AIC. Arthur Newton served in five Australian armies, the AMF/Militia, the PMF, the 2nd AIF, the Interim Army and the ARA. Newton's article is not simply a record of his service, but includes the insights and opinions of the author concerning the life and future of the AIC. In his concluding remarks, Arthur Newton dismisses the notion of re-establishing the Corps, writing:

> To me it appears unnecessary, if not an impossibility to group all warrant officers in one corps ... there appears little reason to maintain even an Army wide seniority list of WOs Class One except to keep the computer happy.[2]

In a similar vein, Newton offers his opinion on the standards of the AIC as a yardstick for the quality of contemporary warrant officers, commenting that, 'I have a theory that since armies existed, old soldiers have always believed that the WOs and NCOs of their youth were far superior to those of the present.' His final words are unequivocal: 'the warrant officers and NCOs [I have] been associated [with] during the 1960s and 1970s at the Infantry Centre were equal or better than their counterparts from the past.'[3]

These are important contemporary viewpoints from an officer who was a principal member of the AIC—and one of its most articulate—particularly in its heyday between the two world wars. Arthur Newton's comments and views neatly lead to the difficult task of assessing the worth of the Corps.

Fig 19. *Warrant Officer (later Lt Col) Arthur Newton, second from the left.*

Support and leadership of the Citizen Army

At a time when Australia's principal land defence was a citizen Army, an Instructional Corps was an essential element in shaping that Army. Leadership and training were in short supply and desperately needed by the citizen Army particularly in the years that were to prove the lead-up to World War II. The corps provided both. Support in training and leadership continued throughout the war for both the AMF/Militia and the 2nd AIF. Analysis of AIC activities and its individual members provides clear evidence that the corps did not fail in its task. However, with the establishment of the ARA, when the Army-wide training task disappeared and examinations were introduced for quartermaster officers, the Army's need for an Instructional Corps disappeared.

The AIC—exemplary soldiers

While the proud record of the AIC speaks for itself, its members are consistently described by those they served as 'magnificent and exemplary soldiers'. Over the more than 50 years since the Corps disappeared from the Army, regular officers and senior NCOs still express admiration for the warrant officers of the AIC. Understanding the reason for this admiration has become more important now that the AIC is part of history.

In 1921, the Inspector General of the AMF, Lieutenant General Sir Harry Chauvel, GCMG, KCB, commented on the tremendous value to the 1st AIF of the leadership and training of the small number of PMF soldiers. Chauvel wrote:

> Because of the fact that our citizen Army did so extraordinarily well during the late war, there is a tendency on the part of the Australian public to discount the value of the professional soldier and to doubt whether he is necessary at all. This is, perhaps, quite natural, as the people did not realise that the framework of the Army, of which they are so justly proud, had been built up for years before the war by the efforts of a small body of professional soldiers.[4]

The Inspector General was commenting on the efforts of the instructional staff sergeant majors such as Captain James Newland, VC, Major Claude Easterbrook, DSO, MC, and Captain Ernest Latchford, MC, who were to become founding members of the AIC.

In 1921 the AIC had inherited all the previous traditions of the soldiers of the Empire. At the same time, they acquired the newly created traditions of Gallipoli and the Anzac Spirit that inspired them as they trained soldiers to fight on the Western Front in France and Belgium. The inherited deeds of an empire Army, captured by Rudyard Kipling in his epic poem *The 'Eathen* resonated strongly with the warrant officers of the newly established AIC: 'the backbone of the Army is the non-commissioned man.'[5] When this eulogy was added to the new traditions of Gallipoli and Anzac, the now updated and strongly Antipodean version of military service traditions was created.

From 1919 onwards the Australian Army would follow and revere these combined old and new traditions. The AIC, as trainers of the Army between the wars, not only inherited these traditions, but also used them to set the example for the new divisional Army. As professional soldiers, admired because they had come through the Great War, they were able to inculcate the new Army traditions into a citizen Army. Throughout the interwar period the members of the AIC generated a toughness in respect, manner, bearing, dress and discipline. It was to these lessons that many former 2nd AIF soldiers ascribe their own survival in World War II.

There is little doubt that the Returned Sailors', Soldiers', and Airmen's Imperial League of Australia (now the RSL) carried the Anzac Spirit forward into the public arena in the interwar period. Equally it is the case that from 1921 to 1939, in the citizen Army, carriage of the Anzac Spirit was by and through the AIC. A large number of the warrant officers of the AIC were veterans of the 1st AIF. They personally carried forward the Anzac Spirit and its traditions, passing these onto the men who were to become the 2nd AIF. Despite the fact that it is now over half a century since the AIC departed into history, modern recruits joining the Army in its second century of service become part of a traditio.n that echoes these traditions of the AIC. This is the catch cry of Army trainees captured by C.J. Dennis in his poem *The Push*: 'An' they've drilled us. Strike me lucky! But they've drilled us for a cert!'[6]

The end of the AIC

The legal end of the AIC came, as did its beginning, in an amendment to the Australian Military Regulations.[7] On 19 May 1955, Australian Military Regulation 68 Sub-Regulation (1) was amended to read: 'The following shall be the Corps of the Army, and their precedence shall be in the order given.'[8] The Sub-Regulation was amended by omitting the words 'The Australian Instructional Corps'. The removal of the title of the corps from the Army Precedence List of Corps brought to an end the AIC's pre-eminent role immediately following the Australian Staff Corps at the head of the Precedence List. The amendment meant that, for the Australian Army, the AIC ceased to exist, slipping quietly away through a simple omission from a list.

While 19 May 1955 was the legal termination of the AIC, the drawdown of the corps had been underway for almost five years. Although in its time the AIC instructors were considered the epitome of Army practical training and were admired throughout the service, over half a century later, the corps is barely remembered and often confused with the Royal Australian Army Educational Corps.

American General Douglas MacArthur provides the fitting conclusion to this history that has focused on the efforts and achievements of the AIC in practical training and leading the Australian Army over its 34-year history. In his 1933 Annual Report of the Chief of Staff, General Macarthur stated that;

> 'In no other profession are the penalties for employing untrained personnel so appalling and so irrevocable as the military.'[9]

CHAPTER THIRTEEN
NOTES

1. The Army does not have a Nominal Roll (or record) of the members of the AIC. Currently, from service records examined there are 1,908 positively identified and confirmed members of the Corps. Thus the approximate figure of 2,000 is based on examination of about 7/8 of the Army records for the lifetime of the AIC.

2. Newton, *The Australian Instructional Corps*, p. 46.

3. Ibid., p. 52.

4. Report of the Inspector General of the Australian Military Forces, Lieutenant General Sir H.G. Chauvel, GCMG, KCB, dated 31 May 1921, item 73, p. 17.

5. Kipling, 'The 'Eathen' in *The Complete Barrack-Room Ballads of Rudyard Kipling*, pp. 74–76.

6. Clarence J. Dennis, 'The Push', *The Moods of Ginger Mick*, Angus & Robertson, Melbourne (rev. edn.), 1982.

7. AMR 52A Statutory Rule 73, 14 April 1921.

8. AMR 68, Sub Regulation 1, 19 May 1955.

9. Annual Report of the Chief of Staff, 1933.

APPENDIX SEVEN
AIC QM POSTINGS 2ND AIF

FAMILY NAME	DOB	AMF RANK.	AIF DATE	RANK	UNIT
H H Downey, MC, 1st AIF	25/10/1891	QM & Hon Capt 1/2/1938	1/5/40	Major 1/5/40	AAOC DADOS
J E Hendry, MBE, VP511 1st Aif	4/6/1890	QM & Hon Capt 1/2/1938	1/5/40	Major 1/5/40	Arty 1 Aust Corps
H M Maughan 1st AIF	16/7/1894	QM & Hon Capt 17/2/1933	7/5/40	Major 7/5/40	AAMC SOMS Ad HQ
E T Lergessner 2155	28/11/1906	T/QM & H/Lt 11/1/1938	13/10/39	Capt 13/10/39	2/1 Inf Bn QM
B S Black NP1018 NX76	29/11/1900	T/QM & H/Lt 1/12/1938	13/10/39	Capt 13/10/39	2/2 Inf Bn QM

		AMF	AIF		
FAMILY NAME	DOB	RANK.	DATE	RANK	UNIT
E Thorne 1762	2/7/1902	T/QM & H/Lt 15/2/1939	13/10/39	Capt 13/10/39	Arty 6 Div QM
J C Holden 882	9/5/1902	T/QM & H/Lt 15/2/1939	13/10/39	Capt 13/10/39	Cav Regt 6 Div
W G Clementson VP2080, VX51	11/11/1907	T/QM & H/Lt 1/8/1939	13/10/39	Capt 13/10/39	Sigs 6 Div QM
W J Guy	20/2/1891	T/QM & H/Lt 1/9/1938	13/11/39	Capt 13/11/39	Arty 6 Div QM
E F Allchin, MM SP15214 SX1429 1st AIF	16/8/1894	T/QM & H/Lt 15/10/1938	13/11/39	Capt 13/11/39	2/10 Inf Bn QM
C H Sweeney 1st AIF	9/9/1893	T/QM & H/Lt 1/12/1938	13/11/39	Capt 13/11/39	2/11 Inf Bn QM
G R V Smith	3/2/1900	T/QM & H/Lt 1/9/1938	4/4/40	Capt 4/4/40	Rly Units Eng
A B S Collins 1st AIF	10/2/1892	QM & H/Lt 1/9/1938	1/5/40	Capt 1/5/40	AAOC
H Fraser, MBE 1st AIF	11/4/1892	T/QM & H/Lt 15/10/1936	1/5/40	Capt 1/5/40	2/16 Inf Bn QM

FAMILY NAME	DOB	AMF RANK.	AIF DATE	RANK	UNIT
C S Richards 2572	30/4/1907	T/QM & H/Lt 15/12/1937	1/5/40	Capt 1/5/40	Arty 2/1 Med Regt
E M Kent	15/7/1902	T/QM & H/Lt 1/11/1938	1/5/40	Capt 1/5/40	1 AA Regt QM
B A Moylan 1st AIF	24/10/1896	T/QM & H/Lt 15/11/1938	1/5/40	Capt 1/5/40	2/27 Inf Bn QM
H G Loveband SP457 QX6169 1st AIF	22/6/1896	T/QM & H/Lt 1/1/1939	1/5/40	Capt 1/5/40	Arty 2/7 Fd Regt
A H J Ross 1027 1st AIF	9/1/1898	T/QM & H/Lt 1/2/1939	1/5/40	Capt 1/5/40	2/2 Pnr Bn Adjt
J L A Kelly NP2692 NX12214	10/3/1907	T/QM & H/Lt 1/10/1939	1/5/40	Capt 1/5/40	2/13 Inf Bn QM
J M L Macpherson, MC NP550 NX422 1st AIF	3/12/1897	T/QM & H/Lt 1/10/1939	1/5/40	Capt 1/5/40	Arty 7 Div 2/5 Fd Regt
H G W Myers 2518 1st AIF	25/6/1903	T/QM & H/Lt 1/11/1939	1/5/40	Capt 1/5/40	Arty 1 Aust Corps

FAMILY NAME	DOB	AMF RANK.	AIF DATE	RANK	UNIT
W W Farquarson 2138	28/1/1904	T/QM & H/Lt 20/11/1939	13/4/40	Capt 1/5/40	Arty 7 Div 2/6 Fd
A G Oglethorpe 2145	4/7/1907	T/QM & H/Lt 15/12/1939	1/5/40	Capt 1/5/40	Arty 7 Div 2/4 Fd
F A Bradford 3522	13/9/1905	T/QM & H/Lt 15/12/1939	1/5/40	Capt 1/5/40	Sigs 7 Div QM
D McNab 2644	26/7/1910	T/QM & H/Lt 15/12/1939	1/5/40	Capt 1/5/40	2/17 Inf Bn QM
W E R Burke 1907	19/11/1906	T/QM & H/Lt 1/4/1940	1/5/40	Capt 1/5/40	Arty 1 Aus C 2/1 Svy
J M Mills 1st AIF	25/1/1896	T/QM & H/Lt 1/2/1940	1/5/40	Capt 1/5/40	AASC 1 Aust Corps
C J Farnington, MBE, DCM VP387 VX27387 1st AIF	31/5/1895	T/QM & H/Lt 20/5/1940	20/5/40	Capt 20/5/40	Aust Gen Base D
D Holt 1581 1st AIF	5/9/1899	T/QM & H/Lt 1/1/1940	20/5/40	Capt 20/5/40	Arty 2/8/ Fd Regt

FAMILY NAME	DOB	AMF RANK.	AIF DATE	RANK	UNIT
C Ladds 1st AIF	10/3/1894	QM & H/Lt 1/9/1939	1/7/40	Capt 1/7/40	2/25 Inf Bn QM
W L Cleland 361 1st AIF	19/4/1894	T/QM & H/Lt 1/7/1939	1/7/40	Capt 1/7/40	2/3 Pnr Bn QM
A V Tunstill 1691	12/7/1901	T/QM & H/Lt 1/10/1939	1/7/40	Capt 1/7/40	2/28 Inf Bn QM
A O McVicar NP731	2/4/1899	T/QM & H/Lt 15/12/1939	24/7/40	Capt 24/7/40	AAOC HQ 1 Aus C
B W C Carroll	21/3/1911	T/QM & H/Lt 1/11/1939	15/3/40	Lieut 15/3/40	21 MG Bn 2nd Reo
L D Cossart	18/11/1906	T/QM & H/Lt 7/9/1938	1/4/40	Lieut 1/4/40	2/9 Inf Bn 3/4 Reo
A J Lyons 2623	1/1/1908	T/QM & H/Lt 15/12/1939	1/4/40	Lieut 1/4/40	2/9 Inf Bn 3/4 Reo
C B Peat 309 1st AIF	14/10/1892	QM & H/Lt 1/2/1940	1/5/40	Lieut 1/5/40	AAOC

APPENDIX EIGHT
A CHRONOLOGY OF THE AIC

1901   The Australian Army established as the 'Commonwealth Military Forces';
        Citizen Force: Militia 16,105 & Volunteers 11,361 + PMF 1,544 (29,010).

1903   *Defence Act* 1903 passed by the Federal Parliament.

1906   Australian Cadet Corps formed (ACC).

1911   Universal Military Training commenced (UMT) *Defence Act* Section 125.
        Royal Australian Navy (RAN) raised (2,111 pers).

1914   Start of The Great War, CMF & UMT called up *Defence Act* Section 60.
        First Australian Imperial Force (AIF) raised,
        Citizen Force: Militia 42,656 + PMF 2,989 (45,645).

1915   Gallipoli Campaign.

1917   The Military Board proposes a Divisional Army.

1918   End of The Great War (11 November),
        Citizen Force: Militia 118,172 + PMF 4,014 (122,186).

1919   Versailles Peace Conference,
        'Swinburne Report'.

1920   'Senior Officers Report',
        Australian Staff Corps established;
        1 & 2nd Schools of Instruction held at Liverpool, NSW.

1921	Australian Instructional Corps (AIC) established: (24 April);
	Military Board created three 'Quartermaster Lists';
	Central Training Depot (CTD), Liverpool, NSW opened;
	Royal Australian Air Force (RAAF) raised (151 pers).
	Citizen Force: Militia 124,781 + PMF 3,179 (127,960).
1922	Washington (USA) Naval Conference;
	Chanak Crisis (Plan 401 evolved);
	Savage cuts to the Permanent Military Forces (PMF);
	CTD, Liverpool, closed;
	Citizen Force: Militia 35,083 + PMF 2,073 (45,645).
1923	'Singapore Strategy' adopted;
	'Suggestions for the elimination of Disabilities and the General Improvement of the AIC': Major A J Coghill.
1925	AIC Command and Control Issues;
	QM & Hon Major W W Tracy & QM & Hon Major F S McLean, DSO & Bar.
1927	Canberra: Duke of York visit; Army encampment Red Hill (9 May).
1928	AIC Establishment: 60 QMs + 540 WOs.
1929	The Great Depression commences in USA;
	Scullin Government suspends UMT *Defence Act* Section 125;
	Commencement of all volunteer 'Militia';
	Citizen Force: Militia 46,176 + PMF 1,755 (45,645)
1931	Scullin Government loses office;
	Financial Emergency Act 1931;
	AIC Badge approved and issued.
1932	Lyons Government institutes 'Raids Policy';
	Financial Emergency Act 1932;
	AIC Establishment: 47 QMs + 432 WOs (AAO 182-1932);
	Citizen Force: Militia 28,285 + PMF 1,536 (29,821).
1935	Five Year Rearmament Policy instituted by Lyons government;
	No.1 Special Course, Feb-Jun, Small Arms School, Randwick, NSW.
1936	No.1 Refresher Course, Feb-Jun, Small Arms School, Randwick, NSW;
	No.2 Special Course, Feb-Jun, Small Arms School, Randwick, NSW;
	No.3 Special Course, Aug-Dec, Small Arms School, Randwick, NSW.
1937	No.4 Special Course, Feb-Jun, Small Arms School, Randwick, NSW;
	'Militia' used to describe the Citizen Army;
	AIC Establishment: 80 QMs + 523 WOs (AAO 42-1937).

1938	No.5 Special Course, Feb-Jun, Small Arms School, Randwick, NSW;
	No.6 Special Course, Jul-Nov, Small Arms School, Randwick, NSW.
1939	No.7 Special Course, Jan-Jun, Small Arms School, Randwick, NSW;
	No.7 Special Course (Artillery), Feb-Jun, Sydney, NSW;
	Second World War Commences;
	Militia called up (3 months full time) *Defence Act* Section 60;
	Second Australian Imperial Force (2nd AIF) raised;
	AIC Establishment: 183 QMs + 774 WOs (AAO 1-1939).
1940	No.8 Special Course, Aug 39-Jan 40 Central Training Depot, Liverpool NSW;
	No.9 Special Course, Mar-Jun, Small Arms School, Randwick, NSW, and, Mar-Jun, at Central Training Depot, Liverpool, NSW;
	No.10 Special Course, July Small Arms School Randwick, NSW (Cancelled).
1941	Japan enters the war (7 December).
1942	UMT conscripts 'in for the duration + 1 year';
	'Militia' becomes Citizens Military Forces.
1943	Australian Jungle Divisions formed (February);
	Citizen Military Force + 2nd AIF (529,674).
1945	VE Day: Victory in Europe (May);
	VJ Day: Victory over Japan (15 August);
	'Interim Army' created (1 October).
1946	Victory march in London;
	British Commonwealth Occupation Forces (BCOF), 34 Aust Inf Bde.
1947	2nd AIF disbanded (30 June) remaining pers. Transferred to 'Interim Army';
	Australian Regular Army (ARA) authorised (13 September).
1948	Citizens Military Forces (CMF) re-raised;
	Citizen Military Forces 8,697 + ARA 10,712 (19,409).
1949	Royal Australian Regiment (RAR) raised in Japan (25 Nov);
	139 Warrant Officers become Lt (QM).
1950	Korean War commences (June).
1951	55 QM (AIC) transferred to other Corps.
1952	'Interim Army' disbanded (14 August).
1953	End of Korean War (July);
	AIC (QM) becomes ARA (QM) & transferred to other Corps, AAO 96-1953;
	Citizen Military Forces 69,061 + ARA 27,180 (96,241).

1955 Australian Instructional Corps (AIC) removed from the Army List of
Corps' (19 May);
Citizen Military Forces 85,177 + ARA 23,098 (108,275).

APPENDIX NINE
SURVIVING WARRANT OFFICERS
INTERVIEWED

AIC Members

Coupland, WO II Frederick James
> (Direct appointment to AIC, NP 8767 AAO 145-1941) *First interview 27 July 2004*

Dawson, Lt. Thomas Arthur
> (8313 WO II, No. 9 Special Course, SAS)
> *First interview 16 November 2001*

Fawcett, Colonel Guy OBE
> (3094 WOII, No.4 Special Course)
> *First interview 3 May 2003*

Guest, Lt.-Col. Frank (Leslie Francis)
> (No. 9 Special Course, CTD, NP5483 T/WOII) *First interview 22 July 2003 First interview 27 July 2004*

Hannell, Colonel Les
> (3406 WOII No. 6 Special Course)
> *First interview 14 January 2002*

McPherson, Colonel Colin W. MM
> (Direct appointment to AIC, 5547 T/WOII, AAO 22-1941) *First interview 25 November 2002*

Newton, Lt.-Col. Arthur James Cahair MBE
> (3707 T/WOII, No.2 Special Course)
> *Author of the only publication on the AIC (Army Journal article)*
> *First interview 1 October 2002*

Pfennigwerth, Lt. Roy
      (Direct appointment to AICAAO 8-1941 T/WOII)
      First interview 18 March 2004
Shields, Major (William). Rupert J.
      (No. 7 Special Course: 3895 WOII)
      First interview 4 May 2003
Wiseman, Lt.-Col. Frank W.
      (No.9 Special Course: 3865 WOII-T/WO1)
      First interview 28 January 2002

Family Members Of AIC Warrant Officers

Dunn, Ms. Irene
      (Father: 2881 Lt.-Col. Robert Norton Whiston)
Etheredge, Mr. Don
      (Father: 273 SSM 2nd Class Alfred Robert Etheredge)
Finney, Mr. Stephen OAM
      (Father: NP 3181, NX165146 RSM Alfred Stephen Finney)
Henrys, Maj. Mike
      (Father: NP 2204 WOII Ernest Henrys)
Laffey, Mr. Kevin
      (Father: NP 9984 QM & Hon Maj Martin Laffy)
      (Uncle: NP 2916 Capt. John Phillip Laffy)
Larkin, Lt.-Col. Bruce R.
      (Father: VP 7500 QM & Hon Capt William Henry Larkin)
Latchford, Maj-Gen. Kevin AO
      (Father: 112 WO1 Ernest Latchford, MBE MC)
Osgood, Mr. George
      (Father: NP 3706 Athol Osgood, POW died in Borneo 1945)
Shearim, Mr. Keith
      (Father: NP 152 James Duguild; King's Medal Winner as champion
      rifle shot of the Army: Buried at Rookwood)
Shearim, WO 1 Peter
      (Grandfather: NP 152 James Duguild Shearim)
Sparrow, Mr. Lionel
      (Father: 538 WOII Raymond Woodall Sparrow)

APPENDIX TEN
LIST OF RESPONDENTS AND CONTRIBUTORS

Over the decade plus it has taken to write this history a great many people have assisted, helped and contributed.

This list is an attempt to express my personal 'thanks'.

Allen, Mr. Jim
> (Research Officer, Central Army Records Office, Melbourne)

Austin, Mr. Ron
> (Slouch Hat Publications)

Bertram, Mr. Jack
> (Sgt, 1st Battalion, Papuan Infantry Battalion)

Cape, The Late Maj.-Gen. Tim CB, CBE, DSO.

Carey, Brig. Phil RFD, ED
> (President, Royal United Service Institute, NSW)

Cullen, The Late Maj.-Gen. Paul AO, CBE, DSO & Bar

de Witt, Major John
> (RAAMC)

Goodall, The Late Mr. Bill
> (Historian, served with 3 Fortress Company, RAE)

Gordon, Maj.-Gen. Ian CSC
> ('The Blamey Oration', RSUI of NSW)

Gower, Maj.-Gen. Steve AO
> (Director, Australian War Memorial, Canberra)

Griffiths, Mr. Anthony (Tony)
  (*A History of the Lithgow Small Arms factory*)
Handel, Maj. Paul RFD
  (*Dust, Sand & Jungle*)
Harper, Mr. Trevor
  (Secretary, 55/53 Australian infantry Battalion, AIF)
Harries, WO II Norm MBE
  (Instructor, Eastern Command, OCTU)
Harrison, Mr. Noel
  (President, United Service Club, Newcastle)
Houston, Lt.-Col. Bill
  (2 I/c, Army History Unit, Canberra)
Hutcheson, Dr. John MC
  (Short History of the School of Military Engineering)
Jackson, Colonel John RFD
  (Oral Historian, Army History Unit, Canberra)
James, Lt. Clarrie
  (Author 'ANGAU' One Man Law)
Jamison, Lt.-Col. Andrew
  RAAOC (2nd AIF)
Johns, Mr. Jim
  (N286304, Pte 36 Australian Infantry Battalion, AMF)
Jooste, Ms L.
  Director-General, Department of Defence, South Africa
Kennedy, Mr. Arthur
  (Artillery Museum, North Head)
Knowles, Mr. Merv
  (work colleague of Theodore Schmedje, MC, No 8 Sp Course)
Kuring, WO 2 Ian
  (*Redcoats to Cams*)
Land, Capt. John
  (Curator, Army Museum, Singleton)
Lee, Mr. Roger
  (Head, Army History Unit, Canberra)
McCarthy, Dr. Dayton
  (*The Once and Future Army*')

McCausland, The Late Brig. Alan ED
    (*A Short History of the Australian Army*)
McGibbon, Dr. Ian
    (Official Historian, Royal New Zealand Army)
McGilvray, Lt.-Col. W. M.
    (AEME, later RAEME)
Maitland. Maj-Gen. Gordon
    (*The Royal NSW Regiment*)
Manera, Mr. Brad
    (President, Military History Society of Australia)
Marsh, Ms Joan
    (Treasurer, The South African Military History Society)
Matthew, The Late Mr. Harry
    (55/53 Australian Infantry Battalion AIF)
Morris, Brig. Roy W. AO (Officer of the Order of Australia)
    (Hon. Colonel Commandant, RAAOC)
Morton, Professor Desmond
    (*A Military History of Canada*)
O'Brien, Brig. Michael CSC
    (The Australian Army Journal)
O'Connor, Mr. John
    (*Shooting Prizes to the Army*)
Opie, Maj. John
    (Curator, Anglesey Barracks Museum, Hobart, Tasmania)
Orchard, Capt Malcolm
    (Curator, RUSI of South Australia)
Palazzo, Dr. Albert
    (*The Third Australian Division*)
Parker, Mr. David
    (Curator, RA Intelligence Corps Museum, Canungra)
Pearson, Mr. Ross
    (Member, RUSI of NSW)
Perrett, Mr. Les
    (Secretary, NSW Military History Society Inc.)
Procter, The Late Mr. Reg
    (N10392 Sergt, 1ˢᵗ Field Brigade, RAA)

Renshaw, Mr John
    (Librarian, RUSI of NSW)
Reynolds, Associate Professor Wayne
    (*Australia's Bid for the Atomic Bomb*)
Ryan, Dr. Alan
    (Editor, *Australian Army Journal*)
Sealey, Lt.-Col. Robert RFD, ED
    (*The Defence Reservist*)
Searle, Mr. John
    (Secretary, 2/13 Australian Infantry Battalion, AIF)
See, Mr. Hugh
    (Secretary, Fort Scratchly Restoration Committee)
Short, Mr. Tom
    (Secretary, Forster Sub Branch, RSL)
Simmons, Mrs. Kaye BA
    (Secondary School History Teacher)
Slater, Brig. R. A.
    (Contributor, *Swan Street Sappers*)
Smith, Mr. Eric
    (2/13 Australian Infantry Battalion, AIF)
Smith, Lt.-Col. Neil AM
    (Mostly Unsung Military Publications)
Smith, WO1 Noel
    (trained by AIC Instructors in 1950)
Snewin, Mr. Chris
    (Editor, *Stand To*, RSL National HQ, Canberra)
Stanley, Dr. Peter
    (Senior Historian, Australian War Memorial)
Stanley, The Late Flt.-Lt. Richard (Dick)
    (Secretary, United Service Club, Newcastle)
Staunton, Mr. Anthony
    (Victoria Cross Winners)
Swifte, The Late Lt.-Col Tim
    (Darwin Mobile Force Commemorative Booklet)
Thomson, Dr. Alistair
    (*Anzac Memories*)

Thompson, WO 1 Wallace OAM
>(first RSM of the Army)

Tongs, Capt. Bede MM
>(2/4 Australian Infantry Battalion, AIF)

Youll, Lt.-Col. Rob
>(*Swan Street Sappers*)

Visser, Lt.-Col (Dr) Deon (
>Chair, Military Studies, University of Stellenbosch)

Waring, Lt.-Col. George
>(Ordnance Officer WWII)

Wedd, The Late Mr. Monty OAM
>(Monarch Military Museum)

Wertheimer, Lt.-Col. E. John
>(Contributor, *Swan Street Sappers*)

Wilcox, Dr. Craig
>(*For Hearths and Homes*)

Williams, Maj.-Gen. R. CB, MBE,
>OStJ, Royal New Zealand Artillery Corps

Wotton, The Late Rev. Roy OAM
>(World War II AIF Chaplain)

Wright, The Late Mr. Peter
>(President, 55/53 Australian Infantry Battalion, AIF)

APPENDIX ELEVEN
ABBREVIATIONS AND ACRONYMS

A & I Staff	Administrative & Instructional Staff
AA Bty	Anti Aircraft Battery (Artillery)
AAMC	Australian Army Medical Corps
AAO	Australian Army Order
AAOC	Australian Army Ordnance Corps
AASC	Australian Army Service Corps
AAVC	Australian Army Veterinary Corps
AAWT	Australian Army Weapon Training (School)
Adjt	Adjutant
ADST	Assistant Director Staff & Training
AE	Australian Engineers
AFA	Australian Field Artillery
AFV	Armoured Fighting Vehicle
AGA	Australian Garrison Artillery
AHQ	Army Headquarters (Melbourne)
AIC	Australian Instructional Corps
AIF	Australian Imperial Force (WORLD WAR I)
ALP	Australian Labor Party
AMF	Australian Military Forces
AMR	Australian Military Regulations
AMR & O	Australian Military Regulations & Orders
ASC	Australian Service Corps (became RAASC)

AWM	Australian War Memorial
Bde	Brigade
Bn	Battalion
Brig.-Gen.	Brigadier General (now Brigadier, One Star)
BSM	Battery Sergeant Major
Cav Div	Cavalry Division
CB	Companion Order of the Bath
CGS	Chief of the General Staff
CMF	Citizens Military Forces (1948-1983?)
	Commonwealth Military Forces (1901-1931)
CO	Commanding Officer
CQMS	Company Quartermaster Sergeant
CTD	Central Training Depot (Liverpool, NSW)
DB	District Base
DCM	Distinguished Conduct Medal
DDMS	Deputy Director Medical Services
DFO	Departmental Finance Officer
DGMS	Director General Medical Services
Dir	Director
Div	Division
DMF	Darwin Mobile Force (1938-1940)
DOB	Date of Birth
DSO	Distinguished Service Order
Fd Tps	Field Troops
FSR	Field Service Regulations
GCMG	Grand Cross Order of St. Michael & St. George
GO	General Order (became Military Order)
GSM	Garrison Sergeant Major
HQ	Headquarters
Hy Bty	Heavy Battery (Artillery)
IG	Inspector-General
Inf Div	Infantry Division
JTC	Jungle Training Centre (Canungra, Queensland)
KCB	Knight Commander Order of the Bath
KFF	Khaki Fur Felt (Slouch Hat)
LH	Light Horse (Regiments)

Lt.-Col.	Lieutenant Colonel
Maj.-Gen.	Major General (Two Star)
MBE	Member Order of the British Empire
MBI	Military Board Instruction
MC	Military Cross
MD	Military District
MHR	Member of the House of Representatives
MID	Mentioned in Dispatches
Mil Sec	Military Secretary
Mixd Bde	Mixed Brigade (contains Infantry & Cavalry units)
MM	Military Medal
MS	Manuscript (also Military Secretary)
MT	Motor Transport
NAA	National Archives of Australia
NCO	Non Commissioned Officer
NP	New South Wales Permanent
NSW	New South Wales
NX	New South Wales Australian Imperial Force Volunteer
OBE	Officer, Order of the British Empire
OC	Officer commanding
PMF	Permanent Military Forces
Q Record	Quartermaster Record (Clothing & items on charge)
QM	Quartermaster
Qr Mr	Quartermaster
RAA	Royal Australian Regiment of Artillery
RAAF	Royal Australian Air Force
RAE	Royal Australian Engineers
RAFA	Royal Australian Field Artillery
RAGA	Royal Australian Garrison Artillery
RAN	Royal Australian Navy
RMC	Royal Military College of Australia (Duntroon)
RMO	Regimental Medical Officer
RN	Royal Navy (Imperial Navy)
RNSWL	Royal New South Wales Lancers
RSL	Returned Sailors' Soldiers' and Airmens' Imperial League of Australia

RSM	Regimental Sergeant Major
SAS	Small Arms School (Randwick, NSW)
Sigs	Signals
SMLE	Short Model Lee Enfield (Rifle)
SSM	Staff Sergeant Major
Svcs	Services
Svy	Survey (Artillery)
Trg	Training
UAP	United Australia Party
UT	Universal Training
VC	Victoria Cross
VD	Volunteer Decoration
VDC	Volunteer Defence Corps
WDSL	War Disability Supernumerary List
WO	Warrant Officer
WO1	Warrant officer Class One
WOII	Warrant officer Class Two
W & NCOs	Warrant & Non Commissioned Officers
WORLD WAR I	World War One
WORLD WAR II	World War Two

APPENDIX TWELVE
AIC NOMINAL ROLL

Highest Known Rank	Surname	Given Name	Regimental Nos	Highest Known Rank	Surname	Given Name	Regimental Nos
T/WOI	Adair	E A	VP 4205	WOII	Alphred	W H	1352
T/WOII	Adams	W D		SSM 3rd Class	Anderson	R B	1699
QM & Hon Capt	Addison	Robert Hamilton	VP 7401, 147	QM & Hon Capt	Anderson	Robert Campbell Newton	VP7404(?)
SSM 3rd Class	Addison	J R G	3903	WO1: BSM	Anderson	H L	628
T/WOII	Addison	G A	2448	T/WOII	Anderson	K	3711
WOII	Aikins	J S		SSM 2, Hon Lt	Andrew, MBE	J	155
WO1	Airey, MM	George Frederick	5975	QM (ARA)	Andrews	George Howard	VP 4253: VX101972
QM & Hon Capt	Aitken	James Hudson	NP9923, 310	T/WOII	Angus	J A (Jack)	3620
SSM 2nd Class	Aldridge	R F	445	WOII	Ansell	H	
T/SSM 3	Alexander	C M		Capt	Appleton	John	NP 1753; 1755
Capt	Allan	John Ross	NP 5453	QM & Hon Capt	Apps	James	
Hon Lt.-Col	Allchin, MM	Edmund Franklin	365: SP 15214: SX1429; 4/22	WOII	Armstrong	K V	QP2408
				T/WOII	Arndt	Q R	5347
Hon Maj	Allison	Robert	WP629; WX33747	T/Capt	Arnold	William Tom	VP 7406: VX 101847: 2034
Capt	Allison	Edward Marley	QP 2336 1/54	QM & Hon Capt	Arnold	H A	
T/WOII	Allison	A D Y	3974				
T/WOII	Allum	R C	3858	T/SSM 3	Arrowsmith	T H	

Highest Known Rank	Surname	Given Name	Regimental Nos	Highest Known Rank	Surname	Given Name	Regimental Nos
T/WOII	Ashdown	C R W	4904	WOII	Barry	V W	VP 3608
WOII	Ashwin	N J	3648	SSM 2nd Class	Bartlett	R W	151
WOII	Atkins	J	15060	Capt (QM)	Bartlett	Eric Leigh John	669; 2/318
T/WO1	Auld	A Mc	2933	WOII	Bartley	E H	
WOII	Austen	F H	2726	SSM 2nd Class	Bashford	R	414
WOII	Austin	O (?) H		T/Capt	Batchelor	Jack Copeland	TP 4840; TX 6421
QM & Hon Capt	Bacon	Norman Edward	144; VP7404	Hon Maj	Bateman, MM	Reginald William	QP 686; QX45291
SSM 1st Class	Bailey	C H	84	T/Maj	Bates	Eric	VP 3528; VX 114026; 3/362
SSM 2nd Class	Bailey	W E	284	T/Lt	Bathurst	Cyril Ernest	SP 6430; SX 26127
T/WO1	Bailey	W B	4733	WOII	Batson	D G	QP2409
WOII	Baker	G J (C J?)	4041	T/WO1	Bauer	C C	4547
WOII	Baker	R C	2800	WOII	Bauer	H W	6453
Lt.-Col	Baker, MBE	George Samuel	VP7408	SSM 2nd Class	Baumann	C W A	35
WOII	Baker, MM	N W	677	WOII	Baxter	W C	4108
WO1A	Balfour	A D	875	Capt (QM)	Baxter	Raymond	2306
SSM 3rd Class	Banks	C H	4804	T/WOII	Baxter	H	1604
T/WOII	Barber	S G	6501	SSM 2nd Class	Bayes	W J	234
SSM 2nd Class	Barchard	F P	231	QM & Hon. Maj	Beale	Kenneth	(VP)76?
T/WOII	Barclay	R W	3783	Hon Capt	Beattie	J P	
WO1	Barham	William Henry	53	Maj	Beatty	Alfred Joseph	201, VP201
T/WOII	Barker	V M	4833	WOII	Beauchamp	W E	3911
SSM 3rd Class	Barker	B M	4833	QM & Hon Maj	Beers	Edward St.John	
QM & Hon Capt	Barker	George Henry	TP339; 345	SSM 3rd Class	Behets	A L	366
WO1	Barker	S	1501	SSM 3rd Class	Bell	B R	1623
T/WOII	Barkley	A	8759	Major	Bell	Arthur Fenton	VP 3569;VX 85287
WOII	Barnes	D H G	15130	T/WOII	Bell	K G	8479
SSM 2nd Class	Barnet	F P	301	SSM 3rd Class	Bell	W J	2609
Capt (QM)	Barnet	Francis Colin	3621; 3/126				
WOII	Barnett	K C	QP2365				
T/WOII	Barnett	P J					
WOII	Barney	W A	4549				
T/WOII	Barrett	J					

Highest Known Rank	Surname	Given Name	Regimental Nos
T/WOII	Bellette	S J	8485
T/WOII	Belmer	R S	2994
T/WOII	Belyea	C C	7299
Lt (QM)	Benbow	Harry Maurice Stephen	WP 4715; WX 32676; 5/73
T/WOII	Bennett	A S	6228
QM & Hon. Lt	Bentley	Stanley Charles	
WOII	Berman	M E	3012
Hon Maj	Berman, MBE, DCM	Donald Frederick	486; NP9962:
WOII	Bernard	L F C	4066
SSM 3rd Class	Bernard	S E	3678
Lt (QM)	Bernard	Hugo Robert Charles	3489
SSM 3 & H/Lt	Bernard	C F W	497
SSM 3rd Class	Berney	J A	1601
T/WOII	Berry	E W	4042
WOII	Berryman	A F	
SSM 2, Hon Lt	Biggsley	J C M	94
T/WOII	Bills	M W	5633
Maj (QM)	Bilton	Sydney Gerald Joseph	VP 3647; VX 133190; 3/372
T/WOII	Bingham	G R	3976
Hon Lt Col	Birch	Ernest Wilfred	378; VP7413; VX85237
SSM 3rd Class	Bird	C R	3622
T/Lt	Birks	Henry Napier	SP 6433; SX 26397
T/WOII	Birrell	B A	
Capt	Bishop	Samuel Herbert	VP 7414; VX 101849
Hon Capt	Bishop	W J	
WOII	Bishop	L G	2179
Maj (QM)	Bizzell	J L	2413; 1/87

Highest Known Rank	Surname	Given Name	Regimental Nos
Capt	Black	Kenneth Henderson	NP2741; DX209
QM & Hon Capt	Black	Bernard Stanislaus	NP1018: NX76
SSM 3rd Class	Blackburn	J M	680
T/WOII	Blackie	J W	5343
WOII	Blackshaw	B B	4043
QM & Hon Capt	Blainey, MC	Arthur R	
SSM 3rd Class	Blair	Alexander Thomas	1008
WOII	Bland	W J	
T/WOII	Bloomfield	R R	7305
T/WOII	Blundell	H N	6947
QM & Hon. Capt	Bohle, MBE	Alan Henry Moorhouse	3080
Capt (QM)	Booth	Bruce Mannering	NP 2755; 2/150
T/WOII	Bostock	M V	5310
T/WOII	Bosworth	G	4708
Maj (QM)	Bourne	Vivian Langston	NP 3015: NX 134871; 2/423
WOII	Bowden	Willie Everett	
SSM 3rd Class	Bowden, MM	E W	541
WOII	Bower	H V	
SSM3	Bower	F C	(NP)181?
WOII	Bowers	T A	4044
T/Lt	Bowey	Francis Thomas	VP 3743: VX 149827
T/WOII	Bowie	R W	3298
WOII	Bowkett	W F R	
SSM 3rd Class	Boyd	R T	1242
T/WOII	Boydell	S	9602
T/WO1A	Boyle	Thomas James	SP 4458
WOII	Braby	George Frederick	VP 7419
T/QM & Hon Lt	Bradford	Frederick Andrew	3522

Highest Known Rank	Surname	Given Name	Regimental Nos
WOII	Bradley	Alfred Edward Arthur	NP 2756
SSM 3rd Class	Bradley	S E	1975
T/WOI	Bradley	W R	2680
WOII	Bradmore	A R	4760
SSM 2nd Class	Brady	William John	461
WO1	Bragg	A F	627
T/WOII	Bramwell	T	3692
SSM 2nd Class	Branch	Russell Benedict	477
T/WOII	Bray	A C	6462
T/WOII	Bray	A E C	9429
Lt (QM)	Brearley	Joseph Thomas	WP 4585: 5/27
Capt (QM)	Bretherton	Peter	1429; 3/155
T/WOII	Brett	S C	4353
Lt	Breydon	R	
T/WOII	Briggs	E J	8681
WO1	Bright, MM	A W	676
WOII	Brinchman	E D	
SSM 3rd Class	Brinckman	Ernest Ferdinand	640
SSM 3rd Class	Brinkley	N C	546
T/WOI	Britten	J H	5480
T/WOII	Brogan	R C	576
Lt (QM)	Bromley	Harry Bowden	2168; 3/342
SSM 2nd Class	Bromley	Charles Edward	424
WOII	Broun	C H	
WOII (SSM)	Brown	F H	1479
T/WOII	Brown	G E J	8483
WOII	Brown	J H	
WOI	Brown	O K	1453
WOII	Brown	Ernest Henry	VP 4313
WOII	Browne	V C	
H/Lt. Col	Browne, MBE	Alfred Allen	103, VP7423

Highest Known Rank	Surname	Given Name	Regimental Nos
T/WOII	Brownsea	E W	7325
Lt (QM)	Bruce	William George	2660: 2/90
T/WOII	Bruce	R T	2169
WOII	Bryan	A D	5306
WOI	Bryceson	G W	412
SSM 3rd Class	Btown	O K	1453
WOII	Buchanan	Charles James Thompson	
T/WOII	Buchanan, MM	H	QP2437
T/WOII	Buckingham	D J	2434
SSM 3rd Class	Bull	J	2125
T/WOII	Burchill	J	QP8542
SSM 3, Hon Lt	Burden	A C M	512
WOII	Burden	G W	6466
WOII	Burgess	Edgar William Wesley	NP 9136
T/WOII	Burgess	G K	4033
SSM 2nd Class	Burgess	W J	334
T/QM & Hon Lt	Burke	William Edmund Richard	1907
SSM 3rd Class	Burkinshaw	R F M	471
WOII	Burrell	Lindsay Gordon	VP 7427
T/WOII	Burrell	L G	3792
SSM 2, Hon Lt	Burrow	S V	116
T/WOII	Burt	H J	6319
Lt (QM)	Burton	Harry Alexander	3717; 3/397
WOII	Burton	C H	NO 1513
SSM 3rd Class	Bushell	A E	
T/WOII	Bussell	Donald Royston	NP 8924

Highest Known Rank	Surname	Given Name	Regimental Nos
T/WOII	Buswell	H W	4543
SSM 3rd Class	Butcher	C S	533
SSM 3rd Class	Butler	Herber Walter	2053
T/WOII	Butler	J A	840
QM & Hon Lt	Buttery	David Ewan	(NP)386
QM & Hon Lt	Button	Joseph John (Joe)	329
T/WOII	Byrnes	L S	8683
T/WOII	Cady	A	3337
Maj (QM)	Callaghan, MBE	Thomas Noel Power	2791; 2/492
WOII	Callcott	W G	
WOII	Cameron	J	916
SSM 3rd Class	Campbell	Drummond Burrows	NP 99973 2654
T/Capt	Campbell	Ernest McKenzie	WP22008 323
SSM 3rd Class	Cann	F	377
QM & Hon Maj	Canning	Bertram	VP7429 352
T/WOII	Canning	B L	4001
WOII	Canterbury	Thomas Charles Kingdom	VP3719 VX85253
Maj (QM)	Carbin	Hilary James Austin	NP 2697; 2/254
WO1	Carder	M C	NP2834: NX567?
Maj (QM)	Cardy	John Allan	5025; 2/338
WOII	Carey	J W	4843
SSM 2nd Class	Carlin	Francis John	437
Lt (QM)	Carloss	Charles	NP 1478
WO 1st Class	Carmody	J B	65
H/Maj	Carmoody	James Burnett	WP22007
SSM 2, Hon Lt	Carnegie	C R	220
WOII	Carpenter	Ian Campbell Gordon	NP9521

Highest Known Rank	Surname	Given Name	Regimental Nos
T/QM & Hon Lt	Carroll	Brian William Benedict	2811
T/WOII	Carroll	T P	4423
SSM 2 & H/Lt	Carroll	B	265
WOII & Hon. Lt	Carroll	A B	
WOII	Carson	John Charles S	NP4974
WO1: MG 3	Carter	C R	623
SSM 3rd Class	Carter	M C	2834
WOII	Cashman	E J	3001: 3110
Hon Lt	Cato	Hilmer Dennis	TP4811 TX6136
WOII	Caudle	Garnet Rex	SP4520 DX804
WOII	Cavanagh	Reginald James	VP3471
T/WOII	Cavanagh	H L	3805
T/WOII	Cawsey	L S	3582
WOII	Chad	T N	NP8757; NX502391
Lt (QM)	Chamberlain	Richard Henry	2723
WOII	Chapman	Frederick Ernest	
WO1	Cheland	W L	
Maj (QM)	Christie	Herbert James	2740; 2/122
T/WO1	Christie	R A	2743
QM & Hon Maj	Christie, DSO	Robert	
Lt-Col	Christie, MBE	Alexander	QP165; VX101927
WOII	Christopher-son	Charles Leslie	QP 8554
WO1	Chumleigh	Harold Vere	
SSM 3rd Class	Clark	J G	3404
WOII	Clark	J	QP2429
WOII	Clarke	D J	4109
T/WOII	Clarke	G G	2844
T/WOII	Clarke	R C	5311
SSM 3rd Class	Clarke	Charles Denis	1573

Highest Known Rank	Surname	Given Name	Regimental Nos
T/WOII	Clarkson	B M	7185
WOII	Cleary	Harry Edward	NP 5826
T/WOII	Cleary	Royal James	NP 2995
T/QM & Hon Lt	Cleland	William Lewis	361
Lt.-Col	Clementson OBE	William George	VP2080: VX51: 2080
T/WOI	Clinghan	F T R	NP 5309
WOII	Clyde	J	
QM & Hon Maj	Coats, MBE	Marmaduke	
T/WOII	Cochrane	G A	8467
WOII	Cochrane	Alfred Edward	TP 6616
Lt (QM)	Codling	Lionel Harry	6407: 4/38
SSM 3rd Class	Cogger	Carl Raymond	423
T/WOII	Coghlan	Walter James	VP 7438; 4045
Maj	Coghill	Arthur John	
SSM 2nd Class	Cole	I S	148
T/WOII	Cole	T J	9230
Capt	Coleman	Thomas Fulton	
SSM 2nd Class	Coller	A C	472
Lt (QM)	Collings	Kenneth Lambert	3520: 3/345
WOII	Collingwood	S	1925
Col.	Collins	Arthur Bligh Smith	310
SSM 2nd Class	Collins	John Joseph Damien	172
T/WOII	Collins	D D	4785
SSM 3rd Class	Colman	H M	4830
T/WOII	Connell	J W	6901
Hon Lt	Connor	M B	
T/WOII	Cook	S B	991
WOII	Cook	D J	

Highest Known Rank	Surname	Given Name	Regimental Nos
Lt.-Col	Cook, DSO MC	Francis	SX1225
QM & Hon Lt	Cooke	D F	290
SSM 3rd Class	Cooke	E R S	1063
Capt (QM)	Cooke	Ralph Sanderson	2/241
T/WOII	Cooke	E L	Not allocated
T/WOII	Cooke	H J	4906
T/WOII	Cooper	S C	8480
SSM 3rd Class	Coppin	Harold Frederick	2265
T/WOIA	Corbett	W J	166
WOII & Hon Lt	Corbett, DCM	E	
T/QM & Hon Lt	Cossart	Leslie Dunlop	
Capt	Cottee	E H	
SSM 3rd Class	Couche	R V	3667
SSM 2nd Class	Couche	John Roy	277
QM & Hon Maj	Couchman, DSO	Frank M	
Lt (QM)	Coughlin	Walter James	3/251
SSM 3rd Class	Coughlin	C H	5781
WOII	Coulter	L	
WOII	Coultham	W C	4067
Lt (QM)	Coulton	Lionel Robert John	QP2792
WOII	Coupland	Frederick James	NP8767: NX116219
SSM 3rd Class	Cousins	E J	358
T/WOII	Coutts	A G	8685
SSM 3rd Class	Coward	H	336
SSM 3rd Class	Cox	G R	4478

Highest Known Rank	Surname	Given Name	Regimental Nos	Highest Known Rank	Surname	Given Name	Regimental Nos
Maj	Cox	Merthyn Stewart Francis	WP4678; VX59547	WOII	Curr	David Thomas	(NP?)887
T/WOII	Cox	W	6981	Maj (QM)	Currow	Melville	VP 3573; 3/383
QM & Hon Lt	Coxhead	Albert David	156	Lt (QM)	Currow	William Albert	3610; 3/445
WOII	Crafter	J G	6448	QM Hon Lt	Currow, MM	Wilfred Lewis (Louis)	987
T/SSgt	Cran	D McK	2351	T/SSM 3	Cutts	R N	
SSM 2, Hon Lt	Creancy	Harold John	99	T/WOII	Dack	W R	6412
WOII	Creed	V K		WOII	Dalby	R W N	15126
Maj (QM)	Crew	Leonard Frank	NP 2724; 2/178	T/WOII	Dale	O S	7297
Lt (QM)	Crew	Henry William Adam	QP 2267; 1/96	QM & Hon Maj	Daley, MC	John James	WP 22010513
WOII	Crompton	Eric Bernard	VP 3609	SSM 3rd Class	Dalgleish	E S	3606
WOII	Cronin	C F	3563	SSM	Daly	J	
T/WO1A	Cropper	S	2950	Lt (QM)	Danson	David Allan	3758
WOII	Cross	G	5239	Maj (QM)	Darcey	William Albert	3063; 2/113
WO1	Cross	William Thomas	QP2312	WOII	Dare	Harold William	QP 2397
WOII	Cross	Leslie Gordon	NP 9151	QM & Hon Maj	Darley, OBE	Thomas Henry	
WOII	Crossan	W	2558	T/WOII	Date	V E M	15002
WOII	Crossart	L D		WOII	Davey	William Glanville	464
CSM	Crotty	L	1635				
T/WOII	Cruden	L G	6318	SSM 3rd Class	Davidson	J J D	2795
SSM 3rd Class	Crute	E W	2857	WO1 & Hon Lt	Davies	E F	192
T/WOII	Cuddihy	G F	(NP?)3106	WOII	Davies	Ian	NP 2924
T/WOII	Cuddihy	A A	5045	T/WOII	Davies	N L	6028
SSM 3rd Class	Cullen	A H H	2452	Lt (QM)	Davis	Claude Stephen	3516
Lt (QM)	Cullen	Richard Cyril	VP 3550;VX 101818; 3/333	T/WOII	Dawes	W G D	3202
				Hon. Lt	Dawson	Thomas Arthur	QP8313
WOII	Cumming	S		QM & Hon Capt	Dawson	Harvey James	420; VP 7449
T/WOII	Cunningham	J	4086	WOII	Dawson	D A	
QM & Hon Lt	Cunningham	M W	370	SSM 2, Hon Lt	Day	J H	178
SSM 3rd Class	Cupitt	B H	3032	QM & Hon Capt	De Campo	Norman Leslie	429; VP 7450

Highest Known Rank	Surname	Given Name	Regimental Nos
SSM 3rd Class	De Lautour	W H	2786
T/WOII	Dearness	T	8320
Lt (QM)	DeGroote	Roger John Ivan	5030
WOII	Dellow	George Kimptom	NP 3037
T/WOII	Delves	W F	4335
SSM 3rd Class	Delves	W P	3906
T/WOII	Delves	Gerald Lewis	VP4006
T/WOII	Dennis	Arthur Reginald	TP 6622
Lt (QM)	Denniston, MBE	James William	2181; 4/31
WOII	Derbidge	Charles Harry	NP 2771
SSM 3rd Class	Derham	B E	508
T/WOII	Dettman	L P	4629
WOII	Devereaux, MM	Wallace O	TP344, 542
QM & Hon Capt	Deves	Charles	298; NP 9979
Maj (QM)	Deveson	Ernest Alfred	VP 3744; 1/65
SSM 3rd Class	Dewar	R	545
T/WOII	Dewar	O B	9384
Lt (QM)	Diamond	Percy	NP 3076; 2/125
T/QM & Hon Lt	Dickinson	Ray Theodore Castle	NP 1034
SSM 2nd Class	Dike	N W P	133
SSM 2nd Class	Dillon	J	433
Capt (QM)	Dingey	John Herbert	VP 7451; 1054; 3/269
T/WOII	Dodd	S	4555
SSM 3rd Class	Donald	J A	3690
SSM 3rd Class	Done, MM	C G A	1940

Highest Known Rank	Surname	Given Name	Regimental Nos
T/WOII	Donegan	J F	3813
T/WOII	Dooley	J D	10703
WOII	Dorrat	R W	6944
Lt (QM)	Dore	Harry Frank	NP 2972
Lt.-Col	Dossetter	Edward (Ted)	4805; 2/205
Lt (QM)	Douglas	R	5038; 2/269
WOII	Dovan	R V	
WOII	Dow	McFarlane William	SP 6405
T/WOI	Dowd	W G M	VP 5961
Brigadier	Dowdy	Vincent Ernest	SP 4502 NX403
SSM 3rd Class	Dowell	M G	2491
T/WOII	Dowling	Alfred Bernard Charles	SP 6401
SSM 3rd Class	Dowling	L E	3584
T/WOII	Down	J D	6475
QM & Hon Maj	Downey, MC	Herbert Hamilton	
WO 1st Class	Dowsett	A G	74
T/WOII	Dowton	F C	9441
WOII	Doyle	W L	
SSM 3rd Class	Doyle	J E	624
T/WOII	Dring	C R	6945
Capt	Drinkwater	Arthur William	
T/WOII	Driver	Errol Christensen	WP 4631
WO1	Druitt	C K	4002 VX85018
SSM 3rd Class	Drummy	J W	519
T/WOII	Duberley	F R	
T/WOII	Duffus	H A	7180
QM & Hon Maj	Duffy, DSO	John	
BSM	Duggan	A E M	2674

Highest Known Rank	Surname	Given Name	Regimental Nos
WOII	Duncan	J L	
QM & Hon Lt	Duncan	George David	102
SSM	Dunn	A	
T/WOII	Dunn	R H	15003
WOII	Durrant	E H	
SSM 3rd Class	Duthie	R J	374
WOII	Duvan	R V	
SSM 3rd Class	Dwyer	J F	534
T/WO1	Dyer	E	5905
SSM 3rd Class	Eagleson	Leslie Arthur James	3095
SSM 3rd Class	Eames	Bertie Victor	563
QM & Hon Maj	East-Almond	Geoffrey Nicholson	
WO1	Easter	A E (Bert)	281
Hon. Col.	Easterbrook MBE, DSO, MC	Claude Cadman	VP7457
WOII	Eaton	T	NP5035
T/WOII	Eddington	P	4766
T/WOII	Eddy	L W	3825
Hon. Lt.-Col	Edgecombe, MBE	Stanley Roy	3722; 3/335
SSM 2nd Class	Edwards	Theodore	344
T/WOII	Edwards	A J	735
WOII	Edwards	A S	6467
WOII	Edwards	Archie Russell	NP 9440
SSM 2, Hon Lt	Edwards, MBE	R F G	135
P/SSM	Edwards, MC, DCM	J H	
Hon. Lt	Edwards	Francis	
WOII	Egan	W C	
T/WOII	Elbourne	A D	4909
SSM 3rd Class	Eldridge	W J	405

Highest Known Rank	Surname	Given Name	Regimental Nos
Lt (QM)	Ellis	Walter William	NP 2687: 2689; 2/421
T/WO1A	Ellis	E L	1232
T/WOII	Ellis	C C	3981
T/Capt	Eltham, MID	Thomas Ivanhoe	4271
SSM 2nd Class	Endacott	G E	110
T/WOII	England	R A	4487
Hon Lt Col	Etheredge, OBE	Alfred Robert	273, VP7463; 3/142
T/WOII	Evans	F N	4337
T/WOII	Evans	A G	8515
T/WOII	Everingham	A G	3429
T/WOII	Everton	S M G	4326
Hon Col	Every, MM	George Edward	NP398; NX130594
T/WOII	Eyres	T H	7101
T/WOII	Facey	L F	3570
T/WOII	Fairbairn	T C	4910
Hon. Col.	Farnington, MBE, DCM	Charles James Wilson	VP387; VX27387; 387; 3/105
WOII	Farquharson	G A	2362
T/QM & Hon Lt	Farquharson	Wallace William	2138
QM & Hon Maj	Farrow	Thomas Joseph	276; 499
Capt (QM)	Farthing	Harold Frederick	2/96
Lt (QM)	Farthing	Allan Charles	NP 2699; 2/225
WOII	Faulkhead	C N	3761
T/WOII	Faulkner	L J	6528
T/WOII	Faull	L N	9474
Colonel	Fawcett, OBE, psc	Guy H	3094
T/WOII	Fentiman	H F	9315
T/WOII	Fenton	J J	

Highest Known Rank	Surname	Given Name	Regimental Nos
SSM 3rd Class	Fenton	J P	382
T/WOII	Ferguson	G S	3760
SSM 3rd Class	Ferguson	J A	2333
SSM 2nd Class	Ferguson	Reginald	421
SSM 3rd Class	Ferguson	Ernest Manning	VP 1032
WOII	Ferres	W	
SSM 3rd Class	Finch	Foster Gladstone	507
WOII	Findlay	J D	15001
SSM 2, Hon Lt	Fishbourne	P J	118
WO1	Finney, OAM	Alfred Stephen	
SSM 3rd Class	Fisher	S J W	3705
WOII	Fisher	H	(NP)2770
WOII	Fisher	Robert Alexander Irving	VP 4334
Lt (QM)	Fishwick	Eric Bertram	NP 3294
MG 3rd Class	Fitzmaurice	M P	612
SSM 2nd Class	Fitzpatrick	T	300
WOII	Fitzpatrick	F	15016
SSM 2, Hon Lt	Flannery	Michael Joseph	167
SSM	Flannery	W	
SSM 2 & Hon Lt	Flannigan	P	247
Lt (QM)	Fletcher	Stanley	3078; 3/187
SSM 2nd Class	Fletcher	S T	443
WOII	Flew	S J	
SSM 2nd Class	Flower	G A	363
Lt (QM)	Flowers	John	2463
SSM 3rd Class	Folland	F L N	4498

Highest Known Rank	Surname	Given Name	Regimental Nos
Lt (QM)	Ford	Alfred Joyce	QP 1606; 1/38
SSM 2nd Class	Forrest	J E	159
T/WOII	Forsyth	J	
SSM 3rd Class	Foster	James Herbert	1006
T/WOII	Foster	R W	5170
Hon Lt Col	Foster, MC	Henry Lawrence	VP7472, 190
Maj (QM)	Fox	Jack	SP 4484; SX 25427; 4/56
WOII	Foxton	P G	4671
SSM 2nd Class	Franklin	A E	427
WOII	Franklin	A B M	
T/WO1	Franklin	J B	2331
T/QM & Hon Lt	Fraser	Hugh	
SSM 3rd Class	Fraser	H	384
QM & Hon Capt	Fraser, MC	Alexander	
T/WOII	Freeman	W S	481
T/WO1	Freeman	Frank	VP 3712
WOII	Freeman, DCM	W	
T/WO1	French	H P	5013
QM & Hon Lt	Friday	W A	441
WOII	Frith	Henry George	SP 6449
T/SSM 3	Frogley	A L	
SSM 3rd Class	Fullbrook	Gordon Harman	553
T/WOII	Fyffe	J L	4004
T/WOII	Gadsden	F H	15123
Capt (QM)	Gahan	Keith Menzies	3612; 2/393
WO1	Gaites	G T	150
Master Gunner 3rd Class	Gallagher	Edward Bernard	792

Highest Known Rank	Surname	Given Name	Regimental Nos	Highest Known Rank	Surname	Given Name	Regimental Nos
T/WOII	Galwey	J H	2814	SSM 3rd Class	Ginn	Roger Gregory	331
WOII	Gapps	J B	NP 2507	WOII	Glance	John Jacob	WP 5962
SSM 3rd Class	Gardener	James Albert	478	QM & Hon Maj	Glasgow, MBE, MC	Daniel Robert	
WOII	Gardiner	G R	6435	WO	Glass		
T/SSgt	Gardiner	K D	3811	T/WOII	Glenny	G W	3523
T/WOI	Gardiner	R P	VP 4068	SSM 3rd Class	Godfrey	E F	543
T/WOII	Gardner	M C	4911	T/WOII	Godkin	H J	3524
BSM	Garland	W A L	516	SSM 3rd Class	Godwin	Sydney Barrett	313
SSM 3rd Class	Garlick	Richard	540	SSM 3rd Class	Goninon	Edward Francis	1539
QM & Hon Maj	Garling	Septimus William		WOII	Good, DCM	L A G (L J A)	4069
WOII	Garnett	T J		T/WOII	Goodman	K C	2288
SSM 3rd Class	Garrard	Norman Frederick	NP 2759	SSM 2nd Class	Goodwin	S B	313
T/WOII	Gaul	Alexander John French	NP 4912	Maj (QM)	Goold	Jack Michael	1192; 4/8
T/WOII	Geary	F R	6335	SSM 2nd Class	Gordon	J P	97
T/WOII	Gee	H F		SSM 3rd Class	Gordon	G L	663
SSM 2nd Class	German	C C	417	WOII	Gordon	N A	
T/WOII	Gibson	J F	4019	T/WOII	Gordon	A A	2517
T/WOII	Gibson	J E	4913	BSM	Gough	A K	2009
WOII	Gibson	J P	2631	T/WOII	Gould	L J	4401
Maj (QM)	Gilbert	Harold Lunn	SP 4481; 4/37	SSM 2nd Class	Goyne	Thomas Alexander	289
SSM 3rd Class	Gilbey	George Alfred	1698	WO1	Grabs	A	403
WOII	Gill	G	6438	T/WOII	Grace	Oswald William	NP 3019
SSM	Gill	M W		T/WO1	Graham	R C	1876
WOII	Gill	John Frederick	WP 5954	SSM 3rd Class	Graham	John William	474
SSM 2nd Class	Gill	W	232	WOII	Graham	C D	3111
SSM 3rd Class	Gillespie	J M	3079	SSM 2, Hon Lt	Graham	T	139
SSM 3rd Class	Gillespie	A C	2271	T/WOII	Graham	William Robert	QP 8647
MG 2nd Class	Gillett	T G	162	T/WOII	Graham	C V	4005
SSM 3rd Class	Gillies	C W	1763				

Highest Known Rank	Surname	Given Name	Regimental Nos
T/WOII	Grant	E C	6410
QM & H/ Capt	Grant	C H	153
SSM 3rd Class	Graves	J W S	4827
WOII	Gray	W A	4206
T/WOII	Gray	K A	5032
SSM 2nd Class	Gray	W	296
WOII	Gray	W M	
WOII	Gray, MC	T W	4270
Maj	Green	James	
T/WOII	Green	W	3970
SSM 2nd Class	Green	T G W	356
SSM 3rd Class	Green	F V	2173
WO1	Green	Arthur William	620
SSM 2nd Class	Green	Sydney Augustus	330
SSM 3rd Class	Green	James John	555
QMS	Greenlees	E	1000
T/WOII	Greer	W	3970
QM & Hon Capt	Grenfell	Cyril James Hilton	193
Lt (QM)	Greville	Sydney Jamison	1055
T/WOII	Grewar	R E	QP2425
QM & Hon Capt	Grieve, MC	Charles Perry	
SSM 3rd Class	Griffiths	Thomas William	552
SSM 3rd Class	Griffiths	H	1692
WOII	Griffiths	T J O	15044
Lt (QM)	Grigg	Clarence Leonard	NP 1819
QM & Hon Lt	Grigson	E D	452
WOII	Grove	Maurice	VP 3745
T/WOII	Grundy	H R	4092

Highest Known Rank	Surname	Given Name	Regimental Nos
QM & Hon Lt	Gubbins	H J	351
SSM 3rd Class	Guest	Cecil Ivor	3073
T/WOII	Guest	Thomas Edward	VP 3680
SSM 2nd Class	Guest	Cecil Ernest	225
T/WOI	Guest	Leslie Francis (Frank)	NP5483
QM & Hon Capt	Guilfoyle, MC	Charles	
T/WO1A	Gurnett	L G	2203
T/QM & Hon Lt	Guy	William James	648
WOII	Guyatt	Harold Clifford	VP 3498
Capt (QM)	Guyer	Stanley James	1416, 5/17
SSM 2nd Class	Gyton	H L	85
T/WOII	Hacker	W H	9144
WO1	Hackfath, DCM	W H	274
T/WOII	Hadley	H	985
WOI	Haigh, MBE	Joseph Rowe	
T/WOII	Haines	W A	3694
Hon Lieut	Hair	W M	157
Lt (QM)	Hales	Edward Karl	4753
SSM 3rd Class	Hales	H G	1026
WOII	Hall	Albert Mafeking	VP 1041 (NP 10049?)
WOII	Hall	C C	3885
SSM 3rd Class	Hall	J E M	3755
T/WOII	Hall	W O	4325
WOII	Hall	G	
T/WOII	Hallam		3226
SSM 3rd Class	Halloway	R A	2822
SSM 3rd Class	Halloway	W J	2803

Highest Known Rank	Surname	Given Name	Regimental Nos
WOII	Halloway	J J	
T/Sgt	Hallsworth	N F D	5785
SSM 2nd Class	Halstead	E	203
T/WOII	Hamilton	A L	6659
WOII	Hamilton-Browne	E G	396
WO 1st Class	Hammond	S	77
T/WOII	Hammond	F G	3657
WOII	Hanger	William Robert	VP 3615
QM & Hon Lt	Hanlin, MBE	John Weir	114
T/WOII	Hann	Wilfred Leighton	SP 6585
Lt (QM)	Hannaby, MBE	Herbert Leonard	1937; 5/45
Lt.-Col	Hannell	Les E	3406
SSM 3rd Class	Hansen	J T	544
Maj (QM)	Hansen	Theodore Andrew Rothwell	VP 4046; VX 101848; 3/269
T/WOII	Hanslow	S B C	5024
WOII	Hanson	Stewart Tasman	VP 4040
WOII	Hanson	D J	4542
T/WO1A	Hanson	F G	2917
SSM 2nd Class	Harding	G E	257
WOII	Hardy	H T	
WO1	Harlin	J W	
T/WOII	Harmer	Sydney George	NP 2884
T/WOII	Hartnett	A L	2368
WOII	Harper	S J	3660
SSM 2, Hon Lt	Harrad	H T	242
WOII	Harriot	G R	1764
Master Gunner 3rd Class	Harriott	G M	176

Highest Known Rank	Surname	Given Name	Regimental Nos
SSM 3rd Claas	Harris	H G	549
WOII	Harrison	J T	
SSM 3rd Class	Harrison	E M	399
T/WOII	Harrison	S R	5312
SSM 3rd Class	Harrison	John Henry	VP 3757
T/WOII	Hart	G L	4915
BSM	Hartnett	Harcourt Lernard	598
QM & Hon Maj	Harvey, MC	John McFarlane	
T/WOII	Hatfield	F B	3543
SSM 3rd Class	Haupt	F K	4496
T/WOI	Havercroft	R	NP 5022
QM & Hon Maj	Hawkey, MC	John Martin	
Lt (QM)	Hawkins	John Russell	4047; 3/400
WO1A & Hon Lt	Hawkins	Leslie Roderick	138
WO 1st Class	Hawkins	A H	175
Capt (QM)	Hayes	Bert George John	2500
WOII	Hayes	B	3529
Lt (QM)	Hayes	George	3902; 5/71
Capt	Hayes, MBE	Thomas Exlesford	QP2251
T/WOII	Hays	G	3902
T/WOII	Haywood	F S T	6033
SSM 3rd Class	Haywood	E V	2010
WOII	Hazzard, MM	P D	4207
T/WOII	Head	J M	4009
Hon Capt	Healy	J E	
Capt	Heap	Desmond A	3426
T/WOII	Hearnes	Geoffrey	VP 6714
Capt	Heath	J H	

Highest Known Rank	Surname	Given Name	Regimental Nos
SSM 3rd Class	Heath	K Le H M	536
WOII	Hedges	J T	
T/WOII	Hemsley	C A	6340
T/SSgt	Henderson	C R	5869
T/WOII	Henderson	W J	15040
T/WOII	Henderson	J S	7304
Lt Col	Hendry, MBE	John Edward	VP511
MG 3rd Class	Hennessey	J T	636
T/WOII	Henricksen	H A O	4389
MG 2nd Class	Henry	J	252
T/WOII	Henry	L D	4048
T/WOII	Henry	Mervyn David	VP 7296
Lt (QM)	Henry	Basil Birks	WP 4638
WOII	Henrys	Irving R	311
Lt (QM)	Henrys	Ernest	NP 2204; 2/234
T/WOII	Henstridge	H D	6408
SSM 3rd Class	Herbert	A R T	3534
WOII	Herden	H R	4489
SSM 3rd Class	Heriot	Stanley Drysdale	585
WOII	Herrod	D S	
WOII	Heslin	P	
SSM 3rd Class	Hewland	Charles James	564
Capt	Heydt	H E	
SSM 3rd Class	Heywood	W S	3907
SSM 2, Hon Lt	Hicks	H T	108
T/WOII	Higginbottom	R A	6409
WOII	Higgs	C P	
T/WOII	Hill	G A	8750
QM	Hill	E M	393; NP9990

Highest Known Rank	Surname	Given Name	Regimental Nos
WOII	Hill	W A J	
WOII	Hillard	L V	2620
WOII	Hillier	A H	
T/WOII	Hillior	E J	4976
QM & Hon. Lt	Hillman	A J	
T/WOII	Hills	S E	4025
T/WOII	Hines	C J	9442
Lt (QM)	Hirst	Arthur Bruce	1881; 3/147
Capt	Hiscock	Cyril	
WOII	Hoar	John Cecil	WP 1520
T/SSM 3	Hocking	A T F	
T/SSgt	Hodge	P J	5629
SSM 3rd Class	Hodgess	Arthur William Percival	732
SSM 2, Hon Lt	Hodgson	William Robb	196
SSM 3rd Class	Hogan	W J	454
Capt (QM)	Hogarth	George Maxwell Lambert	4576; 5/76
T/WOII	Hogg	T R	4309
T/QM & Hon Lt	Holden	John Cletus	882
SSM 3rd Class	Holdsworth	W T	2769
T/WOII	Holgate	James Edwin	
T/WOII	Holland	J C	6343
T/QM & Hon Lt	Holt	David	1581
T/WOII	Home	S E	8484
SSM 2nd Class	Hook	Charles Peel	308
SSM 3rd Class	Hook	Charles Leslie	3074
SSM 3rd Class	Hope	Adrian Frederick	426
WOII	Hopkinson	L R C	
T/WOII	Horsey	S G	3775

Highest Known Rank	Surname	Given Name	Regimental Nos
WOII	Horton	A	297
SSM 3 & H/Lt	Horwood	J	504
T/WOII	Hosken	B G M	9287
WOII	Hosking	Hubert Arthur James	2775
SSM 3rd Class	Houghton	M K	2013
WOII	Houston	R G	4285
SSM 3rd Class	Howard	G F W	809
Lt (QM)	Howells	Arthur Edwin	3691
T/WOII	Huck	C	6075
BSM	Hudson	R C	931
T/WOII	Hudson	K	3083
SSM 2, Hon Lt	Hudson	A J	95
T/WOII	Huggins	A M F	4919
WOII	Hughes	James	VP1619
WO1	Hulme	J	646
MG 3rd Class	Humphreys	H F	616
Capt (QM)	Hunt	Herbert James	NP 1372; 2/231
T/WOII	Hunter	J G	5484
WOII	Hunter	D	932
Hon Maj	Hunter, MM	Robert Alexander	372: QP372
T/WOII	Hunting	W J	3765
WOII	Hurley	F J	4049
WOII	Huston	R G (Happy)	
T/WOII	Hutchins	A G	6574
WOII	Hutchinson	John Norman Cuthill	NP 1128
QM & Hon Capt	Hutchison, MBE	John	182
SSM 3rd Class	Hutton	Norman Ernest	NP 979
WOII	Huxley	I F	1706
WOII	Ide	H J	
WO1	Ikin	T J	548

Highest Known Rank	Surname	Given Name	Regimental Nos
T/SSM 3rd Class	Iles	A E	10714
QM & Hon Maj	Inglis, MC	William	
WOII	Ingram	F J	2??7
T/WOII	Ivermee	E F C	4294
Lt-Col	Ives, OBE	Cecil	NP3271
SSM 3rd Class	Jabobson	R H P	3500
SSM 3rd Class	Jack	J J	632: 6332
T/WOII	Jack	T	
WOII	Jackson	A D	6468
T/WO1	Jackson	Arnold Wray	SP4462
T/WOII	Jackson	E	
WOII	Jacobson	R H P	VP3500
SSM 3rd Class	James	W T	346
T/WO1	James	A	2783
WOII	James	J	
Lt (QM)	James	Edgar Ernest	NP 2746; QP 2746; 1/42
Lt (QM)	James	Vincent Friedlien	3672
SSM 3rd Class	James	F	487
Lt (Hon Capt)	James, MC	William Walter	
WOII	Jamieson	D R	6415
T/WOII	Jamieson	H L	2598
SSM 3rd Class	Jamieson	Sydney Thomas Blair	338
SSM 2nd Class	Jamieson	W W	276
WOII	Jeanneret	Alan Francis	TP4842
WOII	Jeffrey	C M	
T/WOII	Jeffrey	H S	9436
QM & Hon Lt	Jerrett	Vincent	197: 3293
SSM 3rd Class	Jessup	Edgar Hugh	2190

Highest Known Rank	Surname	Given Name	Regimental Nos
T/WOII	Johns	S C	6665
T/WOII	Johnson	H H	6817
WOII	Johnson	Kenneth Albert	TP6620
T/WOII	Johnson	W J	718
QM & Hon Lt	Johnson	George Alexander	VP3535; VX101813
WOII	Johnson	Alexander Wallace	NP 3197
T/WOII	Johnson	W P	8673
SSM 2, Hon Lt	Johnson	C H	229
QM & Hon Lt	Johnston	G A	3293
Lt (QM)	Johnston	Robert Walter	2338; 1/85
WOII	Johnston	G A	3535
WOII	Jones	W K	462
WOII	Jones	T P	
WOII	Jones	R T	
T/WOII	Jones	R N	3793
SSM 3rd Class	Jones	E C	4831
Capt (QM)	Jones	Edward Brendon	1030; 3/222
SSM 2nd Class	Jones	W P	464
WOII	Jones	H	
SSM 2nd Class	Jones	Albert Ernest	343
WOII	Jones	J	QP2436
Capt	Jones	A H	
WOII	Jones	H E	
WOII	Jones	? (Taffy)	
QM & Hon Lt	Jordan	William Patrick	1528
T/QM & Hon Lt	Jordon	W P	
SSM1A & Hon Lt	Joyce	A E	191
SSM 3rd Class	Kaglund	E S D	568

Highest Known Rank	Surname	Given Name	Regimental Nos
Lt (QM)	Kay	Ernest Edward	678; 5/67
SSM 3rd Class	Keats	R S	700
T/SSM 3rd Class	Keft	J H	
WOII	Keirnan	L J	687
WOII	Kelley	Hector McNash Samuel	WP5959
T/WOII	Kelly	F M	2284
SSM 3rd Class	Kelly	A T	2254
T/WOII	Kelly	J J	5112
WOII	Kelly	Ernest Sydney Handley	QP2427
Lt Col	Kelly, DSO, MID	Joseph Lawrence Andrew	NP2692; NX12214
WOII	Kelsey	Alfred William	SP4474
SSM 2nd Class	Kemm	Percival John	442
T/WOII	Kemp	W J	6949
SSM 3rd Class	Kendall	C W	2322
SSM 2nd Class	Kennedy	J C A	143
WOII	Kennedy	J A	4921
T/WOII	Kennedy	K W or K V	4922
QM & Hon Maj	Kennedy, MBE, MC	William	
SSM 2, Hon Lt	Kenney	A S A	233
SSM 3rd Class	Kent	R J	
WOII	Kent	J	
T/QM & Hon Lt	Kent	Edward Martin	837
WO1 & Hon Lt	Kenyon	T R	
WOII	Keogh	R F	4832
SSM 3rd Class	Kerr	George	3759

Highest Known Rank	Surname	Given Name	Regimental Nos
SSM 2, Hon Lt	Keyon	T R	216
QM & H/ Maj	Kidd	A C	
Lt (QM)	Kidston	Richard	QP2319; 1/82
SSM 3rd Class	Kiernan	L J	687
QM & Hon Maj	Kimber	Lewis Joseph	
SSM 3rd Class	King	N F C	2690
WO1	King	G R	348
SSM 3rd Class	King	A D A	2068
SSM 3rd Class	Kingston	J C	4569
WOII	Kinrade	T H	3914
T/WOII	Klaws	Harry Albert	VP4095
T/WOII	Knee	L W	3085
T/WOII	Knight	J A	4923
T/WOII	Knight	Sidney John	VP3823
SSM 3rd Class	Knight	H A	455
WO1	Knudsen	C M	380
T/WOII	Kollias	J E	2776
Lt (QM)	Kollias	Norman Hector	2702; 5/42
Lt (QM)	Korff	Jack Earlston	2918; 2/414
SSM 2nd Class	Labeska	Louis Lushington	363
Lt (QM)	Lacey	Reginald Gordon	1882; 3/408
T/QM & Hon Lt	Ladds	Charles	268
Capt	Laffy	John Patrick	2916
QM & Hon Lt	Laffy	Martin John Joseph	344: 617
RSM	Lake	John William	278
WOII	Lake	William James	966
T/WOII	Lambert	L H J	QP2431
WOII	Lambert	H T	S32756

Highest Known Rank	Surname	Given Name	Regimental Nos
T/WOII	Lancaster	G W H	9390
T/SSgt	Langworthy	P E	5535
SSM 3rd Class	Lannan	L M	NP645
WOII	Larequi	Hermin Richard	NP 8760
Hon Maj	Larkin	Henry William	262, VP7500
T/SSM 3rd Class	Larsen	E F	
Hon Col	Latchford, MC, MBE	Ernest William	112, VP112
WOII	Law	W B	4841
WOII	Lawes	W J	3683
T/WOII	Lawn	B E	3842
SSM 2nd Class	Lawrence	H P	245
Lt (QM)	Lawson	Robert Shaw	1909; 3/178
SSM 3rd Class	Lazarus	F H	485
Capt (QM)	Le Serve	Sydney Alfred Moore	2610
WO1	Leach	A W	631, 2926
T/WOII	Leach	W J E	6946
Lt (QM)	Leach, MBE	Sydney Ronald	3092; 2/177
SSM 3rd Class	Leamon	E H	1773
SSM 2nd class	Leamon	G H	145
SSM	Leaworthy	S	
T/WOII	Lee	S T P	5630
T/WOII	Lee	Albert William	VP3802
SSM 3rd Class	Leeson	J L	VP683
CSM	Leggett	Victor Lancelot	992
T/WOII	Leigh	W A	NP8702
SSM 2nd Class	Leigh	W J	389
WOII	Lenton	William Levi	QP2307
Hon Lt Col	Lenton, OBE	Roy Mandeville	79, TP72, 70

Highest Known Rank	Surname	Given Name	Regimental Nos
T/QM & Hon Lt	Lergessner	Ernest Thomas	2155
Maj	Leworthy	Seymour Harold	432; 3/348
WOII	Lindsell	F W	
CSM	Locke	John Robert	562
WOII	Locke	H J	
T/WOII	Long	F H	2344
SSM 3rd Class	Loughton	H L	4662
T/WOII	Love	A W	4256
Hon Lt Col	Loveband, MM & Bar	Howard Gordon	SP457; QX6169
Hon Lieut	Lovejoy	H R	
T/WOII	Lovell	A V	9331
WOII	Low	D R	6411
WO1	Lowery	C M	NP3042
SSM 3rd Class	Luff	J H	244
SSM 3rd Class	Luke	Joseph Aberdeen	1426
WOII	Lukeman	E S	
T/WOII	Lyall	J V	4291
T/WOII	Lyall	J	8344
T/WOII	Lynch	P J	4097
SSM 2nd Class	Lyon	William John Gibson	463
SSM 3rd Class	Lyon	L H	4604
SSM	Lyons	W	
T/QM & Hon Lt	Lyons	Albert John	2623
T/WOII	Lythe	K	3697
T/WOII	Macauley	L H	
WO1	MacDonald	W L	106
QM & Hon Maj	MacKay, MBE	William Martin	
WOII	MacKell	J S	2896
SSM 3rd Class	Mackenzie	K M	3167
WOII	Macklow	K	2591

Highest Known Rank	Surname	Given Name	Regimental Nos
T/WOII	Mackrell	J S	7374
Capt	Maclennan	W J	
Hon Maj	MacPherson MC, C de G	Jack MacHattie Lord	NP550; NX422
T/WOII	Macquarie	I	6244
T/WOII	MacWilliams	J F	4003
WOII	Maddigan, MM	C C	
WOII	Maddocks	E W	2802
SSM 3rd Class	Madigan	R J	4504
T/WOII	Magarry	R W	2345
QM & Hon Maj	Magenis, DSO	George Charles	205, 6463
WOII	Maguire	H M	2510
SSM 3rd Class	Maher	C E	2987
SSM 3rd Class	Maher	C A	2472
Lt (QM)	Mahon	John Lawrence	2363
SSM 3rd Class	Main	J G	2599
SSM 3rd Class	Main	J M	2563
WOII	Male	L W	3706
T/WOII	Maloney	L J	9424
SSM 3rd Class	Maloney	J	2845
T/WOII	Maloney	R A	3157
WOII	Manley	J R	3814
Lt (QM)	Mansom	Dudley James	SP4542; 4/71
WOII	Manterfield	A	2031
SSM 3rd Class	Marinier	V H J	3574
T/WOII	Mark, MM	W J	
QM & Hon Lt	Marnie	William Kermack	505
Hon Maj	Marsden, DSO	T Roy	
SSM 3rd Class	Marsh, OBE	Jack Edward	NP3408; NX39

Highest Known Rank	Surname	Given Name	Regimental Nos
SSM 2nd Class	Marshall	George William Joseph	258
T/WO1	Marshall	Leonard Albert	WP5904
WOII	Marshall	J C N	588
Lt (QM)	Marshall, MM	Ernest Walter	5910; 3/370
SSM 2nd Class	Martin	Sydney Ernest	415
SSM 3rd Class	Martin	H S	1185
SSM 3rd Class	Martin	H L	3125
T/WOII	Martin	A J	4051
T/WOII	Martin	A I	3652
WOII	Martin	John Henry	NP 5832
WOII	Martin	Lawrence Frederick	WP6205
T/WOII	Maslen	A T	4254
WOII	Mason	E F	S28145
SSM 2nd Class	Mason	T	408
T/WO1	Mason	H V	5909
T/WOII	Mason	R R	6951
SSM 3rd Class	Mason	K T G	4472
WO1	Masters	H B	101
WOII	Masters	H W	2977
WOII	Mathews	P H F	4208
SSM3	Mattewry	L B	
SSM 2nd Class	Matthews	R	51
T/QM & Hon Lt	Matthews	Walter William	169
T/WOII	Matthews	O C	4935
QM & Hon Capt	Maughan	Harold Melville	89
T/WOII	May	E B	NP8732
T/WOII	Mayberry	L P	6063
Hon Lt	Mayes	Charles Aiken	

Highest Known Rank	Surname	Given Name	Regimental Nos
T/WO1	Mayfield	Joseph John Thomas	QP2335
SSM 3rd Class	Mays	C S	3571
SSM2, Hon Lt	Mays	G P	68
WOII	Mazzesoni	J	
T/WOII	McAdoo	N N	9438
QM & Hon Maj	McArthur, DSO	John	
WO1	McArthur, MM	T A	394
SSM 3rd Class	McBain	Douglas John	2104
SSM 2nd Class	McBride	A	227
SSM 3 & Hon Lt	McCabe	J	611
T/WOII	McCabe	F M	3846
WOII	McCaffrey	F	1316
Maj (QM)	McCallum	Douglas Clarence Roy	294; 1/29
QM & Hon Lt	McCardie	I	
QM & Hon Maj	McClean	F S	
SSM 3rd Class	McCombe	L D A	VP3791
Lt (QM)	McCormick	Leslie Rutherford	VP7514: 5911; 3/249
QM & Hon Lt	McCredic	Thomas	105
WOII	McCrickard	R F	
SSM 3rd Class	McCulloch	J H	3081
WOII	McCulloch, MM	J B	4763
WOII	McDermott	T	
T/WOII	McDermott	H V	4927
WOII	McDonald	J E	
SSM 3rd Class	McDonald	E G	2876

Highest Known Rank	Surname	Given Name	Regimental Nos
T/WOII	McDonald	C	1758
WOII	McDonald	A G	
T/WOII	McDonough	A E	6952
SSM 3rd Class	McEachern	A W D	607
QM & T/ Maj	McFarlane	R A	
T/WOII	McGee	G W	4824
WOII	McGee	J T	
WOII	McGlone	T	
Capt	McGrath	John Francis	303; 2/161
SSM 3rd Class	McHenry	L B	1707
T/WOII	McIlloy	V A	4307
QM & Hon Capt	McIlroy	Robert	4052
Hon Lt Col	McInnes, MBE	Allan Cedric	288; NP9988; NX117487
WOII	McKay	L W	15131
T/WOII	McKay	M D	9421
SSM 3rd Class	McKenna	J P	2859
WOII	Mckenzie	A I	
Lt (QM)	McKenzie	Grant Stewart	3882; 3/274
T/WOII	McKenzie	J A	3653
T/WOII	McKenzie	A J	7301
SSM 3rd Class	McKenzie	J B	491
MG 3rd Class	McKinlay	D J	639
Maj (QM)	McKinna	Andrew Agnew	SP4541; 4/43
WOII	McLaws	R C	
SSM 3rd Class	McLean	J M	1014
T/WOII	McLean	I J	905
QM & Hon Maj	McLean, DSO & Bar	Frederick Stephen	
WOII	McLennan	J A	
SSM 3rd Class	McLennan	Angus Douglas	WP1005

Highest Known Rank	Surname	Given Name	Regimental Nos
Lt (QM)	McLennan	Neil Fraser	VP3857; VX101844; 3/415
QM & Hon Maj	McLennan, MBE	Kenneth	
WOII	McLeod	H I	6436
T/WO1A	McLeod	Norman Thomas	618
SSM 3rd Class	McLeod	J	2028
T/WOII	McMahon	A J	7303
SSM 1A	McMahon	P	113
Capt (QM)	McMillan	Robert Victor	3880; 3/193
WO1	McMullan	A V	643
WOII	McMurray	S	698
T/QM & Hon Lt	McNab	Duncan	2644
SSM 2nd Class	McNamara	L J	391
Lt (QM)	McNamara	Ronald David	NP3409; 3/310
QM & Hon Lt	McNamara	S J	
SSM 3rd Class	McNaught	Douglas James McNeil	666
SSM 3rd Class	McNaughton	Neil John	VP1971
SSM 2nd Class	McPherson	J W	128
Colonel	McPherson, MM, psc	Colin W	5547
Maj (QM)	McQuade	Peter Merlin	NP2704; 2/324
SSM 3rd Class	McRobb	J G	170
Lt.Col.	McVicar	Alfred Oscar	NP731
T/WOII	McWilliam	J F	4003
Lt (QM)	Meadows	Jack Arthur	2703; 2/417
SSM 3rd Class	Meadows	F C A	2649
SSM 3rd Class	Mee	R	431
T/WOII	Meech	L E	4756

Highest Known Rank	Surname	Given Name	Regimental Nos	Highest Known Rank	Surname	Given Name	Regimental Nos
Capt (QM)	Mellor	Arnold	NP 2608; 2/200	SSM 3rd Class	Monish	L W	3575
SSM 3rd Class	Mellor	W O	1781	WOII	Monk	H O	3475
				WOII	Monk	L I	VP 3596
SSM 3rd Class	Merrick	David Stanislaus	672	T/WOII	Moody	T I	5978
SSM 3rd Class	Merry	E O	2051	T/WOII	Moody	F	2442
				T/WOII	Mooney	D W	2953 2593?
SSM 2nd Class	Metcalf, DCM	Jock	328	Maj	Moore	Harry Hearne	275; 3/231
WOII	Metcalfe	T W		T/WOII	Moore	K E	4937
SSM 3rd Class	Middleton	W D	4628	Lt (QM)	Moore	Walter	3510
				WOII	Moore	John Walter	VP3892
T/WOII	Milford	C F	2361	QM & Hon Lt	Moore	Frederick William	496
T/WOII	Miller	R	2939				
T/WO1	Miller	James Clive Knowles	VP1051	WOII	Moore	Stanford Marcus	NP5530
T/WOII	Miller	Ian Keith	NP9595	QM & Hon Maj	Morgan	Albert Edward Llantrisant	
T/SSM 3	Mills	N		SSM 3rd Class	Moricre	E G	3661
T/WOII	Mills	S E	4023	Maj	Morley	Charles	
T/WO1A	Mills	G R	3703	T/WOII	Moroney	M M (or H H)	QP8497
Maj	Mills, MBE	John Martin	342; 2/70	SSM 2nd Class	Morrell	Francis Gordon	198
QM & Hon Maj	Mills, OBE	Christopher John (Charles)		SSM 3rd Class	Morris	Frederick James	502
T/WOII	Millynn	R H	2860	Capt	Morris	Charles	
Lt (QM)	Minchin	Bertram Francis	TP4751	SSM 2nd Class	Mortimer	Arthur Harold	286
T/SSgt	Minnis	V L	4936	T/SSM 1	Mortimer	A T	318
WOII	Minster	Trevor Edward Leslie	VP7171; VX101853	T/WO1	Morton	R M	3688
				T/WOII	Moseley	E J	3312
SSM 3rd Class	Mitchell	D A	3633	WOII	Mouchmore	J	
WO !st Class	Mitchell	H	72	WOII	Mowbray	S P	2078
SSM 3rd Class	Mitchell, MM	W J	285	Maj	Moylan	Bertie Alexander	435; 4/23
WOII	Moffatt	J S		QM & Hon Lt	Moylan	J G	
T/WOII	Moffatt	A G		T/WOII	Moylan	F W	3893
T/WOII	Mofflin	P	5939	T/WOII	Mulholland	P V	
T/WOII	Molloy	V A	4307	T/WOII	Mulligan	M	5472
MG 1st Class	Moncrieff	E W	937				

Highest Known Rank	Surname	Given Name	Regimental Nos	Highest Known Rank	Surname	Given Name	Regimental Nos
T/WOII	Mummery	H B	5902	T/WOII	Nichol	William Quentin Archibald	3898
T/WOI	Munro	V L	4973				
SSM 3rd Class	Murdoch	J K	4705	WO1A: MG 3	Nicholls	Harold Arthur	613
Maj (QM)	Murphy	Walter Vivan	3075; 2/149	WO1 & Hon Lt	Nicholson	W R B	
WOII	Murphy	T					
T/WO1	Murphy	Sydney Vincent	VP3687	T/QM & Hon Lt	Nicholson	Thomas Cornelius	
T/WOII	Murphy	A J	6245	T/WOII	Nicholson	E G	3732
T/WOII	Murray	J W	6948	T/WOII	Nicholson	W H	4053
T/WOII	Murray	W B	4938	SSM 2nd Class	Nickel	J W C	52
T/WO1A	Murray	J	2943				
T/WO1A	Murry	H J	354	SSM 3rd Class	Nicol	W Q A	3898
QM & Hon Lt	Myers	Harold George William	2518	T/QM & Hon Maj	Nix	H J	134
Capt	Naghten	Harry		T/WOII	Nolan	F	3087
WO1	Nairn	William Percival	WP22073	T/WOI	Norgrove	R P	NP 3093
WO1	Nathan	Percy John Henry	123	QM & Hon Lt	Norman	J H	QP2428; 168
T/WOII	Neal	J E	5486	T/WOII	Norris	J H	6057
WO1	Neels	G	127	QM & Hon Capt	Norris, MBE, MC	Arthur Randolph	184
Maj (QM)	Neels, MBE	Norman	2826; 2/370				
WOII	Neil	J R	15020	Capt (QM)	Nugent	James Alexander	VP689; 3/277
T/WOII	Nelson	J W	2984	T/WO1	Nyman	R J	5907
WOII	Nelson	A V O	2273	SSM 3rd Class	Oakley	C O	469
T/WOII	Newing	Charles Wilfred	NP 5014	QM & Hon Lt	Oates	W H	
QM & Hon Maj	Newland, VC	James Ernest		T/WOII	O'Brien	J L	
SSM 3rd Class	Newman	David Alexander	3613	T/WOII	O'Brien	E J	5850
SSM 2nd Class	Newman	Charles John	304	SSM 2nd Class	O'Connor	A	395
T/WOII	Newman	R D	4940	T/WO1	O'Connor	Clement Charles	SP4461
T/WOII	Newnam	J	2327	T/QM & Hon Lt	O'Donnell	F	NP9927; 1261
WOII	Newton	W E		Lt (QM)	Ogle	John William	1/15
WOII	Newton	R D		T/QM & Hon Lt	Oglethorpe	Allan Geoffrey	2145
Lt.-Col	Newton, MBE	Arthur James Cahir	3707	WOII	O'Grady	P F	
T/WOII	Nichol	T	3777				

Highest Known Rank	Surname	Given Name	Regimental Nos	Highest Known Rank	Surname	Given Name	Regimental Nos
WOII	O'Halloran	E		WOII	O'Sullivan	J P	1600, 832
WOII	O'Halloran	A		WOII	O'Toole	F H	
SSM 3rd Class	O'Hanlon	A P	2334	SSM 3rd Class	Owen	George Harry	2082
WOII	O'Hannery	M J		WOII	Owens, DCM	F P	
Maj (QM)	O'Hea	Robert Stuart	2940; 159				
SSM 1A	Ohma	J R	91	T/WOII	Page	K B	3442
SSM 3rd Class	Okey	C	302	T/WOII	Pain	J C	2980
				T/WOI	Palmer	E R C	5471
T/WO1	O'Leary	James Murray	3603; VP4544	WOII	Palmer	B R	1315
Hon Capt	Olifent	W R		WOII	Palmer	F N	4110
SSM 3rd Class	Oliver	A E	340	WOII & Hon Lt	Pamphilon	F	
WOII	Olsen	O B		Lt	Pantlin	Frederick William	
SSM 2nd Class	Olsson	C O	280	T/WOII	Paris	William James	NP2954
WOII	O'Malley	A G		WOII	Parker	W L	
WO1	O'Mara	J A	473	T/WOII	Parrett	E J	9433
WO1	O'Meara, MM	W	664	WOII	Parsons	Arthur Henry	VP7295
				Hon Maj	Partridge, MM	John Lester (Leslie)	365; SP15161
WO1A	O'Neil	W B	104	T/WOII	Pattison	H J	QP2435
SSM 2nd Class	Oram	William	282	T/WOII	Patton	A J	2707
T/WOII	Oram	F	5703	QM & Hon Maj	Paul, DSO	John Keating	
WOII	Orantlin	A E					
QM & Hon Maj	Ordish, DSO	Harold		Lt (QM)	Payne	Noble Edward	NP1854; 2/315
WOII	Orme	C J	4939	QM & Hon Capt	Pearce	Henry Christian	
SSM 3rd Class	Ormsby	W L	3899	WOII	Pearn	H W	
				T/WOII	Pearson	G H	4404
T/WO1A	O'Rourke	Herbert Bede Francis	2564	WO1	Pearson	Amos Robert	401
SSM 2nd Class	O'Rourke	John Peter Patrick	339	T/WOII	Pearson	A E	1722
T/WOII	Orr	R B	4630	T/QM & Hon Lt	Peat	Clarence Bertram	309
SSM 3rd Class	Orton	W C	3872	T/WOII	Peddey	E F	4054
T/SSgt	Osborne	H H	2183	QM & Hon. Lt	Peddle	Thomas Henry	554
WO1	Osgood	Athol	3072	SSM 2nd Class	Pegg	J	410
WOII	O'Shea	Joseph Ambrose	VP3901; VX101846	T/WOII	Pelmear	T	8370

Highest Known Rank	Surname	Given Name	Regimental Nos	Highest Known Rank	Surname	Given Name	Regimental Nos
T/WOII	Pemberton	J H	4336	T/WOI	Porter	W H	NP 5031
T/WOII	Perkins	W V		WOII	Potter	J D	6457
SSM 3rd Class	Peters	Harold Egbert	VP986	SSM 2nd Class	Powell	A E	253
SSM 3rd Class	Peters	L B	2291	SSM 2nd Class	Power	F H	448
T/WOII	Pfennigwerth	R E		SSM 3rd Class	Power	K	2635
SSM 3rd Class	Phelan	E T	333	T/WOII	Pownall	G B	5635
T/WOII	Phillips	E H		T/WOII	Powys	A	5251
Maj	Phillips	Henry Thomas	440; 3/234	Capt	Pratt	William Herbert	
SSM 3rd Class	Phillips	M J	413	SSM 3rd Class	Preddey	H L	2456
T/WOI	Phillips	H G	5459	WOII	Preddy	Henry llwson	
WOII	Phillips	I O	2156	Lt (QM)	Presgrave	Ewan Cave	SP4464; SX20133
WOII	Phillips	W G		SSM 3rd Class	Priddie	R E	1025
T/SSgt	Philip	A	6031	WOII	Priddle	Roy Edward	
Maj (QM)	Pickburn	Fredrick George Alexander	2274; 1/106	WOII	Prior	Robert Henry	VP7069
SSM 3rd Class	Pickering	R C	527	SSM3	Prior	J H	406
SSM 3rd Class	Pickett	A W	373	WOII	Pritchard	William Rees	VP3650
Lt (QM)	Pillow	Leslie Charles	4055; 1/106	WOII	Probert	Ernest	VP7203
Lt (QM)	Pipkorn	Conrad Carl Oswald	VP3762	Maj	Protheroe	Frank Leslie	332; 3/301
WOII	Pippard	G T	1578	WOII	Pryce	H R	QP2407
SSM 3rd Class	Pleydell	H L	630	Lt (QM)	Pullar	William Albert	VP3588; 3/243
SSM 2nd Class	Pluck	R	416	WOII	Punch	Leslie	NP8963
T/WOII	Pollard	C T	QP8643	WO1	Purcell	C J	
T/WOII	Pollard	L T W	9437	T/WOII	Purdue	E W	2087
SSM 3rd Class	Pontey	R M	3112	WOII	Purton	H D	3675
T/WOII	Poole	H J	6984	SSM 3rd Class	Purves	William Winter Home	2188
WOII	Pope	Victor Stuart	4544	WOII	Purves	M E H	3449
SSM 2, Hon Lt	Pope, MBE	W E	149	WOII	Quirk	Edward Valentine	
T/WOII	Porteous	J A G	5482	Hon Lt	Quirke	D	27
				WOII	Raffan	Alfred James	468
				Lt	Raisebeck	J J	

Highest Known Rank	Surname	Given Name	Regimental Nos
SSM 2nd Class	Ramsay	F D	321
Hon. Maj	Randle, MBE	William	VP7559
Col	Ransom, MID	Neville Franklin	1634
SSM 2, Hon Lt	Ransom	H F	230
SSM 2nd Class	Rawson	George	267
WOII	Rayment	F	QP2340
SSM 3rd Class	Raymer	Henry William	984
T/WOII	Rayner	C P	5532
T/WOII	Read	Evelyn Frederick	8780 NX69250
CSM (WOII)	Read	A C	
WOII	Reaney	W	5231
T/WOII	Reardon	J T	
WOII	Redhead	Theodore John	VP6989
T/SSgt	Reece	I G	8720
SSM	Reed	L	
Lt (QM)	Rees	Edward Douglas	2252
WOII	Reid	H H	6452
WOII	Reid	H W	6452
SSM 3rd Class	Reid	L T	2785
T/WO1	Reid	S G	3314
Capt (QM)	Reid	James	QP2202; 1/48
T/WOII	Reid	A	7034
WOII	Reidy	S H	5964
T/WO1	Reidy-Crofts	T B	6347
WOII	Reimers	C R	QP2439
WOII	Reordan	T L	QP2367
Lt (QM)	Resuggan	Francis Edward	1877; 2/427
T/WO1	Rhoades	E R	5450
QM & Hon Lt	Rice	George Lawrence	1997
T/WOII	Richards	T R	2426

Highest Known Rank	Surname	Given Name	Regimental Nos
SSM 3rd Class	Richards	Llewellyn	1782
QM & Hon Lt	Richards	Clarence Samuel	2572
WOII	Richardson	A C	NP5520; 3491
WOII	Richardson	G	379
WOII	Riches	A	4056
T/WOI	Riding	John	NP3382
WO1	Ridley	A E	270
WOII	Ridley	Charles Adrian	2652
SSM 3rd Class	Rimington	G A	VP3658
WOII	Ritchie	Alexander	VP4289
T/WOII	Ritchie	J	1618
Capt	Roach	John Henry	
Hon Col	Roberts, MC	Arthur Leslie	VP7565
WOII	Roberts	A G	4209
Capt	Roberts	Albert Edward	
WOII	Roberts	W R	3558
WOII	Robertson	William Edward	VP3931
Maj	Robertson	Maxwell (Max) Kenneth	10704
WOII	Robeson	William Frederick	NP5039
T/WOII	Robinson	N	5643
Lt (QM)	Robinson	Charles John	NP2577; NX120167; 2/427
WO1	Robinson	J	55
T/WOII	Robson	Gerard John	VP1362
QM & Hon Maj	Roche	William	
SSM 3 & H/Lt	Roddick	W S	503
SSM 2nd Class	Rodham	T	419
T/WOII	Roger	F C G	2443
WOII	Rogers	L J	
WO1	Ronald	H W	625

Highest Known Rank	Surname	Given Name	Regimental Nos	Highest Known Rank	Surname	Given Name	Regimental Nos
SSM 3rd Class	Roney	D J	2083	WOI & Hon Lt	Scanlon	C R	238
SSM 3rd Class	Rose	H K	1411	Maj	Schmedje MC	Theodore James	4057
SSM 3rd Class	Rosee	F J	3077	SSM 3rd Class	Scholes	Hugh Rischie	VP3766
SSM 3rd Class	Rosengrave	T D	1181	SSM 2nd Class	Scholtz	C L	179
QM & Hon Capt	Rosevear, MC	George		SSM 3rd Class	Scott	A R	4503
Capt (QM)	Ross	Albert Henry John	1027; 3/212	Capt (QM)	Scott	F A M	933; 5/22
SSM 3rd Class	Ross	E H	3856	SSM 3 & Hon Lt	Scott	R W	638
T/WOII	Ross	R K	5903	SSM 3rd Class	Scott	W L	1247
WOII	Ross	R J		Capt (QM)	Scott	Robert Martin	1786; 3/229
WOII	Ross	W S		SSM 3rd Class	Scroggins	D W R	3615
WOII	Rossiter	F M S	4269	Lt (QM)	Seabert	Leslie Robert	1935; 3/302
T/WO1	Rouse	D L	2332	Lt (QM)	Seller	Daniel Lawson	1/68
WO1	Rouse	H L	140	WOII	Sellick	P	5458
Lt (QM)	Rowell	Norman Howard	3069; 3/398	T/WOII	Semmens	A A	15037
T/WO1	Rozzolli	E R	NP 5028	SSM 3rd Class	Serisier	F W	981
QM & Hon Maj	Ruddock	William Charles Gentry	TP13	WOII	Serisier	A P (A F?)	2806
WO1	Rumney	H J	647	T/WOII	Seymour	W F	5481
WOII	Russell	E A	4106	SSM 3rd Class	Seymour	A F	2670
SSM 2nd Class	Ryan	L J	126	Hon Capt	Seymour, MC	L	
WOII	Ryan	J B		Hon Lt Col	Shalders, MC	Henry Richard	VP7579 183
Hon Capt	Ryan	T J		Maj	Shalless	E J	261; VP261
T/WOII	Ryan	L	5021	T/WOII	Shannon	J H	4058
SSM 3rd Class	Salter	C J	194	Lt (QM)	Shannon	George William	4048; 3/430
WO1	Salthouse	J F	376	Capt	Shappere	Harry	
SSM 3rd Class	Sanderson	D	3070	QM & Hon Maj	Sharp	William	
WOII	Saunders	C H	4071	WOII	Sharpe	Osso Stewart Morrison	WP22057
SSM 2 & Hon Lt	Saunders	J	206	SSM 3rd Class	Shaw	James Arthur	NP2721
Brigadier	Savage, OBE	Bernard S	4944				

Highest Known Rank	Surname	Given Name	Regimental Nos
T/WOII	Shaw	E A	3598
SSM	Sheahan		
WO1	Shearim	James Dugild	152
Lt (QM)	Sheedy	Laurence Joseph	3617; 3/196
Lt (QM)	Sheldrick	Alfred George	3565; 3/242
T/WOII	Shepherd	W J	6344
WO1	Sheppard	W A	121
T/WOII	Sheppard	R D	8314
QM & Hon Capt	Sheppard, DCM	Albert	506
SSM 3rd Class	Sherlock	H D	721
SSM 2nd Class	Shields	R W	109
Maj	Shields	William Rupert John	VP3895; VX101852
Lt (QM)	Shimeld	John Arthur	2900; 2/326
Capt	Shipley	G F C F	
T/WO1	Short	B H	2957
QM & Hon Maj	Shreeve	James William	1723
WOII	Shrewe	J W	
QM & Hon Lt	Sibthorpe	G R	254
T/WOII	Silcock	H I	4947
Lt (QM)	Silcox	Gordon William	2865
T/WOII	Simons	B R	6406
T/WOII	Simpson	J	4338
Lt (QM)	Simpson	Stanley Alexander	2533
WO1	Simpson	A D	353
T/WOII	Simpson	J W	5080
T/WOII	Sitters	H H	4532
T/Capt	Skerrett, MC	William Charles	VP1737
QM & Hon Capt	Skinner, DCM, MM	Andrew	381
WO1	Slater	J S	522
T/WOII	Slater	E E	9490

Highest Known Rank	Surname	Given Name	Regimental Nos
QM & Hon Maj	Sloan	Hannibal	
T/WOII	Slow	G	3504
QM & Hon Lt	Small	Donald William Francis	2764
T/WOII	Smiles	Jack F	3088
SSM 3rd Class	Smiley	J I	2653
T/WOII	Smith	G L	4008
T/WOII	Smith	A J	4060
T/WOI	Smith	C E	2199
WOII	Smith	W A	
T/WOII	Smith	I S J	7331
MG 3rd Class	Smith	W H	2166
WOII	Smith	J F	4210
SSM 3rd Class	Smith	George William	NP1951
WOII	Smith	Frederick Walburton	NP8741
WOII	Smith	S O	
SSM 2nd Class	Smith	A F	447
T/WOII	Smith	M D	
SSM 3rd Class	Smith	I H	3089
Capt (QM)	Smith	George Robert Vernon	3/145
SSM 3rd Class	Smith	T	531
T/WO1A	Smith	H J	559
T/WO1	Smith	C D	2828
SSM 2nd Class	Smith	R M	129
SSM 3rd Class	Smith	H	537
WOII	Smith, MC	D	
T/WOII	Smithers	S	3213
QM & Hon Lt	Smyth	William	614
T/WOII	Smyth	Frank Miles	4949

Highest Known Rank	Surname	Given Name	Regimental Nos	Highest Known Rank	Surname	Given Name	Regimental Nos
T/WOII	Smythe	S R		QM & Hon Lt	Stanton	Cecil Richard	96
T/WOII	Snelling	C	8650	Capt (QM)	Starkey	C A R	3521; 2/330
SSM 2, Hon Lt	Solomon	H I	136	T/WOI	Starling	Harry Clarence	NP2117
T/WOII	Somerville	W S	5493	WOII	Starling	N R G	2847
WOII	Sommerville			WOII	Stead	A E J	3969
QM & Hon Lt-Col	Sorensen	Soren Frank		WOII	Stead	S S	QP2410
WOII	Spark	J I	4211	SSM 3rd Class	Steele	G	3477
BSM	Sparkes	R	786	WO1	Steele, DCM, MM	Joseph Beck	TP641
Lt.-Col	Sparrow	Raymond Woodall	538; 3/129	T/WOII	Steer	P G M	4387
T/Col.	Speckman, MBE, MC	Carl Rudolph	VX13549	WO1 & Hon Lt	Stefanson	Allan Stefanus	
WOII	Spence	R J E	425	WOII	Stenson	A C	
WOII	Spence	K	4950	QM & Hon Lt	Stephen, DCM	Andrew Barkley	530
Maj (QM)	Spence	F M	2568; 3/153	T/WOII	Stephens	V H	5868
T/WO1	Spence	E H	4548	Maj.	Stephens	A J	306; 4/25
WO1A: BSM	Spencer	J H	610	WO1	Stevens	H A	635
WO1	Spencer	F W	158	WO1 & Hon Lt	Stewart	W	
SSM 3rd Class	Spencer	H B	834	WOII	Stewart	A A	
Lt (QM)	Spencer	Claude Henry George	NP5020; 2/345	T/WO1	Stewart	A C	422
SSM 3rd Class	Spencer	V E C	2099	QM & Hon Lt	Stewart, DCM	G	488
WOII	Spicer	J H		SSM 3rd Class	Stillman	G C	3638
T/WOII	Spratt	F A		SSM 3rd Class	Stimpson	O R	557
WOII	Spring	M C	4072	WOII	Stingemore	P D	4650
Lt (QM)	Sproule	Jack McLean	2/88	Hon Capt	Stinson	W J P	
WOII	Spruzen	E	661: 1235	T/WOII	Stocker	R W	8682
WOII	Squire	L S	4480	WOII	Stone	R J	3330
Capt	Squire	E		Capt	Stone	A J	295; 2/172
WOII	Stagg	J A	N661	SSM 3rd Class	Story	E	1884
T/WOII	Stallman	John William	QP8482	SSM 3rd Class	Strahan, MM	J L	528
T/WO1A	Stammer, MM	F E	459	WO1	Strange	H A	633
SSM 3rd Class	Stanfield	J	409	T/WOII	Strange	C W	3178

Highest Known Rank	Surname	Given Name	Regimental Nos	Highest Known Rank	Surname	Given Name	Regimental Nos
T/WOII	Stratton	N P	2350	SSM 2nd Class	Talbot	R J	326
WOII	Streater	F		Maj (QM)	Tanner	R	5/26
T/WOII	Street	R T	4952	WOII	Targett	C L	
T/WOII	Street	T G	7067	WO1	Tate	J W	
Lt (QM)	Streitberg	Oswald Charles Reid	VP 3754; 3/310	Maj	Taylor	B	357; 1/36
SSM 2nd Class	Strong	G V	411	SSM 3rd Class	Taylor	R	357
WOII	Styles	J T		T/WOII	Taylor	L	4020
T/WOII	Sugars	E L	6484	T/WOI	Taylor	W H	NP 5109
WOII	Suller	D L	QP2303	T/WOII	Taylor	W L	4020
T/WOI	Sullivan	J L	NP 3043	SSM 3rd Class	Taylor	C S	3518
SSM 3rd Class	Sullivan	T E	204	SSM 3rd Class	Taylor	A H	2829
WOII	Summers	J		Lt.-Col.	Taylor, MBE, MC	Albert William	VP7598
WOII	Surplice	R W	6459	SSM 3rd Class	Taylor, MM	H G	453
SSM 2nd Class	Sutton	H	430	Maj (QM)	Tedder	Norman Henry O' Neil	1892; 2/208
T/WO1	Sutton	G J	2055	WOII	Telfer	John Andrew	NP5579
T/WO1	Swain	H B	4212	T/WOII	Telford	L K	6032
WOII	Swann	Robert Charles		SSM 2nd Class	Thomas	C H	259
WOII	Swann	E	15019	Lt (QM)	Thomas	John Francis	4839; 6/47
SSM 3rd Class	Swanson	H J	1447	WOII	Thomas	E P	458
T/QM & Hon Lt	Sweeny	Clarence Henry	341	QM & Hon Maj	Thomas, MBE MC	William Henry	NP9995 486
Lt (QM)	Swifte	Kenneth Bernard Lenthal	2033; 2/187	Maj (ARA)	Thomas, OBE, MC, MID	Kevan Brittan	4757, TX885, 6/11
WOII	Sydes	F	2343	Maj (QM)	Thompson	George William Hunt	QP2268; 1/97
Lt (QM)	Sykes	Leonard Thomas	1637; 3/287	T/WOII	Thompson	W	
QM & Hon. Major	Sykes	George E.		T/WOII	Thompson	T J	6480
WOII	Syme	R		T/WOII	Thompson	C F	6541
SSM 2nd Class	Tackaberry	A E	269	T/WOII	Thompson	H J	
QM & Hon Maj	Tait	John Stewart	VP7596	WOII	Thompson	W R	2337
SSM 2nd Class	Talbot	G S	400	WOII	Thompson, MM	Walter	NP9366

Highest Known Rank	Surname	Given Name	Regimental Nos
T/WO1	Thomson	W J	3980
T/QM & Hon Lt	Thorne	Edward	1762
Lt (QM)	Thornhill	Charles Edgar	2578
T/WOII	Till	J J	6055
SSM 3rd Class	Tindale	W B	547
QM & Hon Lt.	Tomkins	H A	340
SSM	Tompkins	H	
T/Capt	Toohey	Stanley	WP22022; 978
T/WO1	Toomey		
Capt	Tootell	Alfred	
T/WOII	Townsend	C G	8481
WOII	Toy	E G	4308
QM & Hon Maj	Tracy, MBE	William Walter	
Maj	Trask, DCM	Frederick Herbert	
Lt (QM)	Travis	Frederick Henry	2627; 2/312
SSM 3rd Class	Trenham	M C	4808
Maj (QM)	Trevan	Keith H	2360
WOII	Trewern	R E	
WOII	Trickey	F C	4061
WOII	Trindley	N C	
T/WOII	Trounce	J R	4406
Lt.-Col	Trounson	Harrold Edwin Oswald	364
SSM 3rd Class	Trythall	C E	2561
T/WOII	Tuchy	T J	6579
SSM 3rd Class	Tufnell	F	960
T/QM & Hon Lt	Tunstill	Alfred Villars	1691
T/WOII	Tuohy	F J	6579
SSM 3rd Class	Turner	F J	3481

Highest Known Rank	Surname	Given Name	Regimental Nos
WOII	Turner	L E	
WOII	Turner	C C	
WOII	Turpie	J W	2830
SSM 2nd Class	Turton	C	228
T/WOII	Twyford-Jones	P K	3208
QM & Hon Lt	Uhe	J U	199
Capt	Umphelby	Douglas Harold	VP 3600; 3/168
T/WOII	Upton	K C	
SSM 2, Hon Lt	Uren	J	154
SSM 2nd Class	Vale	S G B	292
SSM 3rd Class	Varley	F A	3113
T/WOII	Vaughan	G S	5018
T/WOI	Vautin	T P	4086
Capt (QM)	Vernon	Charles Henry	943; 5/44
WOII	Vole	S	
Lt.-Col	Wade, MBE	Leonard Charles	510
WO1	Wainwright	H M	57
WOII	Waite	H E G	2694
Lt (QM)	Wakefield	John Clement	QP826; 1/26
SSM 2nd Class	Wakenshaw	G A	434
WOII	Walker	J F	
WO1	Walker	Ruben Seymour (John)	
T/WOII	Walker	J R	2863
WOII	Walker	C F	
WOII	Wall	R F	
T/WOII	Wallace	R (J)	QP8658
SSM 3rd Class	Wallis	M J A	3634
WOII	Walsh	J J (A?)	4515; 4514

Highest Known Rank	Surname	Given Name	Regimental Nos
SSM 3rd Class	Walsh	D J H	3507
T/WOII	Walters	S	5578
T/WOII	Walton	John Geoffrey Hinch	SP6465
T/WOII	Ward	F E	1887
WOII	Ward	S	3465
WOII	Wardrop	William Robert	NP2642
WOII	Ware, DCM	W J	
WOII	Warham	R E	4957
WOII	Warhurst	Tom	SP6423
WOII	Warren	F	
T/WOII	Warren	L C	4062
SSM 3rd Class	Warren	G R	3601
Lt (QM)	Warren	Jack Theodore	4482; 4/72
T/WOII	Warren	H J	8749
Lt (QM)	Washington	Edward Alexander	3/334
T/WOII	Waters	H H L	4063
SSM 2nd Class	Watson	A H	327
Maj	Watson, MBE	Geoffrey James (Fango)	4765
T/WO1	Watson	H N	4575
BSM	Watson	L C	945
SSM 3rd Class	Watson	C Y	2304
WOII	Watson	Cecil Leslie	WP22055
SSM 3rd Class	Watters	E	3071
Maj	Watts	Keith Avery	NP2148 NX34920
SSM 3rd Class	Watts	C A	2027
T/WOII	Watts	V H	4064
WOII	Waugh, MBE	Noel Nicholas Ross	NP5507 NX108156
WOII	Webb	H G	

Highest Known Rank	Surname	Given Name	Regimental Nos
SSM 3rd Class	Webb	L G	324
WO1	Webb	A R	649
T/WOII	Webb	J W B	S28763
WO1	Webber	Richard Bird	59
T/WOI	Webster	R R	NP 2819
T/WOI	Webster	David Ross	NP4975
Hon Lt Col	Webster, DCM	George	NP9920 264
WOII	Weight	F V	5017
Maj.	Welch, MBE	Sydney Hamilton	272; 2/62
Lt (QM)	Wellbelove, MC	John James (Thomas)	QP2366
WOII	Wellington	B P	
QM & Hon Maj	Wells	John Maurice	
T/WO1A	Wells	A W	3618
WO1	Wells	J J	
QM & Hon Maj	Wells, MC	Walter	
WOII	Welsh	S H	
WOII	Wenham	Thomas William	VP 4290
Hon Maj	Werner	William Charles	NP9946 255
T/WOII	Westall	D C	5478
WOII	Westbrook	E C L	
T/WOII	Wheatley	T W	6403
WOII	Wheeler	H B	
Lt.-Col.	Whiston	Norton (Robert / Bob)	NP2881
Lt (QM)	Whitaker	Harold Dunham Knott	VP 3508; VX 85045; 3/174
QM & Hon Maj	Whitbourn	Wesley Armstrong	
WOII	White	Richard	WP6073
Lt (QM)	White	Albert Norman	VP 3509; 3/300
Sgt	White	Frederick Edward	VX110546

Highest Known Rank	Surname	Given Name	Regimental Nos
T/WOII	White	A L	3677
SSM 3rd Class	White	A E	3905
T/WOII	Whitehouse	R J	2807
WOII	Whiting	A H A	4107
WOII	Whittakers	Evans Dawson	VP3871
Maj (QM)	Whittle	Gordon Charles	SP4473; 4/55
WOI	Whitton	A A	4820 TX10815
WOII	Whitty	C P	
WOII	Wiese	Albert Adolph	SP6404 (6406?)
Lt (QM)	Wigley	William Ernest	NP4486; 4/69
WOII	Wigley	C H	6431
T/SSM 3	Wilbraham	W T	
SSM 3rd Class	Wilkinson, MC	W T	1700
T/WOII	Williams	D M	5559
QM & T/ Capt	Williams	George Herbert	185
SSM 2nd Class	Williams	F T	235
SSM 3rd Class	Williams	W L	1374
WOII	Williams	Gerald Claude	NP2668
WOII	Williams	E E	3645
SSM 3rd Class	Williams	H J	1463
T/WO1	Williams	C E	3557
WOII	Williams	B J	
SSM 3rd Class	Willis	F L	2535
SSM 2, Hon Lt	Willshire	J D	180
Maj (QM)	Wilson	Thomas Robert McLay	4516; 3/295
Lt.-Col	Wilson	Les H	1846
WO1	Wilson	N U	418
T/WOII	Wilson	D	3008

Highest Known Rank	Surname	Given Name	Regimental Nos
T/WOII	Wilson	E L	3714
WO1	Wilson	Hugh	NP2174
WOII	Wilson	W	
QM & Hon Capt	Wilson	Ernest Simeon	
T/WOII	Wilson	T H	5772
WOII	Wilson	J J	6456
Hon Capt	Wilson, MBE	B	
T/Capt	Winchester	William Owen	NP9978 248
SSM 2nd Class	Winter	H	111
Lt.-Col.	Wiseman	Frank W	3865
WOII	Withington	Edward Alexander	VP 7620; 4065
T/WO1	Wood	G J	3410
WOII	Wood	K D	3264
QM & Hon Capt	Wood	Clifton Loris	171; 495 WP22033
WOII	Wood	George Maurice Fitzgerald	VP 4168
SSM 3rd Class	Wood	C	1702
Hon Lt	Woods	Arthur William	VP 4327 4237
Hon Lt	Woods	Thomas Joseph	VP6797
WOII	Woodward	G A E	5027
T/WOII	Woodward	D P	
SSM 3rd Class	Wooley	Archibald Fullarton	NP1004
T/WOII	Work	D A J	8592
WOII	Worman	A W	
WOII	Worner	J C E	3411
Maj	Worthington	Lesley George	317; 3/233
Maj (QM)	Wright	George William	4639; 5/10
T/WOII	Wright	D E	6712
T/WOII	Wright	Charles Wilber	NP4485
Maj (QM)	Wright, MBE	Frederick James	SP4513; 4/51

Highest Known Rank	Surname	Given Name	Regimental Nos
QM & Hon Maj	Wright, MBE, MC	Charles Robert Victor	
T/WOII	Wyatt	A F	9600
Hon Lt	Wybrow	Campbell Murton	VP7056
T/WOII	Wynn	W (?) F	8348
T/WOII	Wynne	W	QP8348
T/Capt	Yarrington	Herny De Carl	NP9951
Capt	Yates	George Henry	5908
T/WOI	Yellowley	Richard (Dick)	QP 2406
WOII	Yeoman	M A	15127
Maj (QM)	Yorke	Kenneth William Russell	2673; 3/241
T/WO1	Young	Matthew	VP 3193; 3913
WOII	Young	W D	
T/WOII	Young	C W	8525

PRIMARY SOURCES

Documents

'Defence Bill 1909, Extracts from the speech of the Hon. Joseph Cook, MP, Minister of State for Defence, 20th September 1910', in The Army Annual 1910.

'Memorandum on the Defence of Australia by Field Marshall Viscount Kitchener, 12 February 1910' in The Army Annual 1910.

Legge J.G., Australia and the Universal Training Law, Reprinted from Army Review January 1913 with permission of Controller of His Majesty's Stationery Office

Churchill, W. S., The Second World War, Volume 1, The Gathering Storm, Cassell & Co., London, 1948

Greenwood, G & C. Grimshaw (eds.), Documents on Australian International Affairs, 1901-1918, Melbourne, 1997

Army Law Manual, Volume 1, 1964, Updated to Amendment No.40, 24 Sept. 1979.

Reports

Report & Summary of Proceedings, Federal Military Conference 1894, Sydney, Charles Potter, Government Printer, 1894.

Report by the Inspector General of the Commonwealth Military Forces, Major General H. Finn for the year 1905, printed 30th July 1906, Melbourne, J. Kemp, Acting Government Printer for the State of Victoria.

Report by the Inspector General of the Commonwealth Military Forces, Major General H. Finn, dated 1ˢᵗ September 1906.

Report by the Inspector General of the Commonwealth Military Forces, Major General J.C. Hoad for the year 1907, printed 2ⁿᵈ April 1908.

Report by the Inspector General of the Commonwealth Military Forces, Major General G. M. Fitzpatrick, dated 30ᵗʰ May 1911.

Report on the Royal Military College 1910-1911, Sydney, W G. Gullick, Government Printer, 1912

Report by the Inspector General of the Commonwealth Military Forces, Major General G. M. Fitzpatrick, dated 30ᵗʰ May 1912, Melbourne, Albert J. Mullett, Acting Government Printer for the State of Victoria.

Committee of Imperial Defence, Report to the House of Commons by the Prime Minister, 25ᵗʰ July 1912.

Report by the Inspector General of the Commonwealth Military Forces, Major General G. M. Fitzpatrick, dated 30ᵗʰ May 1913, Melbourne, Albert J. Mullett, Government Printer for the State of Victoria.

Report to the Minister of Defence on 'Certain Matters of Defence Policy' by the Committee chaired by Hon. G Swinburne, Melbourne, June 30ᵗʰ, 1919.

Report on the Military Defence of Australia by a Conference of Senior Officers of the Australian Military Forces 1920, Melbourne, Albert J. Mullett, Government Printer, 6ᵗʰ February 1920.

Report on the Royal Military College 1919-1920, Sydney, William Applegate. Gullick, Government Printer, 1920

Report of the Inspector General of the Australian Military Forces, Lt.-General Sir H. G. Chauvel, GCMG, KCB, dated 31ˢᵗ May 1921, Melbourne, Albert J. Mullett, Government Printer for the State of Victoria.

Report of the Inspector General of the Australian Military Forces, Lt.-General Sir H. G. Chauvel, GCMG, KCB, Part 1, dated 31ˢᵗ May 1922.

Report of the Inspector General of the Australian Military Forces, Lt.-General Sir H. G. Chauvel, GCMG, KCB, Part 1, Melbourne 31ˢᵗ May 1923, Printed and Published for the Government of the Commonwealth of Australia by Albert J. Mullett, Government Printer for the State of Victoria.

Report for the Inspector General of the Australian Military Forces, by Lt.-General Sir H. G. Chauvel, GCMG, KCB, Chief of the General Staff, Part 1, Melbourne 31ˢᵗ May 1924.

Report for the Inspector General of the AMF, by Lt.-General Sir H. G. Chauvel, GCMG, KCB, Chief, Gen. Staff, Part 1, Melbourne 31 May 1925.

Report for the Inspector General of the AMF, by Lt.-General Sir H. G. Chauvel, GCMG, KCB, Chief of the General Staff, Part 1, Melbourne 31ˢᵗ May 1926.

Report for the Inspector General of the Australian Military Forces, by Lt.-General Sir H. G. Chauvel, GCMG, KCB, Chief of the General Staff, Part 1, Melbourne 31ˢᵗ May 1927, Printed and Published for the Government of the Commonwealth of Australia by H. J. Green, Government Printer for the State of Victoria.

Report for the Inspector General of the AMF, by Lt.-General Sir H. G. Chauvel, GCMG, KCB, Chief of the General Staff, Part 1, Melbourne 31ˢᵗ May 1928.

Report for the Inspector General of the AMF, by Lt.-General Sir H. G. Chauvel, GCMG, KCB, Chief of the General Staff, Part 1, Melbourne 31ˢᵗ May 1929.

Report for the Inspector General of the AMF, by General Sir H. G. Chauvel, GCMG, KCB, Chief of the General Staff, Part 1, Melbourne 15ᵗʰ April 1930.

First Report by Lieutenant-General E. K. Squires, CB, DSO, MC, Director-General of the Australian Military Forces 1938, AWM 54, 243/6/58

Statement by The Hon. G. A. Street, MC, MP, Minister for Defence on First Report by Lieutenant-General E. K. Squires, CB, DSO, MC, Director-General of the Australian Military Forces, 14ᵗʰ March 1939, Melbourne, Acting Government Printer.

The Clowes Report, The Battle of Milne Bay 1942, Loftus, NSW, Australian Military History Publications, 1995.

Australian Military Forces, *Report on the Royal Military College of Australia for the period 1.1.1942 –31.12.1942,* L.F. Johnston, Commonwealth Government Printer, Canberra.

Australian Military Forces, *Report on the Royal Military College of Australia for the period 1.1.1943 –31.12.1943.*

Australian Military Forces, *Report on the Royal Military College of Australia for the period 1.1.1944 –31.12.1944.*

Australian Military Forces, *Report on the Royal Military College of Australia for the period 1.1.1945 –31.12.1945,* L.F. Johnston, Commonwealth Government Printer, Canberra.

Australian Military Forces, *Report on the Royal Military College of Australia for the period 1.1.1946 –31.12.1946.*

Australian Military Forces, *Report on the Royal Military College of Australia for the period 1.1.1948 –31.12.1948.*

Australian Military Forces, *Report on the Royal Military College of Australia for the period 1.1.1950 –31.12.1950.*

Australian Military Forces, *Report on the Royal Military College of Australia for the period 1.1.1951 –31.12.1951.*

Training Publications

Instructions for Armourers 1931, Supplement No.2 and No.3, London, HMSO.

Instructions for Training, Australian Military Forces & Cadets, H.J. Green, Government Printer, 1933 (AMR & O 1587).

Australian Military Forces, Training Establishments & the Organization and location of Units of the Militia Forces, *H.J Green Govt. Printer Melbourne, 1937.*

Field Service Regulations, Volume II, Operations –General 1935, (Reprinted with amendments 1939), London, His Majesty's Stationery Office, 1939.

Army Training Memorandum (War) Australia No.1, August 1941, By Authority: Victorian Railways Printing Works.

Army Training Memorandum (War) (Australia) No.2, September 1941,

Army Training Memorandum (War) (Australia) No.5, December 1941,

Army Training Memorandum (War) (Australia) No.7, February 1942,

Army Training Memorandum (War) (Australia) No.18, December 1942,

Army Training Memorandum (War) (Australia) No.25, 27th September 1943, By Authority: Wilks and Co. Pty. Ltd., Printers, 19-47 Jeffcott Street, Melbourne.

Army Training Memorandum (War) (Australia) No.26, 25th October 1943

Army Training Memorandum (War) (Australia) No.29, 17th January 1944

Army Training Memorandum (War) (Australia) No.31, 13th March 1944

Army Training Memorandum (War) (Australia) No.32, 10th April 1944

Army Training Memorandum (War) (Australia) No.33, 5th June 1944, (With Supplement: Six Lectures on Epidemic Control in War)

Army Training Memorandum (War) (Australia) No.34, 3rd July 1944

Army Training Memorandum (War) (Australia) No.35, September 25, 1944

Army Training Memorandum (War) (Australia) No.37, December 18, 1944

Australian Military Forces, Army Training Memorandum (War) (Australia) No.38, January 31st 1945

Australian Military Forces, Army Training Memorandum (War) (Australia) No.39, April 30th 1945

Schedule Showing Allied Landforces Schools as at 29 February 1944, ADFA 254612 M778.

Army Training Memorandum No.45 November 1946, Melbourne, Department of

Defence, AHQ, Military Board.

Army Training Memorandum No.46 December 1946-January 1947.

Army Training Memorandum No.47 February-March 1947.

Army Training Memorandum No.49 June-July 1947.

Army Training Memorandum No.51 October-November 1947.

Cadet Training, Volume II (to Certificate A Part II Standard) 1956, London, The War Office.

Infantry Training, Volume 1, Infantry Platoon Weapons, Pamphlet 11, Trained Soldiers (All Arms), Exercises, Weapons handling 1955, *London, The War Office.*

Infantry Training, Volume 1, Infantry Platoon Weapons, Pamphlet 3B, The 7.62-mm Self-Loading Rifle & Bayonet (All Arms) 1961, Printed & modified for Australia.

Australian Military Forces, Infantry Training, Volume 4, Part 2, The Platoon (Provisional) 1964.

Staff and Graduation Lists

Staff and Regimental Lists of the Australian Military Forces, 1ˢᵗ January 1914, By Authority, Albert J. Mullett, Government Printer, Melbourne.

Officers' List of the Australian Military Forces, Part 1, Active List, 1ˢᵗ July 1917.

Officers' List of the Australian Military Forces, Part 1, Active List, 1ˢᵗ April 1920.

Officers' List of the Australian Military Forces, Part 1, Active List, 1ˢᵗ Dec. 1922.

The Army List of the Australian Military Forces, Staff List, 1ˢᵗ July 1925, By Authority, H. J. Green, Government Printer, Melbourne.

The Army List of the Australian Military Forces, Part 1, Active List & AAMC Reserve, 1ˢᵗ January 1926.

The Army List of the Australian Military Forces, Part 1, Active List & AAMC Reserve, 1ˢᵗ January 1927.

The Army List of the Australian Military Forces, Part 1, Active List & AAMC Reserve, 1ˢᵗ January 1928, By Authority, H. J. Green, Government Printer, Melbourne.

The Army Staff and Gradation List of the Australian Military Forces, 1ˢᵗ Aug. 1932.

The Army List of the Australian Military Forces, Part 1 Active List, 1ˢᵗ August 1935.

The Army List of the Australian Military Forces, Part 1 Active List, 1ˢᵗ August

1937.

The Army Staff and Gradation List of the Australian Military Forces, Part 1 Active List, 1st February 1939.

The Army Staff and Gradation List of the Australian Military Forces, Part 1 Active List, 1st February 1940.

The Australian Imperial Force, Staff, Regimental, and Gradation Lists of Officers, No.2, 1st August 1940, By Authority: Brown, Prior, Anderson Pty. Ltd., 430 Little Burke Street, Melbourne, C1.

Provisional Regimental Lists of the Australian Military Forces, April 1942.

Gradation List of Officers of the Australian Military Forces, Volume 1, The Active List, 18th January 1945.

Australian Military Forces, Regimental Lists & Manning Tables, Officers on Active List, No.3, 1st October 1945, Part 1, P.M. Forces, General & Special Lists.

Australian Military Forces, Command, Staff & Extra-Regimental Appointments, List No. 8, 1st November 1945.

Gradation List of Officers of the Australian Military Forces, Volume 1, The Active List, 7th March 1946.

Australian Military Forces, Appointments, Promotions Etc, Lists Nos. 161-180 Inclusive, Volume 16, 28 Nov 1946-24 July 1947.

Australian Military Forces, Appointments, Promotions Etc, Lists Nos. 181-186 Inclusive, Volume 17, 1st December 1947.

The Army List of Officers of the Australian Military Forces, Volume 1, The Active List, 1st October 1950.

The Army List of Officers of the Australian Military Forces, Volume 1, The Active List, 1st April 1953.

The Army List of Officers of the Australian Military Forces, Volume 1, The Active List, 1st August 1956.

The Corps List of Officers of the Australian Regular Army and Regular Army Special Reserve, 1st July 1958.

The Army List of Officers of the Australian Military Forces, Volume 1, The Active List, 1st September 1962.

The Army List of Officers of the Australian Military Forces, Volume 1, The Active List, 1st March 1966.

The Corps List of Officers of the Australian Regular Army and Regular Army Special Supplement, 1st September 1964.

The Corps List of Officers of the Australian Regular Army and Regular Army Special Supplement, 31ˢᵗ March 1967.

Military Orders/Australian Army Orders

Military Orders 1903

MO 230-1903 Instructional Staff, Officers, Warrant and Non Commissioned Officers

Military Orders 1906

MO 293-1906 Ranks and Classification, Warrant and NCOs, Instructional Staff.

Military Orders 1911

MO 52-1911 Special School of Instruction for the training of candidates for appointment to the Instructional Staff (W. & NCOs), Defence Act, Section 21B

Military Orders 1920

MO 167-1920 Instructional Staff (W & NCOs), Qualified at No.1 and No.2 Special Schools of Instruction at Liverpool, NSW

Military Orders 1921

MO 344-1921 Transfer of Quartermasters of the Permanent Military Forces to the Australian Instructional Corps.

Military Orders 1922

MO 321-1922 Permanent Forces-Annual Establishments 1922-23, (i) Australian Instructional Corps.

Military Orders 1923

MO 422-1923 Permanent Forces-Annual Establishments 1923-24, (i) A I Corps.

Military Orders 1924

MO 37-1924 Australian Instructional Corps; Promotions (2), Appointments (2), Discharges (2) and Amendment (1).

Australian Army Orders 1925

AAO 161-1925 Qualifications governing increments required to be obtained by Warrant Officers (II) AIC.

Australian Army Orders 1926

AAO 47-1926 Australian Instructional Corps, Struck off Strength (deserter).

Australian Army Orders 1927

AAO 432-1927 Permanent Forces-Annual Establishments 1927-1928, (i) A I Corps.

Australian Army Orders 1928

AAO 89-1928 Australian Instructional Corps, Promotion (Bandmaster).

Australian Army Orders 1932

AAO 182-1932 Permanent Forces-Annual Establishments 1932-33, Australian Instructional Corps, Table 1 Quartermasters, Table 2 W & NCOs.

Australian Army Orders 1933

AAO 219-1933 Permanent Forces-Annual Establishments 1933-34, Australian Instructional Corps, Table 2 Quartermasters, Table 3 W & NCOs.

Australian Army Orders 1935

AAO 26-1935 Permanent Forces-Annual Establishments 1935-36, Australian Instructional Corps, Table 2 Quartermasters, Table 3 W & NCOs.

AAO 155-1935 Appointment to Australian Instructional Corps, No.1 Special Course of Instruction, Small Arms School (held from 12/2/35 to 12/6/35)

Australian Army Orders 1936

AAO 153-1936 Small Arms School, Cavalry and Infantry Wing, No.2 Special Course for appointment to Australian Instructional Corps (held from 4/2/36 to 13/6/36)

AAO 154-1936 Small Arms School, Cavalry and Infantry Wing, No.1 AIC General Refresher Course (held from 4/2/36 to 13/6/36)

Australian Army Orders 1937

AAO 42-1937 Permanent Forces-Annual Establishments 1936-37, Australian Instructional Corps, Table 2 Quartermasters, Table 3 W & NCOs.

AAO 24-1937 Small Arms School, Cavalry and Infantry Wing, No.3 Special Course for appointment to Australian Instructional Corps (held from 1/8/35 to 12/12/36)

AAO 148-1937 Small Arms School, Cavalry and Infantry Wing, No.4 Special Course for appointment to Australian Instructional Corps (held from 9/2/37 to 12/62/37)

Australian Army Orders 1938

AAO 28-938 Permanent Forces-Annual Establishments 1937-38, Australian Instructional Corps, Table 2 Quartermasters, Table 3 W & NCOs.

AAO 151-1938 Small Arms School, Cavalry and Infantry Wing, No.5 Special Course for appointment to Australian Instructional Corps (held from 8/2/38 to 11/62/38)

AAO 290-1938 Small Arms School, Cavalry and Infantry Wing, No.6 Special Course for appointment to Australian Instructional Corps (held from 4/7/38 to 23/11/38)

Australian Army Orders 1939

AAO 1-1939 Permanent Forces-Annual Establishments 1939-40, Australian Instructional Corps, Table 2 Quartermasters, Table 3 W & NCOs.

AAO 178-1939 Small Arms School, Cavalry and Infantry Wing, No.7 Special Course for appointment to Australian Instructional Corps (held from 16/1/39 to 17/6/39)

Australian Army Orders 1940

AAO 47-1940 Australian Instructional Corps, 1 Appointments (9), 2 Temporary Promotions (24). 3Allotments (26), 4 Discharges (5).

Australian Army Orders 1941

AAO 21-1941 Australian Instructional Corps, 1 Temporary Appointments (8), 2 Appointments (18) 3 Promotions (No.8 Special Course), 4 Confirmations (53).

Australian Military Forces, Appointments, Promotions etc, Part Lists 1-10 Inclusive, Volume 1 October-December, 1943 Part II
    Permanent Military Forces, Australian Instructional Corps, Appointments (3).

Allied Land Forces in South-West Pacific, General Orders, 30 June 1945

GO 54-1945 Australian Instructional Corps, 1 Promotions (4), 2 Confirmations (10), 3 Discharges (79), 4 Reversions (16), 5 Corrigenda (2)

Australian Army Orders 1947.

AAO 59-1947 Australian Instructional Corps, 1 Promotions (145), 2 Discharge (1), 3 Corrigendum (1).

Australian Army Orders 1948

AAO 14-1948 Australian Instructional Corps, Promotions (89).

Australian Army Orders 1949

AAO 110-1949 Australian Instructional Corps 1 Promotions (3), 2 Discharges (8).

Australian Army Orders 1950 (Issued with AAOs dated 30th June 1950).

Permanent Military Forces, Australian Instructional Corps, *To be Lieutenants (Quartermasters), 1st July 1949.*

Australian Army Orders 1951.

AAO 17-1951 Pay in lieu of Furlough

(2/75 Maj (H/Lt.-Col.) S.B. Goodwin (Maj (QM) AIC) 7-½ months

Australian Army Orders 1951(Issued with AAOs dated 30th November 1951).

Australian Regular Army, Australian Instructional Corps,

The following Quartermasters are to be transferred to...Royal Australian Engineers, Royal

Australian Medical Corps, Royal Australian Ordnance Corps, Royal Corps of Australian Electrical and Mechanical Engineers, Royal Australian Army Provost Corps, 1ˢᵗ September 1951.

Australian Army Orders 1953.

AAO 96-1953 Australian Regular Army, Quartermasters—Allotment to Corps. The following officers, who hold the position of Quartermaster in the Australian Regular Army, are allotted to Corps shown to date 14ᵗʰ August 1953, *Royal Australian Armoured Corps, Royal Australian Artillery, Royal Australian Engineers, Royal Australian Corps of Signals, Royal Australian Infantry Corps, Australian Intelligence Corps, Royal Australian Army Service Corps, Royal Australian Army Medical Corps, Royal Australian Army Ordnance Corps, Royal Australian Corps of Electrical and Mechanical Engineers, Royal Australian Army Provost Corps.*

National Archives of Australia (NAA)

AIC Badge Design, 1930, B1535, 716/2/182.

AIC Civic Activities 1934, B1535 859/16/298.

AIC, Commissions AMF & AIF 1943, MP742/1 248/1/15.

AIC commissioned in AIF, Amend of Aust Mil Regs, 1944, MP742/1 248/1/15.

AIC appointments 2ⁿᵈ AIF, 1941, SP1048/8 S/2/193.

AIC Cadre, 2 Div-Cavalry 1941, MP385/3 27/20/280

Annual Establishment—Australian Instructional Corps 1930 (B1535 716/2/182.).

Annual Establishment–Australian Instructional Corps 1940-41(MP 358/3 27/20/820).

Annual Establishment—Australian Instructional Corps, 4MD 1941, D844 55/3/29.

Application, Commission, AIC, 1938, Edmund F. Allchin, MM, B1535 859/16/1500.

Application for a Commission, C J Robinson, 1942, MP508/1 248/708/738.

Beale, WO K, AIC, Grievance 1923, MP367/1 559/15/3146.

Brown, C H, AIC, Meritorious Service Medal not awarded 1931, B1535 701/12/101.

Carson, AIC, WOII J C S, Court Martial 1945, A471/1 70929.

Coghill, Maj A J, Complaints, A2653 1923 Volume 2, Mil Board Meetings 22-33.

Court of Inquiry, Name withheld, Stores discrepancy 1939, B1535 751/2/177.

Curr, WOII David Thomas, AIC, Charge against 1935, B4717 Curr/DT.

Darwin Housing 1933, B1535 869/31/82.

Dawes, W G D, Injury sustained No.8 Course, 1938, B1535 729/3/628.

Discharge, Name withheld, Suspected subversive activities 1938, B1535 751/2/148.

Dowdy, QM & Hon Lt V E, Transfer, Armidale/Lismore 1940, SP1008/1 512/7/956.

Downey, QM & Hon Lt H H, New Guard Activities 1933, S33/1/30.

Enlistment in No.5 Special Course, E M Kent, 1938, B1535 859/16/1257.

Establishment—Instructional Staff (M.B. Agenda 347/1920), A2653/1 1920 Vol 2.

Farrow, QM & Hon Maj T J, Court of Inquiry 1926, MP367/1 452/1/246.

Gardener, WOII A J, Car accident on duty 1935, B1535.729/3/606.

Gray, WO W M, Enlistment 2/4 Bn AIF 1940, SP459/1 512/24/33.

Gill, W, Injury, Court of Inquiry, Newcastle 1931, B1535 729/3/240.

Hughes, WOII James, MM, Discharge 1925, B4717 Hughes /J.

Johnson, WOI G A, New Caledonia Defence Forces 1941, SP1048/7 544/1/98.

Jones, R T, Medically discharged 1931, B1535 738/4/38.

Kent, WOII R J, Medical discharge 1932, B1535 738/3/120.

Latchford, Ernest William MC, Personal records 1934, SP196/3 L3.

LeServe, Sydney A M, Recoupment of medical costs 1939, B1535 738/3/452.

Lowrey, WOI C M, Court of Inquiry, Motorcycle accident 1942, SP459/1 429/5/5296.

McHenry, L B, War Disability Supernummary List 1933, B1535 827/14/11.

McLean, F.S. Hon.Maj. (Dispute, Presidency Court of Inquiry), MP367/1 409/3/2010.

Nathan, P J H, Medical Report 1937, B1535 751/2/125.

No.8 Special Course (AIC), MP385/3, Item 27/20/719.

No.9 Special Course (AIC), MP385/3, Item 27/20/807.

No.10 Special Course (AIC), MP385/3, Item 27/20/808.

Pearson, A R, Reimbursement of medical costs 1935, B1535 912/3/94.

PMF W&NCOs holding AIF Commissions (MBAgend 30/1920) A2653/1 1920Vol 2.

Quartermaster Selection, A & I Staff (M.B. Agenda 347/1920), A2653/1 1920 Vol 2.

QMs Power of Command, (QM & Hon Maj W W Tracy) MP367/1 409/3/2000.

Reinforcement Officers AIF—Consideration of AIC Personnel, SP459/1 430/4/2275.

Seniority of Warrant Officers, 1923 SP 1008/1 524/2/3

Sparrow, R W, Payment of Surgical Fees 1941, A472/6 W3141.

Sheppard, W A, Death, Payment of leave due 1938, B1535 729/5/34.

Thomas, 611 Major Kevan Brittan OBE MC, B2458 611.

Transfers, AIC, 2 Div, WOIIs Fisher & Silcox, 1939, SP1008/1 512/9/1631.

Warrant Officers, AIC attached Army Schools & Coast Defences, MP742/1 248/1/15.

Watts, WOII K A, Armour training in England 1937, B1535 929/21/185.

Australian War Memorial (AWM)

AWM 27 303/297, AAMC Course, AIC (CMF).

AWM 41 1099, Maj G E Sykes, AIC, Personal Narratives 1923.

AWM 49 183, Broadmeadows Camp, 8 Bde Artillery Shoot 1938, AIC cadre.

AWM 60 253/1/62, Warrant Officers AIC–Posted to VDC Bns, AMF N Comd. 1942.

AWM 61 411/1/2, NSW Citizen Rifle Shoot, AIC Duty Officer.

AWM 61 411/6/8, Boy Scouts parade, AIC to judge marching competition.

AWM 61 507/4/370, AIC Appointments, 2nd Div 1937.

AWM 61 532/4/370, Training Abroad, WO K A Watts.

AWM 62 63/1/601, Annual Establishment—Australian Instructional Corps 1938-39.

AWM 62 112/6/359, Annual Establishment—Australian Instructional Corps 1927-28.

AWM 62 112/6A/361, M G L Hogarth, Personal Records 1936.

AWM 62 112/6/646, Appointment of Staff Sergeants Major 1st Class 1936.

AWM 62 112/6A/498, Application to join AIC, 1939.

AWM 62 112/6/679, AIC Cost of Transfers 1936.

AWM 62 112/6/813, Promotion, QM & Hon. Lt, 1939.

AWM182 (7), Staff Corps and other corps.

AWM 182-8, AIC and Tech Units (QMs & Hon Lts) ledger.

AWM 182-10, AIC and Tech Units (QMs & Hon Lts) ledger, A-M.

AWM 182-11, AIC and Tech Units (QMs & Hon Lts) ledger, N-Z.

SECONDARY SOURCES

Books

Addison, Paul and Angus Calder (editors), *Time to Kill, The Soldier's Experience of War in the West 1939-1945,* Pimlico (Random House), London, 1997.

Alexander, Fred, *Australia since Federation, A Narrative and Critical Analysis,* Nelson, Perth, Reprinted 1982.

Andrews, Eric, *A History of Australian Foreign Relations,* Cambridge University Press, Melbourne, 1979.

Andrews, Eric, *The Anzac Illusion, Anglo Australian Relations during WWI,* Cambridge University Press, Melbourne, 1993.

Andrews, Eric, *The Department of Defence,* Melbourne, Oxford University Press, 2001.

Baden-Powell, B. F. S & Brunker, H. M. E., *The Army Annual & Year Book 1910,* William Clowes and Son, London, 1910.

Baker, Kevin, *Paul Cullen, Citizen and Soldier, The life and times of Major-General Paul Cullen, AC, CBE, DSO and bar, ED. FCA,* Rosenberg Publishing, Sydney, 2005.

Ball, Desmond (ed), *Strategy and Defence, Australian Essays,* George Allen and Unwin, Sydney, 1982.

Barcan, A, T. Blunden, A. Dwight, S. Shortus, *A Nation Emerges,* The Macmillan Company of Australia, Melbourne, 1974.

Barclay, Glen St.J., *The Empire is Marching, A Study of the Military Effort of the British Empire 1800-1945,* Weidenfeld and Nicholson, London, 1976.

Barnett, Correlli, *Britain and her Army 1509-1970, A Military, Political and Social Survey,* Allen Lane The Penguin Press, London, 1970.

Barrett, John, *Falling In: Australians and 'Boy Conscription',* Hale & Iremonger, Sydney, 1979.

Barrett, John, *We Were There; Australian Soldiers of World War II tell their stories.* Penguin Books, Melbourne, 1988.

Beaumont, Joan, (ed) *Australia's War 1939-1945,* Allen and Unwin, Sydney, 1996.

Beaumont, Joan, (ed) *Australian Defence: Sources & Statistics,* Oxford University Press, Melbourne, 2001

Bell, Coral, *Dependent Ally, A study in Australian Foreign Policy,* Oxford University Press, Melbourne, 1988.

Bennett, H. Gordon, *Why Singapore Fell,* Sydney, Angus and Robertson, Sydney, 1944.

Bergerud, Eric, (ed) *Touched by Fire, The Land War in the South Pacific,* Penguin Books, Melbourne, 1997.

Bet-El, Ilana, *Conscripts: Lost Legions of the Great War,* Sutton Publishing, Guildford, England, 1999.

Brodie, S and L, *Australia's Prime Ministers,* Sydney, Australian Knowledge, Sydney, 1985.

Brunker, H. M. E., *The Army Annual & Year Book 1912,* William Clowes and Son, London, 1912.

Budden, F. W., *That Mob—The story of the 55/53 Australian Infantry Battalion, AIF,* F. W. Budden, Sydney, 1973.

Burch, Ian, *History of the School of Artillery 1885-1996,* Development Wing, School of Artillery, Manly, NSW, 1996.

Burns, Paul, *The Brisbane Line, Political opportunism verses national security 1942-1945,* Allen and Unwin, Sydney, 1998.

Byrnes, G.M., *Green Shadows, A War History of the Papuan Infantry Battalion, 1 New Guinea Infantry Battalion, 2 New Guinea Infantry Battalion, 3 New Guinea Infantry Battalion, 1940-1947,* G. M. Byrnes, Brisbane, 1989.

Cannon, Michael, *Australia, Spirit of a Nation. A Bicentenary Album,* Currey O'Neill, Melbourne, 1988.

Carroll, Brian, *Between the Wars, An illustrated history of Australia 1919-1939,* Cassell Australia, Sydney, 1980.

Clark, Manning, *A history of Australia, Volumes V, The people make Laws, 1888-1915,* Melbourne University Press, Melbourne, Reprinted 1999.

Clark, Manning, *A history of Australia, Volumes VI, The Old Dead Tree & The Young Tree Green, 1916-1935,* Melbourne University Press, Melbourne, Reprinted 1999.

Clark, Mavis Thorpe, *No Mean Destiny, The story of the War Widows Guild of Australia 1945-1985,* Hyland House, South Yarra, 1986.

Cole, D. H., *Imperial Military Geography,* Sifton Praed & Co, London, Sixth Edition 1931.

Collins, June, *Bandy's Boys, The Darwin Mobile Force,* Joan Collins, Melbourne, 1989.

Connell, Daniel, *The War at Home, Australia 1939-1949,* ABC Enterprises, 1988.

Coulthard-Clark, C. D., *Duntroon, The Royal Military College of Australia, 1911-1986,* Allen & Unwin, Sydney, 1986

Coulthard-Clark, C. D., *The Diggers, Makers of the Australian Military tradition,* Melbourne University Press, Melbourne, 1993.

Coulthard-Clark, *Soldiers in Politics, The Impact of the military on Australian Political Life & Institutions,* Allen & Unwin, Sydney, 1996.

Cowie, Donald, *An Empire Prepared: A Study of the Defence Potentialities of Greater Britain,* George Allen & Unwin, London, 1939.

Crowley, Frank (editor), *A New History of Australia,* William Heinemann, Melbourne, 1974.

Cubis, Richmond, *A history of 'A' Battery, New South Wales Artillery (1871-1899), Royal Australian Artillery (1899-1971),* Elizabethan Press, Sydney, 1978.

Cumpston, I. M., *Defence Policy 1901-2000,* I.M. Cumpston, Canberra, 2001

Davies, Norman, *The Isles: A History,* Macmillan, London, 2000.

De Landa, Manuel, *War in the age of intelligent machines,* MIT Publishing, Third Printing, Cambridge Massachusetts, 1994.

Dennis, Clarence J., 'The Push', *The Moods of Ginger Mick,* Angus & Robertson, Melbourne, Revised Edition 1982.

Dennis, Peter; Jeffrey Grey, Ewan Morris, and Robin Prior, *The Oxford Companion to Australian Military History,* Oxford University Press, Melbourne, 1995.

Divine, David, *The Blunted Sword,* Hutchinson & Co., London, 1964.

Edwards, T. J., *Standards, Guidons and colours of the Commonwealth Forces,* Gale and Polden Ltd, Aldershot, 1953.

Faulkner, John & Macintyre, Stuart, *True Believers,* Allen and Unwin, 2001.

Fairclough, H, *Equal to the Task, Par Oneri, The history of the Royal Australian Army Service Corps,* F.W. Cheshire, Melbourne, 1962.

Festberg, Alfred N., *Australian Army Lineage Book,* Military Historical Society of Victoria, Melbourne, 1965.

Festberg, Alfred N., *The Lineage of the Australian Army*, Allara Publishing, Melbourne, 1972.

Fielding, Jean and O'Neill, Robert, *A select bibliography of Australian military history 1891-1939*, Australian National University, Canberra, 1978.

Fricke, Graham, *Profiles of Power: The Prime Ministers of Australia*, Houghton Mifflin Australia, Melbourne, 1990.

Gammage, Bill, *The Broken Years: Australians in the Great War*, Australian National University Press, Canberra, 1974.

Golding, D. J., *The Emigrant's Guide to Australia in the Eighteen Fifties*, The Hawthorne Press, Melbourne, 1973 (1856)

Greenwood, Gordon, *Australia, A Social & Political History*, Angus & Robertson, Sydney, Reprinted 1978.

Grey, Jeffrey, *A Military History of Australia*, Cambridge University Press, Melbourne, 2000.

Grey, Jeffrey, *The Australian Army*, Oxford University Press, Melbourne, 2001

Grey, Jeffrey, *Australian Brass, The Career of Lieutenant General Sir Horace Robertson*, Cambridge University Press, Melbourne, 1987

Hay, David, *Nothing over Us, The Story of the 2nd/6th Australian Infantry Battalion*, Australian War Memorial, Canberra, 1984.

Hay, Ian, *Arms and the Men*, HMSO, London, 1977.

Handel, Paul, *Dust, Sand & Jungle, A History of Australian Armour During Training & Operations*, RAAC Memorial & Tank Museum, Puckapunyal Victoria, 2003.

Handel, Paul, *The Vital Factor, A history of the 2nd/6th Australian Armoured Regiment 1941-1946*, Australian Military History Publications, Sydney, 2005.

Hartwell, R. M., *The Industrial Revolution & Economic Growth*, Methuen & Co., London, 1971.

Haswell, Jock, *The Citizen Army*, Peter Davies, London, 1973.

Homes, Richard, *Redcoat, The British Soldier in the age of Horse and Musket*, HarperCollins, London, 2001.

Horner, David Murray, *The Gunners, A history of Australian artillery*, Allen and Unwin, Sydney, 1995

Horner, David Murray, *Inside the War Cabinet, Directing Australia's War effort 1939-1945*, Allen and Unwin, Sydney, 1996

Hughes, Colin, *Mr. Prime Minister, Australian Prime ministers 1901-1972*, Melbourne University Press, Melbourne, 1976.

Hunt, Arnold D & Thomas, Robert P., *For God, King and Country: A study of the attitudes of the Methodist and Catholic Press in South Australia,* Salisbury College of Advanced Education, Salisbury, South Australia 1979.

Jackson, P. J., P. Cade, J. Huston, & K. Moses, *White over Green, 2nd/4th Battalion AIF,* Angus & Robertson, Sydney, 1963.

James, Clarrie, *ANGAU, One Man Law,* Australian Military History Publications, Sydney, 1999.

Johnson, D. H., *Volunteers at Heart: The Queensland Defence Forces 1860-1901,* University of Queensland Press, Brisbane, 1975.

Kelly. L.B., (ed) *Military of the Hunter: Citizen Defence Forces Newcastle and Hunter Valley. A history 1855 to 2005,* Reserve Forces Day Hunter Region Council Inc, Newcastle NSW, 2008,

Kipling, Rudyard, 'The 'Eathen' in *The Complete Barrack-Room Ballads of Rudyard Kipling,* ed. Charles Carrington, Methuen & Co, London, 1973.

Kuring, Ian, *Redcoats to Cams: A History of Australian Infantry 1788-2001,* Australian Military History Publications, Sydney, 2004.

Laffin, John, *Tommy Atkins, The story of the English Soldier,* Cassell, London, 1966.

Lee, J. E., *Duntroon, The Royal Military College of Australia, 1911-1946,* Australian War Memorial, Canberra, 1942

Legg, Frank, *The Gordon Bennett Story: From Gallipoli to Singapore,* Angus & Robertson, Sydney, 1965.

Lewis, A. N., *Australian Military Law,* Cox Kay & Co., Hobart, 1936.

Lodge, A. B., *The Fall of General Gordon Bennett,* Allen & Unwin, Sydney, 1986.

Long, Bob, *'Z' Special Unit's Secret War, Operation Semut 1, Soldering with the head-hunters of Borneo,* B. Long Publications, Bayswater, Western Australia, Second Edition 1999.

Long, Gavin, *Australia in the War of 1939-1945, Series 1 (Army), Volume 1, To Benghazi,* Australian War Memorial, Canberra, 1952.

Long, Gavin, *Australia in the War of 1939-1945, Series 1 (Army), Volume II, Greece, Crete and Syria,* Australian War Memorial, Canberra, 1953.

Long, Gavin, *The Six Years War,* Australian Government Publishing Service, Canberra, 1973.

Luvaas, Jay, *The Education of an Army, British Military Thought 1815-1940,* University of Chicago Press, Chicago, 1964.

Macintyre, Stuart, *A Concise History of Australia,* Cambridge University Press, Melbourne, 1999.

MacGregor-Hastie, Roy, *The Mechanics of Power, Government in spite of the People,* Frederick Muller, London, 1966.

McCarthy, John, *Australia and Imperial Defence 1918-1939: A Study in Air and Sea Power,* University of Queensland Press, Brisbane, 1976.

McCausland, W.J.A., *Short History of the Australian Army,* Unpublished, 1971.

McGibbon, Ian (ed), *The Oxford Companion to New Zealand Military History,* Oxford University Press, Auckland, 2000.

McKernan, M & Browne, *Australia Two Centuries of War and Peace,* Australian War Memorial, Canberra, 1988.

McNaughton, I.D., 'Colonial Liberalism, 1851-1892' in Greenwood, Gordon, *Australia, A Social & Political History,* Angus & Robertson, Sydney, Reprinted 1978.

Makepeace-Warne, Antony, *Brassey's Companion to the British Army,* Brassey's, London, 1995.

Mediansky, F. A. *The Military and Australia's Defence,* Longman Cheshire, Melbourne, 1979.

Meaney, Neville, *In Search for Security in the Pacific 1901-1914: Volume 1, A History of Australian Defence and Foreign Policy, 1901-1923,* Sydney University Press, Sydney, 1976.

Millar, T. B., *Australia in Peace and War, External Relations 1788-1977,* Australian National University Press, Canberra, 1978.

Millar, T. B., *Australia's Defence,* Melbourne University Press, Melbourne, 1965.

Millar, T. B., *Defence,* Melbourne University Press, Melbourne, Second Edition 1969.

Moremon, John,' Most Deadly Jungle Fighters?': Australian Infantry in Malaya & Papua 1941-'43, (BA (Hons) thesis, University of New England, 1992).

Mordike, John, *An Army for a Nation, A history of Australian military developments 1880-1914,* Allen & Unwin, Sydney, 1992.

Morton, Desmond, *Ministers and Generals, Politics and the Canadian Militia,* University of Toronto Press, Toronto, 1970.

Morton, Desmond, *The Canadian General, Sir William Otter,* Hakkert, Toronto, 1974.

Morton, Desmond *A Military History of Canada,* McClelland and Stewart, Ontario, 1992.

Murphy, J.E., *History of the Post War Army,* Unpublished, 1955 (AWM 113, Item 10)

Neumann, Claude, *Australia's Citizen Soldiers, 1919-1939; A Study of Organisation,*

Command, Recruiting, Training & Equipment, Master of Arts thesis, Department of History, Faculty of Military Studies, University of New South Wales at Duntroon, 1978.

Nicholls, Bob, *The Colonial Volunteers, The defence forces of the Australian colonies 1836-1901,* Allen and Unwin, Sydney, 1988.

O'Connor, John, *Shooting Awards and Prizes to the Australian Military Forces,* John O'Connor, Sydney, 2002.

O'Connor, Michael, *To live in Peace, Australia's Defence Policy,* Melbourne University Press, Melbourne, 1985.

O'Neill, Robert, 'The Military and Australia's Defence', *The Military and Australia's Defence,* F. A. Mediansky (ed), Longman Cheshire, Melbourne, 1979.

Paull, Raymond, *Retreat from Kokoda,* William Heinemann Ltd, Melbourne, Reprinted 1958.

Palazzo, Albert, *Defenders of Australia, The Third Australian Division 1916-1991,* Army History Unit, Department of Defence, Canberra, 2002.

Palazzo, Albert, *The Australian Army, A History of its Organisation 1901-2001,* Oxford University Press, Melbourne, 2001.

Pears, Maurie and Fred Kirkland, *Korea Remembered, The RAN, ARA and RAAF in the Korea War of 1950-1953,* Doctrine Wing, Combined Arms Training and Development Centre, Sydney, Reprinted 2002.

Perry, F. W., *The Commonwealth Armies: Manpower & Organisation in two World Wars,* Manchester University Press, Manchester, 1988.

Pratten, Garth, 'Under rather discouraging circumstances; The Citizens' Military Forces in Melbourne's Eastern Suburbs between the Wars, 1921-1939', BA Hons thesis, University of Melbourne, 1995.

Radi, Heather, '1920-1929', *A New History of Australia,* Frank Crowley (ed), William Heinemann, Melbourne, Reprinted 1980.

Rayner, Robert J., *The Army and the Defence of Darwin Fortress,* Southwood Press, Marrickville, NSW, 1995.

Reese, Trevor R., *Australia in the Twentieth Century, A short political history,* F.W. Cheshire, Sydney, 1964.

Robertson, John R, '1930-1939', Frank Crowley (ed), *A New History of Australia,* William Heinemann, Melbourne, 1974.

Robson, L. L., *The First A.I.F., A study of its recruitment 1914-1918,* Melbourne University Press, Melbourne, 1982.

Ross, Andrew T., *Armed and ready, Industrial Development and the Defence of Australia 1900-1945,* Turton & Armstrong, Sydney, 1995.

Ross, Jane, *The Myth of the Digger: The Australian Soldier in Two World Wars,* Hale & Iremonger, Sydney, 1985.

Sharpe, Robert, *The Last Day, The Last Hour, The Currie Libel Trial,* Carswell, Scarborough, Ontario, 1985.

Smith, Alan G. R., *The Emergence of a Nation State: The Commonwealth of England 1529-1660,* Longman, London, Second Edition 1997.

Smith, Ian K., *Records of War, A guide to military history sources at the Australian War Memorial,* Australian War Memorial, Canberra, 1996.

Smith, Hugh, 'The Determinants of Defence Policy', *The Military and Australia's Defence,* F. A. Mediansky (ed), Longman Cheshire, Melbourne, 1979.

Solomon, G.D., *A Poor sort of Memory, A personal memoir of the Royal Military College, Duntroon,* Roebuck, Canberra, 1978.

Spencer-Chapman, Freddie, *The Jungle is Neutral,* Chatto & Windus, 1949, London, Third Impression 1953.

Spencer, W.B., *In the footsteps of Ghosts, With the 2nd/9th (Australian Infantry) Battalion in the African desert and the jungles of the Pacific,* Allen and Unwin, Sydney, 1999.

Starr, Joan & Christopher Sweeny, *Forward, The History of the 2nd/14th Light Horse (Queensland Mounted Infantry),* University of Queensland Press, Brisbane, 1989.

Stanley, Peter, *The Remote Garrison: The British Army in Australia 1788-1870,* Kangaroo Press, Kenthurst, NSW, 1986.

Starke, J.G., *The ANZUS Treaty Alliance,* Melbourne University Press, Melbourne, 1965.

Sutton, Ralph, Ken Thompson, & Bill Storer, *Military Forces in New South Wales: An Introduction, Part 1 1788-1904,* The Army Museum Sydney Foundation, 3rd edition, Sydney, 2000.

Sweeney, Tony, *Malaria Frontline, Australian Army Research During WWII,* Melbourne University Press, Melbourne, 2003.

Swifte, L.B., *Darwin Mobile Force: 40th Anniversary Celebrations,* Victoria Barracks Commemorative Edition Booklet, Sydney, 1978.

Tanner, Thomas W., *Compulsory Citizen Soldiers,* Alternative Publishing Co-Operative Ltd., Sydney, 1980

Trigellis-Smith, Syd, Sergio Zampatti, & Max Parsons, *Shaping History, A Bibliography of Australian Army Unit Histories,* Max Parsons, Cheltenham, Victoria, 1996.

Turrell, Norman, *Never Unprepared, A history of the 2nd/ 6th Australian infantry Battalion (AIF) 1939-1946,* 26th Battalion Association, Sandringham, Victoria 1992.

Tylden, Major G, *The Armed Forces of South Africa,* City of Johannesburg Africana Museum Frank Connock Publication No.2, Johannesburg, 1954.

Tyquin, Michael, *Little by Little, (A history of the RAAMC),* Army History Unit, Department of Defence, Canberra, 2003.

Union War histories (Civil), Box 168, File ref. Narep-Unfo: 23, *S.A. Instructional Corps. History (1912-1942)*

Unknown authors, *24th Australian Infantry Battalion, Australian Imperial Force, Pictorial History,* Unknown publisher, 1946.

Usher, George, *Dictionary of British Military History,* Bloomsbury Publishing, London, 2003.

Vasenry, George, *A Short History of the Australian Army,* Unpublished, 1984.

Voyle, Maj.-Gen. G. E., *A Military Dictionary,* William Clowes and Sons, London, Third Edition, 1899.

Watt, Alan, *The Evolution of Australian Foreign Policy 1938-1965,* Cambridge University Press, Cambridge, 1967.

Whiston, Robert Norton, Another Whiston Matter, Unpublished autobiography manuscript, 1996.

Wigmore, Lionel & Harding, Bruce, *They Dared Mightily,* Australian War Memorial, Canberra, 1963 (Second edition 1986).

Wilcox, Craig, *For Hearths and Homes, Citizen Soldiering in Australia 1854-1945,* Allen & Unwin, Sydney, 1995.

Wintle, Justine (ed), *The Dictionary of War Quotations,* Hodder & Stoughton, London, 1989.

Withers, Glenn, *Conscription Necessity and Justice, The case for an all-volunteer Army,* Angus and Robertson, Sydney, 1972.

Youll, Rob, (ed), *Swan Street Sappers, A history of the Engineer Training Depot, Swan Street, Melbourne and of Sappers in Victoria, 1860-1996,* HQ Logistic Support Force Engineers, Melbourne, 1995

Conference Publications

Ball, Desmond (ed), *Strategy & Defence, Australian Essays,* George Allen & Unwin, Sydney, 1982.

Ball, Desmond, The Role of the Military in Defence Hardware Procurement', *The Military and Australia's Defence*, F. A. Mediansky (ed), Longman Cheshire, Melbourne, 1979.

Ball, Desmond, 'The Role of the Military in Mobilisation', *The Military and Australia's Defence*, F. A. Mediansky (ed), Longman Cheshire, Melbourne, 1979.

Bland, Douglas L., (ed) *Backbone of the Army, Non-Commissioned Officers in the Future Army*, McGill-Queens University Press, Kingston, Ontario, 1999.

Cheeseman, G. L. & K. R. Sydney, 'The Requirements of the Australian Military Profession Today', *The Military and Australia's Defence*, ed. F. A. Mediansky, Longman Cheshire, Melbourne, 1979.

Coulthard-Clark, Chris, 'The Role of Military Survey: Benefiting the Army & the Civil Community and the Army' in *A Century of Service: 100 years of the Australian Army*, Peter Dennis & Jeffrey Grey (eds), Army History Unit, Canberra, 2001.

Dennis, Peter; & Jeffrey Grey, (eds); *The Australian Army and the Vietnam War, 1962-1972*, The 2002 Chief of Army's Military History Conference, Army History Unit, Department of Defence, Canberra, 2002.

Evans, Michael, (ed), *Changing the Army: The roles of Doctrine, Development and Training*, Land Warfare Studies Centre, Canberra, 2000.

Evans, Michael, *'From Deakin to Dibb: The Army & the making of Australian Strategy in the Twentieth Century'*, Land Warfare Studies Centre, Working Paper 113, Canberra, June 2001.

Gammage, Bill, 'The Role of the Army in Shaping the Australian Nation to 1939', *Armies & Nation Building: Past Experience—Future Prospects*, David Horner (ed), Strategic & Defence Studies Centre, Australian National University, Canberra, 1995.

Horner, David, 'The Australian Army and nation Building 1939-1972' in *Armies & Nation Building: Past Experience—Future Prospects*, David Horner (ed), Strategic & Defence Studies Centre, Australian National University, Canberra, 1995.

Horner, David, Strategy & Generalship: Strategic & Operational Planning for the 1943 Offensive, in Peter Dennis, & Jeffrey Grey (eds); *The Foundations of Victory & the Pacific War 1943-1944*, The 2003 Chief of Army's Military History Conference, Army History Unit, Department of Defence, Canberra, 2004.

Jans, N. A., 'Generalism, Specialism and Career Development of Army Officers', *The Military and Australia's Defence*, F. A. Mediansky (ed), Longman Cheshire, Melbourne, 1979.

Langtry, J O, 'The Development of the Australian Defence Force', Ball, Desmond (ed), *Strategy and Defence, Australian Essays*, George Allen and Unwin, Sydney, 1982.

Mediansky, F. A. (ed), *The Military and Australia's Defence*, Longman Cheshire, Melbourne, 1979.

Mediansky, F. A. 'The Role of the Military in Strategic Policy', *The Military and Australia's Defence*, F. A. Mediansky (ed), Longman Cheshire, Melbourne, 1979.

Mench, Paul, 'The Education of Officers: Problems and Praxis', *The Military and Australia's Defence*, F. A. Mediansky (ed), Longman Cheshire, Melbourne, 1979.

Millar, T. B., 'The Political-Military Relationship in Australia' in Ball, Desmond (ed), *Strategy & Defence, Australian Essays*, George Allen & Unwin, Sydney, 1982.

Palazzo, Albert, 'Organising for Jungle Warfare', *1943-1944 The Foundations of Victory in the Pacific War*, Peter Dennis & Jeffrey Grey (eds), Army History Unit, Canberra, 2003.

Pearn, John, 'Medicine at War: The Pivot Years of 1943 & 1944 in the New Guinea Campaign' in Peter Dennis, & Jeffrey Grey (eds); *The Foundations of Victory & the Pacific War 1943-1944*, The 2003 Chief of Army's Military History Conference, Army History Unit, Department of Defence, Canberra, 2004.

Ryan, Alan, 'Back to the Future' *A Century of Service: 100 years of the Australian Army*, Peter Dennis & Jeffrey Grey (eds), Army History Unit, Canberra, 2001.

Sligo, Graeme, 'The Development of the Australian Regular Army, 1944-1952', *The Second Fifty Years, The Australian Army 1947-1997*, Peter Dennis & Jeffrey Grey (eds), School of History, University College, University of New South Wales, Australian Defence Force Academy, Canberra, 1997.

Sligo, Graeme, 'The Development of the Australian Regular Army' in *A Century of Service: 100 years of the Australian Army*, Peter Dennis & Jeffrey Grey (eds), Army History Unit, Canberra, 2001.

Stanley, Peter, 'Anzac and Army, Reflections on Army and Society in Australia 1895-1995', *Armies & Nation Building: Past Experience—Future Prospects*, ed. David Horner (ed), Strategic & Defence Studies Centre, Australian National University, Canberra, 1995.

Stanley, Peter, 'Broken Lineage: The Australian Army's Heritage of Discontinuity', *A Century of Service: 100 years of the Australian Army*, Peter Dennis & Jeffrey Grey (eds), Army History Unit, Canberra, 2001

Journal Articles

Anon. (Directorate of Military Training, AHQ), 'The Basis of Expansion for War' in *Australian Army Journal*, No.12, May 1950, Canberra.

Anon. 'Memories of Kokoda' in *Reveille, RSL of NSW magazine*, Sydney, 2002.

Buller, Steve, 'Kokoda, A Japanese Tragedy' in *'Wartime (Official Magazine of the Australian War Memorial',* Issue 20, 2002.

Bunbury, W St. Pierre, 'The Beginnings of the School of Gunnery at Middle Head, Sydney, in *The Army Journal*, No. 288, May 1973, Directorate of Military Training, Canberra.

Dickey, B., 'The Development of Australia's Military Roles in World War II' in *Army Journal No.309 February 1975.*

Evans, Michael, 'Gallipoli and the Military Revolution of World War 1' in *United Service, RUSI of NSW,* Vol. 54, No.1, 2002.

Evans, Michael, 'Towards an Australian Way of Warfare' in *United Service, RUSI of NSW,* Vol. 53, No.4, 2002.

Francis, Hon. Jos, 'The Citizen Military Forces' in *Australian Army Journal*, No. 41, January 1952.

Francis, Hon. Jos, 'The Army Yesterday and Today (1953)' in *Australian Army Journal*, No. 44, January 1953.

Graham, Stuart, 'Tanks against Japan', *Army Journal, Volume 1, Number 2,* June 1955.

Horner, David, 'Kokoda' in *'Wartime (Official Magazine of the Australian War Memorial',* Issue 20, 2002.

Hutcheson, J. M., 'The School of Military Engineering', in *The Army Journal*, No.264, May 1971, Directorate of Military Training, Canberra.

Hutton, Geoffrey, 'Lessons of New Guinea' in *SALT, Australian Army Journal*, Vol. 5, No. 5, 9 Nov 1942.

Kertesz, J. L., 'Australia's Capacity for War in September 1939' in *RMC Journal*, Volume Five: 1976.

McCarthy, J. M., 'Australia and the Sudan War: some contemporary issues in an old setting', in *RMC Journal*, Volume One, March 1972.

Newton, Arthur J. C., 'The Australian Instructional Corps', in *The Army Journal*,
    No. 267, August 1971, Directorate of Military Training, Canberra.

Newton, Arthur James Cahill, 'The Australian Instructional Corps', *Australian
    Infantry Magazine*, October 2013-April 2014.

Parsons, M. C., 'Was Australia's contribution to World War 1 in her national
    interests?' in *RMC Historical Journal*, Vol. 2, 1973.

Perry, Warren, 'Hubert John Foster, An Early Instructor of the AMF', in *United
    Service Quarterly*, Vol.8 1954, Sydney, United Services Institution of
    NSW.

Perry, Warren, 'Lieutenant-General Sir Edward Hutton, The Creator of Australia's
    Post Federation Army', in *The Army Journal*, No. 291, August 1973,
    Directorate of Military Training, Canberra.

Trevan, K. H., 'The Darwin Mobile Force', in *The Army Journal*, No. 275, April
    1972, Canberra: Directorate of Military Training.

Watt, A. D., 'The School of Artillery', in *Australian Army Journal*, No.92, January
    1957, Directorate of Military Training, Canberra.

Wilcox, Craig, 'Relinquishing the Past: John Mordike's An Army for a Nation',
    Australian Journal of Politics and History, Vol. 40, No.1, 1993

Wilcox, Craig, 'Australia's Boer War 1899-1902' in *'Wartime (Official Magazine of
    the Australian War Memorial'*, Issue 21, 2002.

Wynter, D.H., 'Defence of Australia and its relation to Imperial Defence', in *Australian
    Army Journal*, No.391 December 1975 (Reprint of address given to RUSI,
    1935).

Miscellaneous

Gordon, I.C., 'The Blamey Oration', 24 June 2003, Royal United Service Institute
    of New South Wales.

'Citizen Soldier', Coronation Issue, June 1937.

'SALT' Vol.2, No 7, 16 February 1942

'SALT' Vol.2, No 9, 2 March 1942

'Australian Infantry', Magazine of the Royal Australian Infantry Corps, April 2005
    (List of School of Infantry Commanders since 1911)

'The Royal New South Wales Regiment, An Introduction', 1992, A handbook for
    all ranks, Department Publications, Canberra, 1992.

'Particulars of Service, Members of the Permanent Forces serving with the AIF,
    AAG 3rd Military District', M30/864, 47334 of 8th October 1981,
    Unpublished, Central Army Records Office, Melbourne.

INDEX

A

B

G

H

M

No.1 Special School of Instruction, xviii, 13, 77
No.2 School of Instruction (Liverpool, NSW), 30, 60, 189

O

Officer Cadet Training Unit (Woodside, SA), 136, 223
Official Training Areas, 79
Oglethorpe, QM and Captain A.G., 250
Olsson, Staff Sergeant Major Class II Carl O., 178
O'Neil, Warrant Officer Class I W.B., 178
Ordish, QM and Hon. Major Harold, 24, 50, 78, 105
Orme, Warrant Officer Class II C.J., 167, 199
O'Rouke, Warrant Officer H.B.E., 184p
Osgood, George, 203
Osgood, Warrant Officer Class I Athol, 119–120, 187, 203–204
O'Toole, T/Warrant Officer Class II J.P., 85, 105, 109
Owen, Evelyn, 191
Owen gun, 191–192

P

Pantlin, Lieutenant Frederick W., 48
Paul, QM and Hon. Major John K., 50
Pearce, Defence Minister George, 9
Pearce, QM and Hon. Captain Henry C., 52
Peat, QM and Lieutenant C.B., 251
Peddle, QM and Hon. Lieutenant Thomas H., 85, 148
Pickburn, QM and Major Frederick G.A., 160
Pollard, T/Warrant Officer Class II C., 207
Power, Warrant Officer Class III Ken, 117
powers of command, 40, 68
Pratt, Captain William H., 49
Provost Training School (Darley, Victoria), 223

Q

Quartermasters
    commissioning of, xxi, 227–229
    corps transfers, 217, 229

establishment numbers, 49, 64, 106–107, 115–116, 134, 147, 187, 233, 238

and honorary commissions, 33–34

role and selection of, 22, 23–27, 45, 232

Quirke, Hon. Lieutenant D., 108

R

Raffan, Warrant Officer Class II A.J., 86

Ransom, Colonel Neville F., 157, 159, 201–202

redundancies, impact of, 59–61, 102, 106

Regimental Quartermaster Sergeants, AIC role in filling, 45

Regimental Sergeant Majors, AIC role in filling, 45, 65, 80, 139

Returned Sailors', Soldiers', and Airmen's Imperial League of Australia, 206, 244

Richards, QM and Captain C.S., 249

Ridley, Warrant Officer Class I A.E., 108

Roach, Captain John H., 24, 48, 171

Roberts, Captain Albert E., 48

Roberts, Hon. Lieutenant Arthur L., 78

Roberts, Tom, 5

Robertson, Lieutenant General Sir Horace, 25, 84

Robertson, Lieutenant Maxwell K., 221–222

Robinson, Staff Sergeant R.E., 230

Robinson, Warrant Officer Class I I.J., 109

Rolf, Sergeant S., 231

Rosenthal, Major General Charles, 35, 41

Rosevear, QM and Hon. Captain George, 53

Ross, QM and Captain A.H.J., 249

Rowell, Warrant Officer Class I, 137

Royal Military College, (Duntroon, Canberra), 21, 22, 26, 28, 32, 37, 49, 59, 77, 78, 82, 87, 88, 106, 118, 122, 131, 149, 156, 157, 218, 222, 224, 225

Ruddock, Major William C.G., 52, 214

S

Salomon, Brigadier Geoffrey, 149

Sangster, Dr, 88–89

Savage, Brigadier Bernard S., 162, 167

Schmede, Major Theodore J., 200

The author.

Roland Herbert Millbank (1938 –) was born and educated in England. He completed a 5 year indentured apprenticeship as a toolmaker in the aircraft industry. He then worked in production engineering in computers and automobiles, until migrating to Australia in 1965. Concurrently he completed 3 years part time service in the Royal Air Force Reserve as a member of the Royal Observer Corps.

In Australia he undertook further technical education while working in the appliance industry, before joining the New South Wales Government as an industrial promotion officer. In this capacity over a number of years he worked in Sydney, Wollongong, Wagga Wagga, Broken Hill and Newcastle. Additionally he undertook promotional visits to Singapore, Malaysia, Indonesia, Korea, the Philippines and Japan.

Enlisting in the Citizens Military Forces/Army Reserve Roland Millbank was commissioned in the Royal Corps of Electrical and Mechanical Engineers, retiring after 16 years peacetime service as a major.

As a mature age student Roland Millbank attended university where he read history. He has a Batchelor of Arts from the University of Newcastle (2001), a Master of Arts (History) from the University of New England (2003) and a Master of Philosophy (Research Honours) from the University of Newcastle (2009).

Military Treasures of Christ Church Cathedral Newcastle was his first published book in 2010.